THE SPORTING LIFE

THE SPORTING LIFE

Victorian Sports and Games

Nancy Fix Anderson

VICTORIAN LIFE AND TIMES
Sally Mitchell, Series Editor

 PRAEGER

AN IMPRINT OF ABC-CLIO, LLC
Santa Barbara, California • Denver, Colorado • Oxford, England

Copyright 2010 by Nancy Fix Anderson

Library of Congress Cataloging-in-Publication Data

Anderson, Nancy F. (Nancy Fix), 1941–
    The sporting life : Victorian sports and games / Nancy Fix Anderson.
        p. cm. — (Victorian life and times)
    Includes bibliographical references and index.
    ISBN 978–0–275–98999–6 (hard copy : alk. paper) — ISBN 978–0–313–07148–5 (ebook)
1. Sports—Great Britain—History—19th century. 2. Sports and state—Great Britain—History
—19th century. 3. Sports—Social aspects—Great Britain—History—19th century. 4. Games—
Great Britain—History—19th century. I. Title.
GV605.A55   2010
796.0941´09034—dc22   2009050891

ISBN: 978–0–275–98999–6
EISBN: 978–0–313–07148–5

14 13 12 11 10   1 2 3 4 5

This book is also available on the World Wide Web as an eBook.
Visit www.abc-clio.com for details.

Praeger
An Imprint of ABC-CLIO, LLC

ABC-CLIO, LLC
130 Cremona Drive, P.O. Box 1911
Santa Barbara, California 93116-1911

This book is printed on acid-free paper ∞

Manufactured in the United States of America

TO CLIFF

CONTENTS

SERIES FOREWORD

Although the nineteenth century has almost faded from living memory—
most people who heard firsthand stories from grandparents who grew up
before 1900 have adult grandchildren by now—impressions of the Victorian
world continue to influence both popular culture and public debates. These
impressions may well be vivid yet contradictory. Many people, for example,
believe that Victorian society was safe, family-centered, and stable because
women could not work outside the home, although every census taken during
the period records hundreds of thousands of female laborers in fields, factories,
shops, and schools as well as more than a million domestic servants—often
girls of 14 or 15—whose long and unregulated workdays created the comfortable leisured world we see in Merchant Ivory films. Yet it is also true that there
were women who had no household duties and desperately wished for some
purpose in life but found that social expectations and family pressure absolutely prohibited their presence in the workplace.

The goal of books in the Victorian Life and Times series is to explain and
enrich the simple pictures that show only a partial truth. Although the Victorian period in Great Britain is often portrayed as peaceful, comfortable, and
traditional, it was actually a time of truly breathtaking change. In 1837, when
18-year-old Victoria became queen, relatively few of England's people had ever
traveled more than 10 miles from the place where they were born. Little more
than half the population could read and write, children as young as five worked
in factories and mines, and political power was entirely in the hands of a small
minority of men who held property. By the time Queen Victoria died in 1901,
railways provided fast and cheap transportation for both goods and people,
telegraph messages sped to the far corners of the British Empire in minutes,
education was compulsory, a man's religion (or lack of it) no longer barred
him from sitting in Parliament, and women were not only wives and domestic
servants but also physicians, dentists, elected school-board members,

telephone operators, and university lecturers. Virtually every aspect of life had been transformed either by technology or by the massive political and legal reforms that reshaped Parliament, elections, universities, the army, education, sanitation, public health, marriage, working conditions, trade unions, and civil and criminal law.

The continuing popularity of Victoriana among decorators and collectors, the strong market for historical novels and for mysteries set in the age of Jack the Ripper and Sherlock Holmes, the new interest in books by George Eliot and Charles Dickens and Wilkie Collins whenever one is presented on television, and the desire of amateur genealogists to discover the lives, as well as the names, of nineteenth-century British ancestors all reveal the need for accurate information about the period's social history and material culture. In the years since the first edition of my book *Daily Life in Victorian England* was published in 1996, I have been contacted by many people who want more detailed information about some area covered in that overview. Each book in the Victorian Life and Times series will focus on a single topic, describe changes during the period, and consider the differences between country and city, between industrial life and rural life, and above all, the differences made by class, social position, religion, tradition, gender, and economics. Each book is an original work, illustrated with drawings and pictures taken from Victorian sources, enriched by quotations from Victorian publications, based on current research, and written by a qualified scholar. All of the authors have doctoral degrees and many years' experience in teaching; they have been chosen not only for their academic qualifications but also for their ability to write clearly and to explain complex ideas to people without extensive background in the subject. Thus the books are authoritative and dependable but written in straightforward language; explanations are supplied whenever specialized terminology is used, and a bibliography lists resources for further information.

The Internet has made it possible for people who cannot visit archives and reference libraries to conduct serious family and historical research. Careful hobbyists and scholars have scanned large numbers of primary sources—nineteenth-century cookbooks, advice manuals, maps, city directories, magazines, sermons, church records, illustrated newspapers, guidebooks, political cartoons, photographs, paintings, published investigations of slum conditions and poor people's budgets, political essays, inventories of scientists' correspondence, and many other materials formerly accessible only to academic historians. Yet the World Wide Web also contains misleading documents and false information, even on educational sites created by students and enthusiasts who don't have the experience to put material in useful contexts. So far as possible, therefore, the bibliographies for books in the Victorian Life and Times series will also offer guidance on using publicly available electronic resources.

British Victorians created the central elements of twentieth and twenty-first century international sporting culture. Schools and colleges agreed on uniform rules for team games so they could compete against one another;

neighborhoods and factories and towns organized teams of their own; professional players began to earn a living through sports; governing bodies established leagues and championships. New pastimes such as swimming and mountaineering became popular. Women took part in both individual and competitive athletics. Even sports well established before 1800, such as cricket, horseracing, and boxing, were codified, regulated, and commercialized. Informal running and jumping contests were disciplined by regularization, training, and record-keeping. England's chief sports spread around the Empire and international contests arose, including the first modern Olympic Games.

In tracing this history, Nancy Fix Anderson also sets it in context, describing the influence of military traditions, religion, industrialization and urbanization. Victorians recognized the link between exercise and health as well as the value of organized sports as an outlet for social unrest. Issues of class, gender, and region all came into play. In addition to its valuable overviews and useful chronology, *The Sporting Life: Victorian Sports and Games* draws on the sporting press (itself a Victorian innovation) for copious illustrations, exciting narratives, and stories of major sporting heroes.

Sally Mitchell, Series Editor

ACKNOWLEDGMENTS

Writing about Victorian sports has been a most enjoyable experience. Victorian that I am, I could rationalize my pleasure in terms of the historical importance of the topic. Certainly adding to the enjoyment has been the tremendous assistance I have received from so many people. I am especially indebted to Sally Mitchell, the editor of the Victorian Life and Times series. Sally's wise guidance, insightful suggestions, warm encouragement, and amazing patience sustained me throughout the project. The staffs of many libraries also helped me greatly in my research. I am particularly grateful to the staffs at the Widener and Houghton Libraries at Harvard University, the Rare Book Room of the Boston Public Library, the Athenaeum Library in Boston, the Trinity University Library, the Humanities Research Center at the University of Texas, the University of Texas Perry-Castañeda Library, and the interlibrary loan office of the San Antonio Public Library.

I could not have written this book without the assistance that Donene Williams gave me in getting access to many of the Victorian periodicals and newspapers, for which I am most appreciative. As I worked through the complexities of Victorian sports, Michael Anderson was a great help and inspiration, especially with his knowledge of and passion for English football. Michael taught me not only to understand, but also to enjoy the game that Americans call soccer, a pleasure augmented by Jackson Anderson's patient attempts to teach me to play the game. I thank them both, and also Abigail Williams and Carter Williams for their humor and understanding when I would talk what must have seemed incessantly about the delights of Victorian sports. I am grateful to Kathryn Anderson and Donald Williams, for the logistical support they gave me as I worked on this book. Most of all, I thank Cliff, my partner in writing this book, and in life.

INTRODUCTION

Victorian sports? An oxymoron? The Victorians, whose dominant middle-class social ethos was shaped by industrial capitalism, are characteristically known as the exponents of values that seem the antithesis of sports. Did a society that espoused work, seriousness, utility, duty, distrust of leisure, and rationality, have the time and motivation to play, much less to exalt sport into a new religion, making it a central part of its culture and way of life? That is indeed what the hardworking, serious-minded Victorians did. They reshaped their traditional sports, eliminating some while modernizing others, and created new sports, with their games so penetrating all layers of their society, that the English became known throughout the world as a sports-playing nation.

What makes the history of sports in nineteenth-century England so fascinating is the way the Victorians were able to use sports to promote their distinctive bourgeois ethos, even as sports subverted those values. The evangelical and utilitarian shapers of these values saw in competitive physical games a means of promoting their goals of virtuous straitlaced living, but in so doing, they inadvertently endorsed an ethic of play that was enjoyed for its own sake. Sports were used as markers of class, but when sports drew participants from mixed economic levels, class segregation lessened. In a society focused on maintaining strictly differentiated gender personalities and roles, sports were used to define masculinity, but as women increasingly by the end of the century began kicking balls and picking up rackets, the definitions of masculinity and femininity were forced to change. Finally, imperial administrators and soldiers used sports as an emblem of their distinctive and presumed superior culture and their right to rule, but when the colonized peoples took up the English games, they challenged English superiority on the playing field even as some would do on the battlefield.

Sports are an important and intriguing subject of study in most cultures, but especially so in nineteenth-century England. Sports provide a prism through which to view the spectrum of Victorian society, offering insights into the complexities of class and gender and the diversities of region. The study of their sports reinforces the caution against overgeneralizations about Victorian society and highlights the tremendous changes during Queen Victoria's long reign, so that what it meant to be "Victorian" in 1837 was profoundly different than in 1901.

In this survey of the development of Victorian sports, the focus will be on England. The Celtic nations in the United Kingdom—Wales, Scotland, and Ireland—will be discussed in Chapter 8, as part of the larger examination of the diffusion of English sports in the empire and throughout the world. The term "British," inclusive of the whole British Isles, is used in reference to the Empire, but even in the discussions of the spread of sports throughout the British Empire, the emphasis is on English sports. To further limit the scope of this vast subject of the Victorian sporting life, in this book the sports that are discussed are those of physical competition—between people, and people against animals (as in hunting, shooting, and fishing), nature (as in mountain climbing), and one's self (such as beating one's own record), and also, using a looser definition, contests between animals (such as cockfighting and bull-baiting). Physical recreations, such as swimming and cycling, are also included, because the Victorians turned these activities into competitions. Nonphysical competitions, such as billiards and chess, are not included, even though the Victorians often considered these games "sports."

Because sports were such an important part of Victorian life, sources for this book abound. With the dramatic expansion of publications in nineteenth-century England, the voluminous number of mainstream journals and magazines as well as the specialized sporting press provide rich and diverse views on the role and meaning of sports in Victorian England. Many of these periodicals are now digitized and online, in collections available usually through subscription. Memoirs and letters, as well as novels and even poetry, are infused with sporting stories and themes. Scholars in Victorian England took sports seriously as a subject for academic study, and their historical, anthropological, and sociological studies provide modern historians with insights into the mind-set and values of the scholars as well as information from the scholars' research. The challenge, therefore, in writing on the sporting life in Victorian England is that there is so much material and the subject is so broad. This book thus aims at synthesizing the major developments in nineteenth-century English sports, presenting the sports as the Victorians experienced them in their play and competitions and showing how the sports both mirrored and changed Victorian society.

Chapter 1 is a survey of the pre-Victorian sporting world, from medieval village recreations to the seventeenth-century English Civil War, in which sports were a significant point of contention between the King and Parliament, Royalists and the Puritans. With the suppression of sports as a defining characteristic of the Interregnum (1649–1660) under the rule of the Puritan Oliver

Cromwell, the celebrations of the restoration of the monarchy in the late-seventeenth century were made all the merrier with the return of the games. Sports in the eighteenth century reflected that Age of Aristocracy, in which the wealthy leisured classes enjoyed their sporting pleasures without guilt, and villagers played without concern for justifications other than fun. One could hunt animals (with the landowners protecting their prey from lower-class interlopers with strict game laws) or indulge the pleasure of vicarious violence and the passion for gambling in watching cockfighting or bull-baiting, pleasures that cut across class lines. Balls could be batted or kicked or bowled on the open village greens, and the use of one's bare knuckles in pugilistic contests could be enjoyed without discord.

Chapter 2 discusses the impact on sports of the economic and social transformations of industrialization and urbanization that began in the late-eighteenth century, and that changed the social milieu as well as physical landscape of England. With the rise of the industrial middle classes, the new ideologies of evangelicalism and utilitarianism, so consonant with the emerging bourgeois values, reshaped English society, creating what is simply called "Victorianism." Even before the young Victoria ascended the throne in 1837, traditional sports were condemned as immoral or a waste of time. In that age of fear of revolution by contagion from France and looming in England in industrial and agricultural protests, sports were seen as dangerous occasions for the gathering of crowds, often unruly and potentially violent. Social pressure and parliamentary laws served to ban many traditional sports, while the loss of green space and working-class leisure in urban areas effectively restricted outdoor play and games. The aristocratic and gentry classes managed to escape the bourgeois condemnation of sports as well as the consequences of urbanization, as they continued to enjoy their rural field sports of hunting foxes and shooting birds, so that well into the nineteenth century the word "sports" implied "field sports." They also had land that they could dedicate to playing fields, in order to continue batting cricket balls, even as they commonly used servants or hired hands for the more menial task of bowling the ball. Furthermore, they continued to enjoy the spectator sport of horseracing, the "king of sports," which gratified not so much the love of equestrianism as the passion for gambling.

Even though the early middle-class Victorians, espousing evangelical ethics and utilitarian values, at first condemned sports, by the late-1830s and 1840s many came to see the moral and utilitarian values of organized, controlled team play. As shown in Chapter 3, these values were first demonstrated in the elite public schools such as Eton and Rugby, where unruly, rambunctious boys were turned into Christian gentlemen through the rigors and discipline of sport. Cricket, football (soccer and rugby), rowing, and other vigorous sports could channel the aggressive and sexual energies of the boys into respectable, controlled behavior. Team sports were also seen as vital in training boys in the leadership and cooperative skills needed for military success. The Duke of Wellington never said that the battle of Waterloo was won on the playing fields of Eton, but he was so often quoted throughout the nineteenth century as saying it, that that justification for sports took on a life of its own.

Chapter 4 examines the ways that, just as sports served to channel youthful energies and sublimate sexual drives, so they did also for adult Victorians. Characteristically racked by anxieties from sexual repression (or the guilt from failure of repression), many Victorians also suffered from religious doubts, the pressures of work in the economic world of laissez-faire industrial capitalism, health concerns that bordered on hypochondria, and other unsettling emotional concerns. Emotionally stressed, one could join the newly formed Alpine Club and go mountain climbing, with exertion and physical challenge calming the restless soul. The sweat from playing on the cricket field or rowing on the Thames could wash away the tensions of daily life. The shooting of birds and other animals or sparring in boxing could deflect strong aggressive feelings that were useful in business but also dangerous if not controlled.

To maintain order and discipline in their play and especially in that of the working classes, middle-class Victorians developed the concept of "rational recreation," which suggested a higher purpose than pure pleasure. One went to the seaside to swim for reasons of health, not to enjoy the exercise. A man should learn to box in case he had to defend himself or a helpless woman from attack. Cricket should be played to develop one's moral character, not to delight in physical play and competition.

One of the most important justifications of sports in mid-Victorian England was the argument that physical competitive exertion strengthened masculinity in men, whom it was feared were weakened by the sedentary lifestyles of modern industrialism. Concerned to maintain sharp differences between men and women, the Victorians were anxious that with machines replacing muscles in doing work, men were becoming effeminate. With women by the mid-century starting to organize to demand more rights and responsibilities in the public sphere, men felt threatened and could use sports as a way to asset their power, physical strength, and right to dominate. Perhaps the most frequently used word to justify sports was "manly." This focus on the manliness of sports, which encouraged male sporting recreations, tended, on the other hand, to inhibit the participation of women in most sports until the last part of the century.

The "manliness" of sports bolstered not just Victorian social but also religious patriarchy. Responding to the concern that Christianity was becoming feminized, and that such ethics as turning the other check were signs of weakness inconsonant with the values of the Victorian economic world, the movement of "Muscular Christianity" was developed. Arguing that Jesus was a "real man," who probably would have excelled on the playing field, muscular Christians linked religion with the ethics of sports. In a practical sense, to counter the increasing temptations of the secular world, churches introduced sports into their social activities as a way to bring more people into the religious fold, and they often fielded their own teams in sports competitions. Organizations like the Young Men's Christian Association (YMCA), founded in London in 1844 to nurture increased spiritual observances especially among the industrial poor, soon included sporting programs in their activities, promoting the ideal of the muscular Christian.

With the tremendous expansion of sporting activity in the 1860s and 1870s, Chapter 5 discusses what has truly been called a "sporting revolution." With the increasing number of sporting competitions, it was necessary that rules be standardized and that governing bodies be established to govern the sports. The rougher sports were also to some extent tamed—for example, the 1867 Marquess of Queensberry rules of boxing required use of gloves rather than bare knuckles and hacking was banned in rugby—but not too much lest they lose their manly appeal.

This sporting revolution was significantly aided by the technological progress of the nineteenth century. Railways allowed players and spectators to travel to competitions outside one's local area. The telegraph provided news about match results which could therefore be known quickly throughout the nation. Improvement in printing presses and paper made possible the expansion of newspapers, which usually had sports sections, as well as the publication of separate sports journals and magazines. The mass production of sporting equipment further promoted standardization and commercialization of sports. With the spread of sporting competitions in organized leagues, the rivalries between teams, and the popular adulation of new sports heroes, all accentuated by hype from the sporting press, promoters came to realize that large amounts of money could be made by enclosing sports arenas and charging admission for spectators. Sports became big business by the late-nineteenth century.

Another aspect of the sporting revolution was the spread of competitive organized sports to the working classes, as players and as spectators. With more leisure time by the 1870s, when bank holidays and half-days of work on Saturday became standard, working-class men could more easily participate in sports. Industries organized factory teams to promote loyalty among the workers. Better to kick the football than to go on strike. The resulting blurring of class lines in sport participation, however, created almost as much anxiety among the propertied classes as did the threat of blurring of gender roles. There was upper-class resentment when easier transport gave urban middle-class men access to the shooting and hunting recreations that had been the province of the landowning classes. More threatening to the class structure, however, was the participation of working-class men in games with or against the privileged, be it cricket, soccer and rugby football, rowing, or other sports.

Unsettling class lines, by the late-nineteenth century sports also caused a revolution in the lives of Victorian women, the subject of Chapter 6. As part of the larger revolt of women against the restrictions of patriarchy, some women came to demand physical as well as legal and political emancipation. Beginning with gymnastics in girls' schools, introduced to counter the disastrous effects on middle-class female health of their restricted lifestyle, girls and then women began to enjoy the pleasures of physical activity and the competition and sociability of sports. Respectable Victorian society approved the first forays into the sporting life, with the introduction of such tame non-contact games as croquet and archery, and then the new game of lawn tennis, which, although competitive, could be played in a ladylike way. But, as the defenders of patriarchy had direly warned, let women walk a block and they will try to run a mile. Some women even played the quintessentially male sports of cricket, rowing, and football (soccer, but rarely rugby.) Most liberating of all was their adoption of the new sporting vehicle of the bicycle. Through sports, women violated the expected social decorum by sweating, struggling, competing, all qualities that had defined manliness. The New Woman of the 1890s was indeed a New Sportswoman.

Working-class sportsmen, with their bank holidays and half-Saturdays, could spectate at sports. It was more difficult, however, with their full-time jobs, to have the time as players to practice, which was increasingly necessary as team competition became more intense. Skilled players, who were recruited for teams eager to win championships, began to demand compensation for lost work time, and then, for the right to be paid for the sporting labor itself. Chapter 7 explains the contentious movement towards professionalization in some sports, and the resistance in others. The privileged classes, defending the ideal of the amateur, were repulsed by the idea of payment for play. Just as unpaid service as a member of Parliament was maintained as the mark of an English gentleman, so also was the ideal of the amateur sportsman passionately if unsuccessfully defended against professional (often a code for working-class) encroachment. Some sports associations—such as the Football Association, regulating "soccer"—gave up and allowed professionalism. Cricket had earlier evolved a compromise in the form of separating players into amateur "Gentlemen" and paid "Players." The Rugby Football Union refused to allow professionals, causing a split and the formation of a separate rugby association that did allow payments. Even amateurs managed, however, often to make a large income from their sport, through product endorsements in advertising, compensation for "lost time," and, the easiest of all to exaggerate, for expenses.

Perhaps the most intriguing and certainly most historically significant development in Victorian sports, the export of the English games throughout the world, is discussed in Chapter 8. Having regulated, organized, innovated, and expanded sports at home in the nineteenth century, making them a central part of their social life, the Victorians then took their games with them on their imperial adventures, which culminated in the 1890s with the New Imperialism. Sports were important for colonial armies to maintain physical fitness and to alleviate boredom. They were also a symbol of national identity. Whether one was in the heart of Africa, or in the Deccan of India, a soldier could don his whites and play cricket with his compatriots, affirming that yes, he is an Englishman. Similarly traders in all parts of the world could entertain themselves and maintain their identity (always with a sense of superiority) by playing English sports. They began, however, to include the colonized elites into their games, as a way of winning allegiance, and then the sports spread to the common populace. It was easy at first to play their games with just the "white" parts of the empire. White Australians playing cricket did not rouse imperial alarms, at least until Australian teams started beating the English ones. But when brown-skinned Indians began playing and winning at cricket, and black-skinned Brazilians (as part of the economic "informal" British Empire), took up with vigor and success the game of soccer football, the English sense of superiority and imperial entitlement was threatened. In the twentieth century, the British Empire declined and eventually fell, but it left a legacy to the world of parliamentary government, common law, and importantly, modern sports. Most of the sports in modern athletic competitions, such as the soccer World Cup, cricket Test matches, and especially the summer Olympic Games, are English in origin, the products of the rationalized, systematized, vibrant, and creative sporting life of the Victorians.

GLOSSARY

FA: Football Association, the governing body of association (soccer) football

GAA: Gaelic Athletic Association

MCC: Marylebone Cricket Club, governing body of international cricket

RFU: Rugby Football Union, the governing body of rugby football

RSPCA: Royal Society for the Prevention of Cruelty to Animals

RYS: Royal Yacht Squadron, prestigious yacht club headquartered on Isle of Wight

W. G.: W. G. Grace, the great cricketer

Ashes: annual cricket match between England and Australia, from 1882

athletics: track-and-field sports, such as running and long jump

bathing machine: seaside dressing-room cabin on wheels, to be rolled into the water

battue shooting: shooters walking in a line towards a covert of game birds

blood sports: sports that involve the maiming or killing of animals

bowler: the cricket player who, with a straight arm, propels the ball, usually on a bounce, towards the batsman

bowls: an outdoor lawn game, in which balls are rolled towards a target

bull-baiting: combat between tethered bull and specially bred fighting dog ("bulldog")

coursing: the pursuit of game, most commonly hares, by greyhounds

covert: covered underbrush haven for game birds

curling: Scottish team sport played on ice

Derby: most prestigious English horse race, run annually at Epson Downs, near London

field sports: hunting, usually on horseback and with dogs; shooting, usually on foot in pursuit of game birds; angling (fishing)

first-class cricket: matches of two innings that are usually played over three or more days, between teams that the MCC ranks as "first class"

fives: an enclosed court sport, similar to modern-day handball

football: called "soccer" in the United States, the game that is governed by the Football Association. Rugby was also called "football," or "rugby football," but by the early-twentieth century, the word "football" was usually dropped, with the game called just "rugby."

game laws: laws that restricted the right to hunt and shoot certain animals

hacking: in mainly rugby football, the kicking of the opponent's shins

Highland Games: traditional Scottish games, that include tossing the caber (log)

hurling: Irish stick-and-ball sport

leaping head: a second pommel added to the sidesaddle in about 1830

Jockey Club: the regulating body of English horseracing

Lord's: cricket field in London that is home to the MCC

Muscular Christianity: a movement linking physical vigor and religious faith

Old Boys: alumni of prestigious public schools and Oxford and Cambridge

pall mall: outdoor lawn game in which balls are hit with mallets towards targets

pedestrianism: walking contests, usually over long distances and sometimes under unusual or bizarre circumstances

prize-fighting: boxing for prizes, usually bare-fisted, without gloves

public house: a tavern licensed to sell alcohol on the premises; nicknamed "pub," it is owned or managed by a publican

public schools: elite historic boarding schools in England and modeled elsewhere

pugilism: boxing and wrestling

Ranji: nickname for eminent Indian cricketer, Prince K. S. Ranjitsinhji

ratting: contest in a pit in which a dog tries to kill as many rats as possible

regatta: boat race, or series of boat races

ride to hounds: foxhunt

rounders: stick-and ball sport, from which American baseball developed

Sabbatarianism: evangelical opposition to all but religious activity on the Sabbath

Test match: international cricket match between England and countries to which the MCC had awarded test status based on the level of skill of their best teams. In the nineteenth century, only Australia and South Africa were awarded Test status.

trudgen: overhand swimming stroke (later, in modified form, known as "Australian crawl")

turnen: German gymnastics

wicket: the three stumps with crosspiece ("bail"), with one wicket at each end of the cricket pitch (the center part of the cricket field)

CHRONOLOGY

1743	Broughton's rules of boxing are issued
1752	rules of cricket are established; later slightly amended
1754	Golf Club of St. Andrews is founded ("Royal and Ancient" later added to name)
1757	Jockey Club is founded
1787	Marylebone Cricket Club (MCC) is founded
1805	first Eton-Harrow cricket match
1811–1820	regency of George, Prince of Wales
1820–1830	reign of King George IV
1826	Braemar Highland Society is founded ("Royal" later added to name)
1829	first Oxford-Cambridge boat race
1830–1837	Reign of King William IV
1831	Game Law establishes a license system for hunting and shooting
	Lord's Day Observance Society is founded, severely restricting sports on Sundays
1835	Parliament makes bull- and bear-baiting illegal
1836	Grand Liverpool (later Grand National) Steeplechase race is established
1837–1901	reign of Queen Victoria
1839	first Henley Regatta boat races
1844	Young Men's Christian Association (YMCA) is founded
1845	Gaming Act makes gambling debts no longer recoverable at law
1849	Parliament makes cockfighting illegal
1853	U.S. defeats England in Royal Yacht Squadron Cup (thereafter America's Cup)

1854–1856	Crimean War: Britain and France against Russia
1857	Thomas Hughes publishes *Tom Brown's School Days* Alpine Club is founded
1860	last significant bare-knuckle prize-fight in England, between Tom Sayers and John Heenan
1861	Salmon Fishery Act forbids the dumping of sewage in waters containing salmon English cricket team travels to Australia for first time
1863	Football Association is founded
1864–1906	W. G. Grace plays first-class cricket
1866	Amateur Athletic Club is founded
1867	Marquess of Queensberry's rules for boxing are published
1868	All-England Croquet Club is founded at Wimbledon ("Lawn Tennis" added to club name in 1877)
1869	Girton College for women founded, as part of Cambridge University
1870	Education Act establishes state elementary schools
1871	Rugby Football Union is formed
1872	Football Association Cup championship is founded Bank Holidays Act creates holidays on four Mondays in the year
1873	County Cricket Championship is founded
1874	Major Wingfield receives patent for *Sphairistike* (renamed "lawn tennis")
1875	Captain Matthew Webb swims the English Channel
1877	first All-England Croquet and Lawn Tennis Club tennis championship for men first Test match (cricket): Australia v. England
1878	Australian cricket team first visits England National Cyclists' Union is founded
1880	Amateur Athletic Association is founded Ground Game Law allows tenants to kill ground animals on their lands National Eisteddfodd Association is founded, to promote Welsh culture
1882	Australia wins cricket Test match in England, starting annual "Ashes" rivalry Amateur Rowing Association is founded
1883	Blackburn Olympic defeats the Old Etonians in the FA Cup final
1884	first All-England Croquet and Lawn Tennis Club tennis championship for women

	National [later "Field"] Sports Protection and Encouragement Assn. founded
1885	Football Association legalizes professionalism
1886	Hockey Association is founded
1888	Football League is formed
1890	"Original English Lady's Cricketers" team plays one season
1891	Humanitarian League is founded
1892	English Lacrosse Association is founded
1893–1920	Prince K. S. Ranjitsinhji plays first-class cricket for Sussex
1895	Badminton Association is founded
	Northern Union (later Rugby League) is founded, allowing professionalism
	British Ladies Football Club plays one season
1896	Olympic Games are revived
1899–1901	Anglo-Boer War

1

English Sports before the Victorians

With industrialization and urbanization rapidly transforming their world, early Victorians sought refuge in nostalgic images of the preindustrial past. Idealized as a tranquil society of happy village life, this romanticized view of a lost world infused English culture in the early- and mid-nineteenth century. From the paintings of John Constable of idyllic rural haystacks and peaceful cathedrals to the German immigrant Karl Marx's idealization in *Das Kapital* of harmonious medieval class relations, the past had a strong hold on people buffeted by too much change. This nostalgia that hardworking stressed Victorians had for traditional village life included a sense that in the preindustrial rural world there had been more time for relaxation, for play, for games. Especially evocative was the popular image of the landscape of rural sports—the village cricket field, the bowling green, the angler's brook. These and other sports were seen as spontaneous, untainted by the market place, and enjoyed by all, qualities lost in the regimented profit-driven Victorian business world.

FIELD SPORTS IN PREINDUSTRIAL ENGLAND: HUNTING, SHOOTING, AND ANGLING

Even with the romanticized distortions filtered out, preindustrial England did in fact enjoy a vibrant sporting culture, although one that was not, as many Victorians imagined, always noncommercial, unregulated, or equalitarian. Sports ranged from many varieties of ball games to equestrian and blood sports involving animals. The most popular elite English sports historically, from the Middle Ages well into the nineteenth century, were the "field sports" of hunting and shooting. Indeed until the 1850s, the word "sport" simply meant field sports, which included also fishing ("angling").[1] In the traditional English usage, hunting usually meant the pursuit on horseback of animal prey, often accompanied with hunting dogs. Shooting was a sport on foot, most commonly to kill game birds, also often with the aid of dogs.

As with many sports, hunting and shooting had utilitarian origins. For the propertied classes, they began as a means of maintaining military preparedness but had by the early-Middle Ages become primarily a source of entertainment. For the poorer classes, the hunting and trapping of animals remained an important means of putting meat on the table, although they suffered increasing restrictions on access to game. The conquering Normans had brought with them in 1066 the hated Forest Laws that reserved certain lands on which only the ruling classes could hunt. These laws continued well into the nineteenth century in the form of game laws that restricted the hunting of deer, wild boar, and later other animals exclusively to the propertied classes. In defiance of these laws, poachers, including the mythical Robin Hood, became folk heroes.

The sports favored by royalty, hunting and shooting (first with bows and later with guns) entertained monarchs from William the Conqueror to Queen Victoria's husband Albert and up to the present royal family. The Stuart Queen Anne in the early-eighteenth century remained throughout her life an avid hunter, even though in her corpulent old age she had to pursue game in a carriage rather than on horseback.[2] The favored prey was deer, but by the late-seventeenth century, overhunted, they became increasingly scarce in the wild. Deer raised in captivity for the hunt had to be carted in and released in hunting grounds, which lessened the thrill of the chase. Deer parks continued on aristocratic estates, for show rather than sport, and as a substitute the hunting of smaller animals became popular. Wild boar had been traditional prey, reserved by the game laws for large landowners, but now pheasants, partridges, and hares were also enthusiastically pursued, and therefore placed under game-law protection. The 1671 Game Law, the first in a series of laws restricting the killing of certain small animals, prevented all freeholders of land-producing income under £100 a year from killing that game, even on their own land. It also forbade the sale of the game (leading to a lucrative black market in game), a law that was expanded in the eighteenth century.

Partridges and pheasants, which had been captured on the ground with nets, were by the early-eighteenth century shot with the new improved muzzle-loading flintlock guns, which were faster loading, lighter, and more accurate than earlier firearms. One of the casualties of the improvement of guns was the old medieval sport of falconry, which involved using trained hawks to kill game birds. Hares—jackrabbits—were less attractive animals, but also became very popular to hunt. They were pursued not just by humans with guns, but also by specially trained greyhounds. In "hare coursing," greyhounds would chase a hare, and the dog that killed the hare was declared the winner. Hare coursing continued as a popular sport well into the twentieth century, when greyhound racing replaced it. Hare coursing was banned in 2002.

As entertaining as it was to hunt hares, the animal that emerged by the early-eighteenth century as the most satisfactory replacement for the vanishing deer was the once scorned lowly fox. Long considered a vermin that should be eliminated, and which, unlike the other popular game was not edible, the crafty speedy fox ironically became a prized object of the hunt. As fox hunts became popular in the eighteenth century, the rituals of the hunt were formalized, with the distinctive costume of red coats and white breeches of the hunters, the pattern of the pursuit, and the entertainments after the hunt. Characteristically a sport for the elites, wealthy landowners usually organized and sponsored the big hunts, often at great expense.

Essential to the success of the fox hunt were the horse and the hound used in pursuit. The breeding of these hunting animals was significantly improved as a result of the intellectual climate of the eighteenth century. Known as the "Age of Enlightenment," it was a time characterized by belief in rationality, order, and progress, when reason and science were applied to the improvement of agriculture and to the scientific breeding of livestock. Horses and dogs for the hunt were also specially bred, to increase their stamina and speed. This breeding was all the more important as the demands on hunting horses as well as their riders became more challenging, with open fields in that age of the "agricultural revolution" enclosed with fences. The horses now not only had to run fast across the countryside, but also had to jump over barriers. Equally if not more important to the hunt were the hounds. In the words of a historian of foxhunting, Raymond Carr, "The speed, the excitements of hunting, and clean killing of a fox depend on a pack with drive, stamina, voice, and nose." Through careful breeding, by the beginning of nineteenth century "a standard, generally admired type of foxhound had emerged."[3]

Aristocratic and gentry women as well as men participated eagerly in the hunts. So also did clergy, with the sporting parson a familiar if often caricatured figure. Usually a single man, whose "dearest action," according to the early-nineteenth-century sports journalist Pierce Egan (1772–1849), "is in the field. Hunting and shooting are the only business of his life." Egan recounts the anecdote about the Duke of Grafton, who was thrown in a ditch during a hunt. A young curate called for him to lie still and jumped with his horse over him and pursued his sport. The Duke, "delighted with an ardour similar to his own," rewarded rather than rebuked the curate. "That man shall have the first good living that falls to my disposal; had he stopped to have taken care of me, I never would have given him any thing."[4]

Certainly the most memorable image of the eighteenth-century sportsmen is that of the fictional Squire Western, in Henry Fielding's 1749 classic comic novel, *Tom Jones*. Squire Western holds most dear "his guns, dogs, and horses." When his beloved daughter Sophia disappears, he goes in search of her but curses that he is missing out on a hunt. "I am lamenting the loss for so fine a morning for hunting. It is confounded hard to lose one of the best scenting days, in all appearance, which hath been this season." Just when he said that, a pack of hounds bark nearby. Forgetting his search for his daughter, he joins the hunt. "The hounds ran very hard, as it is called, and the squire pursued over hedge and ditch, with all his usual vociferation and alacrity, and with all his usual pleasure; nor did the thoughts of Sophia ever once intrude themselves to allay the satisfaction he enjoyed in the chase."[5]

The eighteenth-century lexicographer and curmudgeon Dr. Samuel Johnson (1709–1784) was ostensibly not as enthralled by the sport. Although he reportedly was a good horseman who went on long hunts, he would never admit to enjoying himself. "I have now learned," his friend Hester Lynch Piozzi quoted him as saying, "by hunting, to perceive that it is no diversion at all, nor ever takes a man out of himself for a moment: the dogs have less sagacity than I could have prevailed on myself to suppose; and the gentlemen often call to me not to ride over them. It is very strange, and very melancholy, that the paucity of human pleasure should persuade us ever to call hunting one of them." Despite Johnson's professed scorn for the sport, he was, Piozzi claimed, "proud to be amongst the sportsmen; and I think no praise ever went so close to his heart as when Mr. Hamilton called out one day upon Brighthelmstone Downs, 'Why Johnson rides as well, for aught I see, as the most illiterate fellow in England.'"[6]

Angling was another popular rural sport that, like hunting and shooting, had begun and for many continued as a means of procuring food. Without the fast pace and high intensity of the other field sports, angling had become by the seventeenth century a sporting contest between human skill and fish evasion. As immortalized by Sir Izaak Walton (1593–1683) in his classic *The Compleat Angler*, first published in 1653, fishing could be a refuge in a world in turmoil. A London ironmonger who supported the losing royal side in the English Civil War (1642–1649), Walton retreated to the brook and stream after the victory of Oliver Cromwell's Puritan army over the royalists, and he concentrated on the therapy of fishing. In *The Compleat Angler*, cataloguing the hundreds of kinds of game fish and the art of fishing each, Walton concludes with the admonition to trust in God's providence "and be *quiet*, and go a *Angling*."[7] A seemingly simple and unremarkable book, *The Compleat Angler* had lasting appeal because of Walton's evocation of a world of sport that could be an escape from the stresses of the everyday world, be they the conflicts of the English Civil War or the later stresses of the nineteenth-century industrial capitalism. The Victorians developed competitions, organizations, and regulations for fishing, as with their other sports. Nevertheless, angling remained a symbol of the bucolic preindustrial sporting world. In tribute to this lost world, a stained glass window with the image of Walton was placed in Winchester Cathedral in 1914.

HORSERACING

In contrast to the simplicity and quietude of angling, horseracing was a widely popular spectator sport. This "sport of kings" featured primarily races held in open fields with no gate fee, and therefore all levels of society could attend. Profits were made from the support services, such as the sale of food and drink. The appeal of attending horse races lay in the excitement of the contest, but even more so in the opportunity it provided to gamble. Many sports have attracted gamblers, but few have been as closely associated as horseracing was and is with the wager.

Gamblers want agreed-upon rules for a sport before they wager, and so appropriately horseracing became in the eighteenth century the first sport to be regulated and standardized. The Jockey Club was formed in 1757 at the racetrack in Newmarket, near Cambridge, to resolve disputes and to set the rules for racing at that racetrack. Composed of the racing elites, the Jockey Club was gradually seen as arbitrator of all racing disputes, as it is up to the present day. The Swiss-French traveler César de Saussure in a letter home to his family described the popularity of English horse races in 1728. "At these horse races crowds of people are to be found. . . . Nothing is more diverting than seeing the farmers of the neighbourhood, all well mounted and making considerable wagers, for they take the greatest interest in this amusement." Commenting on the speed of the horses, de Saussure pointed out that "English horses—more especially those used for racing and hunting— are renowned everywhere, and one cannot help admiring them, for they are excellent."[8]

The speed of the horses could be measured all the more precisely by the introduction by the mid-eighteenth century of the stopwatch. As with hunting horses and dogs, the race horses got faster through scientific breeding, usually between English mares and imported Arabian stallions. King Charles II in the late-seventeenth century was responsible for the importation of the first of the Middle-Eastern stallions. A Victorian sports enthusiast praised the Merry Monarch, who "has strong claims to the nation's gratitude. . . . If he offended the nation by his partiality for French mistresses, he also deserved its thanks for his judicious importation of the oriental mares. He cared little for his subjects' liberties, and was suspected to be indifferent to their religion; but he well understood and took a lively interest in horse-flesh."[9] By the end of the eighteenth century, an official registry of pedigrees was created, the General Stud Book, "a kind of Burke's Peerage of breeding which established the genealogical criteria of the Thoroughbred."[10]

Until the mid-eighteenth century, owners tended to ride their own horses in races, which were usually a distance of about four miles. Races then became shorter, about two miles long, for less predictability and better gambling opportunities. The usually portly aristocratic and gentry horse owners could not successfully compete at that distance, so, to better the odds of winning, professional jockeys usually from the lower classes were hired. Although most of the races were local in that age before railroads were developed that could easily transport horses and spectators, by the end of the eighteenth century the now classic English races were established: St Leger at Doncaster Racecourse in Yorkshire in 1776, the Oaks at Epson Downs in Surrey in 1779, and most notably, the Derby, also at Epsom Downs, in 1780.

A mass spectator sport by the late-eighteenth century that attracted rich and poor alike, horseracing had as its most important patron the profligate sports-loving Prince of Wales, who became Prince Regent for his mentally disturbed father, King George III, in 1811, and who succeeded his father as King George IV in 1820. The presence of the prince gave the races an aura of prestige, making them important social as well as sporting events. The prince did not, however, always receive respect and deference at the track. The *New Sporting Magazine* recounted in 1840, long after his death and happily with the virtuous Victoria on the throne, that in 1791 the prince had entered a horse in a race at Newmarket, whose jockey was accused of riding to lose. The Jockey Club refused to allow the jockey to ride again. The prince, in anger at the club and with loyalty to his jockey, refused to enter horses in races for several years.[11] After his pique faded, the Prince of Wales resumed his patronage of the track as racehorse owner and as gambling spectator.

WATER SPORTS: ROWING AND YACHTING

Befitting a nation surrounded by water and blessed with many navigable rivers, water sports were also popular in the eighteenth century. Spectators enthusiastically watched and wagered on rowing races on the Thames River, originally between professional watermen whose job was to ferry people across the river. By about 1800, the elite schools that had access to rivers, such as Eton and Westminster, and then in 1829 the universities of Oxford and Cambridge, began regular races, which became popular events of the sporting life of the early-nineteenth century through the Victorian age and up to the present day. As the dominant world naval power, it was appropriate that England also had an active yachting tradition. Composed of wealthy elites, the Yacht Club was formed in 1815, with the Prince Regent its most important member. When the prince became king, the word "royal" was added to the name (and renamed in 1833 the Royal Yacht Squadron). Reflecting the class attitude of being above the fray, the Yacht Club did not engage at that time in competitive racing. The Thames Yacht Club (later the Royal Thames Yacht Club under the patronage of King William IV in 1830) was therefore formed in 1823 to sponsor races.

LAWN SPORTS: ARCHERY, BOWLING, PALL MALL, QUOITS, AND FIVES

Among the popular land sports, the one with the richest history was archery. Originally military soldiers rather than sportsmen, English archers with their longbows received mythologized fame in the 1346 Battle of Crécy, in the Hundred Years' War against the hated French, who used their less effective crossbows. By the late-seventeenth century, however, gunpowder had replaced the arrow as a military weapon, and archery survived in tamer form as a peaceful sport. As with many other sports in the pre-Victorian age, women as well as men played and competed as archers. In his *Sporting Anecdotes*, Pierce Egan listed women as among the best archers in England, even though he then called archery "a manly, national, and amusing sport."[12]

Like archery, bowling was also a favorite lawn sport for the upper classes. Although today the entertainment of rolling a ball down a lane to knock over pins is primarily an indoors, mechanized sport of ordinary folk, bowling traditionally was played outdoors on the lawns of the landowning classes, with bowling greens as important parts of the estate landscape. The most well-known avid bowler was the hero of the Elizabethan seas, Sir Francis Drake, who, perhaps according to history and not just legend, was in the midst of a bowling game in Plymouth in 1588 when he was informed that the huge Spanish Armada was approaching, threatening the invasion of England. He reportedly finished his game before boarding his ship to lead the attack, the success of which lead to English domination on the seas for many centuries thereafter.

Pall mall, similar to bowling as a popular lawn sport enthusiastically played by the eighteenth-century elites, is no longer played today except as an antiquarian sport. A predecessor of the game of croquet, popularized in the nineteenth century, pall mall was played on an alley of about one-half mile in length, hollowed out in the center, with arches across the ground. The object was for players with mallets to hit wooden balls down the alley, using as few strokes as possible. At the end of the pall mall alley was the hardest target of all, an arch elevated on a pole, through which the ball was to be hit. In late-seventeenth-century London, the newly restored and fun-loving King Charles II delighted in playing the game and had a pall mall lane laid out in St. James Park. As interest in the sport waned by the end of the eighteenth century, the lanes were converted to other uses. The one in St. James Park is now the fashionable avenue known simply as the Pall Mall. Other pall mall lanes were converted to promenades with shops along them—hence the name "mall."

The sport of quoits, akin to modern-day horseshoes, with flat rings of iron or clay pitched at a pole, entertained the landed classes as a lawn sport, and also the working classes as a pub game. Fives was a popular upper-class ball sport. Like modern handball, it was played against a wall, sometimes outdoors and sometimes in enclosed courts, with players hitting a ball against the wall with their hand (the five fingers giving the name to the sport). Sometimes a racket rather than the hand was used, similar to modern racquetball. It was a game praised by Egan as "the finest exercise for the body, and the best relaxation for the mind .... He who takes to playing at Fives is twice young. He feels neither the past nor future 'in the instant.'" He does not worry about "debts, taxes, domestic treason, foreign levy, nothing can touch him further,"[13] which is perhaps a good argument for all sports.

FOOTBALL AND ROUNDERS

In addition to sports played on the expansive lawns of the landed classes, there were endless forms of sports played by the more common folk on the greens and nearby fields of the villages. These sports were diverse and varied from one village to another, played spontaneously and often in conjunction with village fairs, cycles in the agricultural season, and holidays. Football, the predecessor of the game which Americans call "soccer," began with village boys and girls kicking around a ball, which was usually made of straw tied with twine or, to be lighter, of pig's skin or intestines filled with air. A rough and tumble game, it was especially popular on Shrove Tuesday as a means to enjoy excess before the beginning of the austere season of Lent. Even before the early Victorians tried to stamp it out as too violent, the sport of football had an uneasy history. In the fourteenth century, King Edward III tried to ban it as a distraction from the then militarily useful archery. Queen Elizabeth I in the late-sixteenth century forbade the play of what was considered too violent a game within the city of London. Football survived these and later attempts at suppression to become in the late-nineteenth century England's most important export and perhaps the most popular world sport.

Many village sports included a stick used as a bat to hit a ball. Rounders was a popular team ball sport that sports historians (but not American patriots) consider the ancestor of baseball. It is usually played with nine players on a team, on a field laid out with five bases in a pentagon shape. The aim of the sport is for a batter to hit a pitched ball far enough so the batter can round the bases and score. Similar games include stool ball, sevens, and other ball games now just of antiquarian interest.

CRICKET

As enjoyable as the other ball sports were, none equaled the enduring popularity and passionate following of cricket. A village game in the seventeenth century (and perhaps earlier), by the early-eighteenth century it was played across class lines and was nearing the iconic status it would reach in the Victorian age as the very symbol of English national identity. Rejecting the conclusions of many linguists that the word "cricket" comes from the Old Flemish or perhaps the French word for "stick," Victorian sports historians insisted that the game in name and play was purely English. As Horace Hutchinson asserted in 1903, cricket had been played for a long while, "not as an imported invention, but as an aboriginal growth."[14]

Mocked by non-cricketers (who were and are usually non-English) for its many complex rules and procedures, cricket in the eighteenth century evolved to close to its present form. The first organized English team game, it was played on a field of varying sizes between two opposing teams that would alternate in batting and in fielding. In the first written cricket rules drawn up in 1727, the number of players on each team was set at 12. By the nineteenth century the number had changed to 11, giving the nickname of cricket teams as simply "the elevens." The game is long and leisurely, often played over two to three days, reflecting the slower pace of eighteenth-century preindustrial life and continuing as an island of slowness in the modern world of speed and haste. Strange to American baseball fans, there are only two innings in a cricket match, and today, as a means of shortening the length of the game, some games have only one innings (the word is always written in the plural). An innings consists of 10 of the 11 players batting until the last one is out, then alternating with the fielding team.

Until the late-eighteenth century, the batter used a bat that was curved like a hockey stick, and the ball was literally bowled underarm across the ground. Behind both the batter and the bowler were two stumps in the ground, with a stick ("bail") positioned across the top, a construction known as the wicket. The stumps at that time were about one foot high. The goal of the bowler was and is to knock down the wicket, and the batter's aim is to protect the wicket and hopefully to hit the ball far enough to run down to the opposite wicket, which then scores a run. If the batter can run back to the first wicket, two runs are scored, and so back and forth if possible. A batter can reach the opposite wicket simply by reaching the bat out to within the area around the wicket (the "popping crease"), which is why the batter runs with the bat extended. One of the many things that makes the game confusing to non-cricketers is that the batter (the "striker") is paired with a non-striker (or a "runner"), who stands at the opposite wicket and has to run between wickets just as the striker does when the ball is hit. The non-striker does not score runs. If the batter hits the ball in the air beyond the boundary of the playing field, six runs are scored. A hit ball that rolls over the boundary scores four runs. Games usually result in hundreds of runs scored, and the most honored achievement for a batter is to score a "century"—a hundred or more runs in a game.

The area between the bowler and the batter is known as the "pitch," 22 yards in length. In the 1752 *Rules of the Game of Cricket Played at the Artillery Grounds, London*, which became standard for all cricket games, the

Cricket, as played in the artillery ground, London, in 1743.

stumps at each end were raised to 26 inches (and then 28 inches in 1947.) A third stump and a second bail were added in 1777, to make the wicket easier to knock down and therefore to shorten what even in the leisurely eighteenth century was sometimes seen as too long a game. With the stumps raised, the ball was no longer bowled along the ground but more commonly "bowled" in the air, still underarm. The curved bat was no longer so effective, so the now familiar flat straight bat was introduced, with a select group of aristocratic and gentry players resolving in 1771 that "four-and-a-quarter inches shall be the breadth of a bat forthwith."[15] And so it is, to the present day. Also in the late-eighteenth century, a rule was added forbidding the "leg before wicket (L.B.W.)." This rule aims at preventing batters from using their legs, and later was expanded to include any body part, from blocking the ball to keep it from hitting the wicket.

The cricket ball is composed of a cork center and leather covering. Its weight was set in 1809 to between 5.5 and 5.75 ounces and it has never since changed. It is slightly heavier but also slightly smaller than an American baseball. In the late-nineteenth century, an enthusiast for the game mused over the history of cricket measurements and weights, concluding that they were arbitrary, yet perfect. "Bat and ball and wicket seem exactly suited to the game. . . . They serve their purpose as no other measurements would."[16]

Modern sports need not only consistent rules but also an organization to make and enforce those rules. As with the Jockey Club for horseracing, so also in the late-eighteenth century a governing cricket organization was founded. Its beginnings actually came from the selection of a cricket field. In 1787 cricketers from the aristocracy and gentry asked entrepreneur Thomas Lord (1755–1832) to find a field in central London on which to play their matches, a tough task in that London's green spaces were rapidly disappearing with the mushrooming urban expansion. Lord leased land in the district of Marylebone and had it enclosed so that admission fees could be charged for the games. The various clubs that played there joined together in that same year as the Marylebone Cricket Club (MCC). The MCC gradually became by common consensus the de facto regulator of the game and arbitrator of its rules, as it has been almost to the present day. The field on which the MCC played was moved in 1814 to the district of St. John's Woods, under new ownership, but it has always been known simply as "Lord's," and, although headquartered at the St. John's site, the name of the governing organization remained the Marylebone Cricket Club.

The most controversial decision the MCC had to make in those early years, and that which became one of the last major changes in the rules of cricket, concerned the legalization of roundarm bowling. When bowlers first tried that style, they were penalized for "throwing" the ball. After great debate, the MCC changed the rules in 1835 to allow roundarm bowling, but opposition to that style continued into the mid-nineteenth century. As one traditionalist direly forecast in 1846, "If the present system [of throwing] be continued a few years longer, the elegant and scientific game of cricket will decline into a mere exhibition of rough, coarse, horse play."[17] He would have been even more dismayed when in 1864 the MCC allowed overarm bowling, which became the standard form up to the present day. For effective bowling, bowlers take distinctive run-ups to the line over which they cannot cross before releasing the ball, they bowl with a straight arm, and they often bounce the ball on the ground on the way to the batter, a peculiar sight indeed to those who are not familiar with cricket.

Since the time Victoria came to the throne in 1837, cricket has continued with very little change to the present day and is considered the quintessentially English game, representing all that is virtuous and upright about the national character. As the Reverend John Mitford declared in 1833, "Cricket is the pride and the privilege of the Englishman alone. Into this, his noble and favourite amusement, no other people ever pretended to penetrate: a Frenchman or a German would not know which end of a bat they were to hold."[18] Frenchmen, Germans, and many others could not "penetrate" cricket largely because of the complex and often confusing rules. César de Saussure affirmed this in a 1728 letter to his family: "The English are very fond of a game they call cricket. For this purpose they go into a large open field, and knock a small ball about with a piece of wood. I will not attempt to describe this game to you, it is too complicated."[19] Even the great late-Victorian cricket player, K. S. Ranjitsinhji (1872–1933), who played competitive cricket in England for many years, lamented that he had not in his youth in India had a chance to umpire so he could learn the rules of the game, which, he said at the height of his distinguished career, he did not know very well.[20]

Part of the historical myth about cricket is that it was unique as a sport because all classes played together. Waxing eloquently but inaccurately on the merits of cricket, the historian George Trevelyan wrote that "If the French *noblesse* had been capable of playing cricket with their peasants, their chateaux would never have been burnt."[21] Certainly there was class mixing, from royalty to the servant class. The Hanoverian Prince of Wales, Frederick Louis (1707–1751), the oldest son of King George II, was a noted cricketer. Concerned about fitting in with the country his German grandfather and then his father ruled, Frederick Louis had cricket bats sent to Hanover where he was educated. When he came to England, he eagerly played the game, although it is not true, as legend says, that his premature death, before he could ascend the throne, was caused by a blow from a cricket ball on his head. Aristocrats and gentry also enthusiastically played the sport, which was, according to Richard Holt, "The first team-game in which the upper classes were expected to exert themselves without the aid of a horse."[22] They usually did the more interesting work of batting, while using their servants to do the harder job of bowling—hardly a model of equalitarianism in sports.

As cricket became more popular in the eighteenth century, so did its importance as an occasion for gambling. High stakes also increased the desire of each team for skilled players, which led to the practice of paying the best, usually working-class players—hence the beginning of professionalism in cricket. Sports enthusiasts condemned the idea of payment for play then as it is now, with romantics idealistically remembering an imaged earlier day when money was not a factor in sports.

At least traditionalists could draw comfort from the class segregation that was maintained in cricket. By the early-nineteenth century, a two-tiered system of players had developed—the "gentlemen" (amateurs, who were usually from the upper classes) and the "players" (mainly working-class paid professionals). Although they would often play together, or in matches on opposing teams of "Gentlemen vs. Players," a contest first played in 1806, they remained socially distinct. Entering the field through different gates, from different dressing rooms, the gentlemen were called "sir" while the players were called only by their surnames. This distinction between the gentlemen and the players remained until finally abolished in 1962.

Along with the amateur gentlemen and professional players, there was another category of avid cricket players in the preindustrial world—women. Although later Victorian writers described the eighteenth-century games among women with such labels as "curiosities of cricket,"[23] women cricketers (and female participation in sports in general) were not uncommon before the restriction of women's sports in the Victorian age. Often unmarried women would play married women, sometimes for large stakes. Such "Amazonian matches," as Victorian sports historians called them, had almost disappeared by the time Victoria came to the throne, not to be resurrected until the late-nineteenth century.

Schoolboys also played cricket, especially in the elite boarding "public" (meaning, fee-charging) schools. Although sports were not central to school life as they would become in the Victorian age (see Chapter 3), games like cricket were played, and competitions between schools fostered a lively rivalry. The most important of these matches was between Eton and Harrow, two of the oldest and most prestigious of the public schools. Among the players for Harrow in the first match in 1805 was perhaps its most famous student— George Gordon, Lord Byron (1788–1824). Lame from birth by a defective right foot, Lord Byron used sports to prove his manliness. The easiest for him because of his lameness was long-distance swimming, and in his young adult years he delighted in such challenges as replicating the feat of the mythical Greek hero Leander in swimming the Hellespont (today known as the Dardanelles), the straits connecting the Black and Mediterranean Seas. As a boy at Harrow, however, cricket was his game. Although Lord Byron was judged to be a poor player, and because of his lameness had to have someone run for him, the cricket games remained for him a happy memory in what was otherwise a dismal school experience.[24]

BLOOD SPORTS: COCKFIGHTING, BULL-BAITING, AND RATTING

In contrast to cricket, considered the representative of the best of the English character, the even more popular blood "sports" were condemned by later humanitarian critics as the worst of human depravity. The preindustrial world not only tolerated but also openly enjoyed a level of violence and infliction of pain that the Victorians and their successors would find unacceptable for civilized society. César de Saussure observed in 1728 that "There is cruelty and even ferocity in some of the pastimes of the people." He described, for example, the popular sport of throwing sticks or stones at roosters: "A cock is taken and fastened by a long cord to a stake, and for a few pence anyone may throw a short, heavy wooden club at him.... It is even dangerous on those days to go near any one of those places where this diversion is being held; so many clubs are thrown about that you run a risk of receiving one on your head."[25]

Cockfighting, which removed human contestants altogether, was even more popular. From medieval and probably even Anglo-Saxon days, pairs of roosters were put in a pit to fight against each other, with usually large amounts of money wagered on the outcome. A sport of the working classes but also one enjoyed by royalty and nobles, there were cockpits throughout the countryside and the towns, including the one built by the seventeenth-century King Charles I at Birdcage Walk in central London. Just as horses were bred for speed and dogs for hunting, so cocks, in that scientific age, were bred for fighting. As reported in the *Monthly Visitor* in 1802, "Cocks of the game, are yet cherished by divers men for their pleasures, much money being laid on their heads, when they fight in pits, wherein some be costly made for that purpose."[26] There was some objection to cockfighting, as reflected in the engravings of William Hogarth (1697–1764), in which in 1751 he shows the torture of cocks as one of the *Four Stages of Cruelty*, and, in his 1759 engraving *The Cock-Pit*, he satirizes the gambling by all classes as much as he does the cruelty of the contest. Until the early-nineteenth century, however, the pleasure of the

Bull-baiting in the early-nineteenth century.

sight of violence and blood, augmented by the opportunity to gamble, kept cockfighting as a very popular English "sporting" entertainment.

Rivaling cockfighting in popularity, although not as commonplace because more expensive to stage, was the very bloody sport of bull-baiting. Attracting large, often-boisterous crowds, the baiting of bulls usually took place at village fairs or on specially designated sites. A bull would be tied to a pillar by his hind legs and attacked by a specially bred "bulldog," with short legs and large powerful jaws. The dog would try to grab hold of the bull's throat or muzzle, with spectators betting on whether the dog would rip out the bull's throat before the bull kicked the dog to death. In such contests, the bulldogs were so determined that "some of the noble-hearted animals, after receiving repeated gores and infuriated tosses, still tottered up to their punisher, and fell under his feet, where they were almost trampled to death, still, however, endeavouring to clutch their terrible opponent by the jowl."[27] The hero of this sport so captured the national imagination that it became the personification of England itself, in the form of John Bull or just simply as the heavy-jowled, tenacious bulldog.

Sometimes bears were used instead of bulls, but bear-baiting, unlike the popular bull-baiting, essentially ended by the early-nineteenth century. Another animal commonly pitted against dogs was the lowly ubiquitous rat. Rats would be turned loose in a pit, and a dog would pounce on them and attempt to kill as many as possible. Wagers were placed on how many rats a dog could kill within a certain amount of time. The most celebrated ratting dog, indeed an early-nineteenth-century sporting hero, was Billy, who set a record in 1822 for killing 100 rats within twelve minutes. After such a notable performance, "Billy was decorated with a silver collar, and a number of ribband bows, and was led off amidst the applauses of the persons assembled."[28] His reputation continued for many years. Even as late as the 1840s, a proud owner bragged that his rat-killing dog was the "exact image" of Billy.[29]

BOXING

Sporting enthusiasts enjoyed watching (and betting on) fighting contests between humans as well as animals. As one of the oldest sports, pugilism, especially in the form of bare-knuckle boxing, achieved enormous popularity in the eighteenth and early-nineteenth centuries. Originating as a form of combat and conflict resolution, boxing was transformed in the Age of Reason into a relatively controlled sporting contest, and one whose popularity was due in large part to the great sums that could be wagered on the matches. The most common site for boxing matches was the public (i.e. drinking) house. The patrons of many traditional sports, including cockfighting and even cricket matches, publicans would designate areas either within or outside the pub to hold the matches. Large prizes were offered, hence the name of "prize-fighting" for bare-knuckle boxing. The boxers were mostly working-class professionals who, when they retired from the sport, often became publicans themselves.

Until the mid-eighteenth century, the boxing match was essentially a free-for-all, with fighters continuing until unable to get up (sometimes because they died). In 1743, the former boxing champion and entrepreneur Jack Broughton, concerned after a fighter in his arena died because of a fight, set forth rules that were generally accepted and which regulated the sport until after Victoria came to the throne. These rules included no hitting a man when he is down, no hitting below the belt, and a 30-second wait when a boxer is down before he is declared defeated. There were no timed "rounds," and the match would last until one of the boxers was down beyond the time allowed.

Boxing became especially popular in the late-eighteenth and early-nineteenth centuries, during the long wars against revolutionary and then Napoleonic France. Just as cricket represented the moral superiority of the Englishman, so boxing symbolized his toughness and manliness. Frequent contrast was made, as would be for other sports throughout the nineteenth century, with what were described as the feminized French who fought with puny swords rather than their own fists. Such rhetoric was especially important as a morale booster after Napoleon defeated the English and their allies at Austerlitz (although not at sea at Trafalgar) in 1805 and established domination over the whole continent. When the author of an 1806 article in the *Weekly Entertainer* recommended pugilism "to all ranks," the words must have resonated strongly in that scary time. Pugilism is, the author said, a "manly exercise. . . . Nothing contributes more to brace the sinews, open the chest, and to impart a firm and vigorous tone to the whole body." Importantly, as a means of defense, "it can be an excellent shield to a weak man against casual and vulgar aggression."[30]

Boxing matches also provided an escape from the troubling war news. Even when Napoleon's forces were positioned on the coast preparing for invasion, people from all social classes flocked to highly publicized boxing matches. Boxing champions received the acclaim evocative of the Olympic victors in ancient Greece, often with more public attention than military heroes. Fanning the flames of popular enthusiasm for boxing, Egan wrote extensively on the sport for the *Weekly Dispatch* and in 1812 began a series of volumes simply entitled *Boxiana*. In 1823 he started his own extremely popular sporting journal, *Pierce Egan's Life in London and Sporting Guide*, which included lively accounts of the sporting people as well as events.

In his preface to the first volume of *Boxiana*, Egan, an ardent defender of the sport until he was later disillusioned by the corruption, declared that this work would have no interest to those "who prefer *effeminacy* to hardihood— *assumed refinement* to rough Nature—and to whom a *shower of rain* can terrify their polite frames suffering from the unruly elements." *Boxiana* is mainly composed of biographical accounts of great boxers, whom Egan elevated to almost mythical status. One of the stars was the Jewish boxer,

Daniel Mendoza (1764–1836), whom Egan described in 1789 as "one of the most elegant and scientific Pugilists in the whole race of Boxers .... The name of MENDOZA has been resounded from one part of the kingdom to the other ... the acknowledged pride of his own particular persuasion, and who, so far interested the *Christian*, that, in spite of his prejudices, he was compelled to exclaim—'MENDOZA *was a pugilist of no ordinary merit!'* "[31] The radical journalist Francis Place (1771–1854), discussing the terrible treatment of Jews in early-nineteenth-century England, suggested that the success of Mendoza and his efforts to teach other young Jews the art of boxing caused Jews to be treated with new respect. "It was no longer safe to insult a Jew unless he was an old man and alone.... But even if the Jews were unable to defend themselves, the few who would [now] be disposed to insult them merely because they are Jews, would be in danger of chastisement from the passers-by and of punishment from the police."[32]

Tom Cribb (1781–1848) was another of early-nineteenth century boxing stars, who is best known for his much published matches against the American former slave, Tom Molineaux. Born on a plantation in South Carolina, Molineaux is said to have won his freedom through boxing. In 1809 he went to England to box and got a match with the great Cribb in 1810. *The Sporting Magazine* reported on the great interest the fight aroused. "Whether this arose from the *nature* of the combatants, from the immense sums pending on the issue of the battle, or from the anticipation of an arduous struggle for victory, I cannot say." Molineaux's race was as much of interest as Mendoza's religion was. It was supposed that "the African race were not endowed with such muscular powers as John Bull. In Molineaux, however, this general defect was amply supplied.... What alarmed the natives most was, the consideration that an African or a *tawney Moor*, was looking forward to the championship of England."[33] The "natives" need not have worried, because Cribb defeated Molineaux, although with questionable judging, and Cribb again scored a victory in a rematch the following year.

Despite the enthusiastic following of such dramatic matches, boxing by the 1820s declined as a major English sport because much of the upper class withdrew their support. There was concern about the brutality of bare-knuckle fights, but the suggestion that boxers wear padded gloves was seen as making the sport too boring. Supporters were unable to rid the game of the corruptions that gambling produced. It is hard to enjoy or bet on a match that one suspects is fixed. Wealthy boxing enthusiasts tried to clean up the sport by establishing the Pugilistic Club in 1814–1815, but it failed to do so. A crushing blow to the sport came in 1824 when a judicial decision ruled against bare-knuckle boxing because it "indulged the propensities of the vicious and encouraged gamblers."[34] The sport continued into the Victorian age, but usually as an underground secretive entertainment. It was not until well into the nineteenth century, with the development of amateurism in the sport and with new rules and practices aimed at making the sport safer and less corrupt, that boxing became popular again with mainstream Victorians.

PEDESTRIANISM

Like boxing, pedestrianism was a popular sport in the late-eighteenth and early-nineteenth centuries but which lost its appeal to most Victorians. This sport involved running and more commonly walking ("fair toe to heel") contests, but it was quite different from the modern "athletics," to use the Victorian term for the track-and-field sports that emerged in the 1850s. Pedestrian contests usually involved long-distance events, arranged ad hoc based on wagers on how much distance could be covered in a certain amount of time or days. The sport probably began with aristocrats wagering how fast their footmen could reach a certain destination. Betting against each other, the nobles began hiring footmen who were fast runners. The sport became popular with the working classes when publicans began sponsoring pedestrian contests, which drew large crowds who would also eat and drink at their pubs. As with most preindustrial (and later) sports, large sums were wagered on the outcome. As *The Sporting Magazine* reported in 1822, at a race track in Newcastle-upon-Tyne, a pedestrian attempted to walk 90 miles in 24 successive hours. "There was an immense concourse of people, amounting to no less than 14,000 or 15,000, who loudly cheered him, and raised a subscription for him." At other events, a man undertook to run 18 miles within two hours and another to walk 40 miles in eight hours. At one event a pedestrian successfully bet 10 guineas that he could go 5 miles in 28 minutes, "which is one of the greatest performances on record."[35]

Although most pedestrians were from the working classes, using their strength and endurance to make money, some noted competitors were from the gentry and aristocracy. The sport for them was a way of maintaining and showing their physical prowess (although they were probably glad also for the prize money). Robert Barclay Allardyce (1779–1854), better known as Captain Barclay, was one of the great pedestrian sporting heroes. A wealthy gentleman living in the Scottish Highlands, he dedicated himself, as his great admirer Pierce Egan said, to "the art of agriculture as the serious business of his life; and the manly sports as his amusement." Delighting in pedestrian contests (with wagered profits), he made such notable achievements as walking in 1789 70 miles in 14 hours; 64 miles in 12 hours, including time for refreshment; and in 1801 he bet he could walk 90 miles in 21.5 hours. He finished early. His most notable achievement was in 1808 to walk 1,000 miles in 1,000 hours, a record which many tried but few succeeded in emulating.

To achieve such pedestrian feats, Captain Barclay developed a rigorous training method that included diet as well as exercise. As Egan described it, Barclay would rise at five in the morning, run a half-mile at top speed uphill, then walk six miles at a moderate pace. He would then have a breakfast of "mutton or steak, underdone, and stale bread and old beer." After breakfast, he would walk for six miles, nap naked for one half-hour, and then walk four miles. His dinner was the same as breakfast. He would conclude his daily exercise by running at top speed for a half-mile, then walk six miles. As tribute to

Barclay's athletic life, Egan dedicated *Boxiana* to him, "as a LOVER AND PATRON OF THOSE SPORTS that tend to invigorate the human frame, and inculcate those principles of generosity and heroism, by which the inhabitants of the English Nation are so eminently distinguished above every other country."[36]

Captain Horatio Ross (1801–1886) was another notable gentleman-sportsman, who also lived in the fitness-inducing Scottish Highlands. Named after his famous godfather, Lord Horatio Nelson, Ross made his reputation throughout Britain especially in the 1820s for his skill as a riflemen, a horseman, and, most notably, as a pedestrian. Although without the rigorous regimen of Barclay, Ross would maintain his fitness by walking 8 and usually 12 miles a day, no matter what the weather.[37]

Race between elderly fat man and man with jockey on back.

Pedestrianism did not continue as a mainstream sport into the Victorian age because increasingly contests did not follow the pure display of athletic achievement as that of Captains Barclay and Ross. Instead, to attract easily bored (wagering) spectators, events became sensational and bizarre. Bets were placed on who could run fastest with wheelbarrows, or backwards on stilts, or carrying a jockey on their backs. By the time Victoria came to the throne in 1837, pedestrianism had become more a circus act than a physical sport, and it was pushed to the margins of the English sporting world.

SPORTS IN POLITICS IN PREINDUSTRIAL ENGLAND

Sports were diverse and popular among all social classes in preindustrial England. Perhaps the best evidence of the importance of sports was their centrality in the seventeenth-century conflicts between the Royalist supporters of the Stuart kings and the Puritan-dominated Parliament. The Puritans, emerging in the sixteenth century in opposition to the Anglo-Catholic compromise that was the Elizabethan Church of England, focused on sinful actions that led one from the Godly Path. Included in their condemnations of what they considered sins were not just sex but also drinking, gambling, and secular distractions other than what was necessary to earn a living, especially when those distractions were on the Sabbath. They therefore targeted popular amusements and sports as barriers to salvation.

When the Scottish Stuart King James I came to the English throne in 1603, the high hopes that Puritans had for reforms were dashed. Converting from the Calvinistic Presbyterianism of his homeland to Anglicanism, King James responded to the Puritan opposition by issuing a *Declaration of Sports* (more commonly known as the *Book of Sports*) in 1618. In the *Declaration*, King James voiced concern that if there were no Sunday recreations after church, people "will be restless and will be tempted to convert to Catholicism." He also made the often repeated argument for sports, then and thereafter, that they had the military value of keeping men fit for war. Moreover, if there were no healthful recreations, people would turn to "filthy tippling and drunkenness." Most dangerously, the lack of recreation "breeds a number of idle and discontented speeches in their ale-houses." He therefore decreed that on the Sabbath, "after the end of divine service our good people be not disturbed, letted, or discouraged from any lawful recreation, such as dancing, either men or women; archery for men, leaping, vaulting, or any other such harmless recreation, nor from having of May-games, Whitsun-ales, and Morris-dances; and the setting up of May-poles and other sports therewith used." Prohibited on Sunday, however, were the blood sports of bull- and bear-baiting, although not explicitly cockfighting, "and at all times in the meaner sort of people by law prohibited, bowling." Those who did not attend Sunday services were forbidden all forms of Sunday sports and recreation.[38]

King James ordered the *Declaration of Sport* to be read from all church pulpits, but he then withdrew the order in the face of fierce opposition. His son and successor, King Charles I, was more rigid and insisted in 1633 that the declaration be read. This, and of course other weighty issues such as taxation, led to the outbreak in 1642 of the English Civil War between the royalists and the parliamentarians, resulting in the defeat and execution of the king in 1649. The victorious Puritans established the New Jerusalem in the form first of a parliamentary Commonwealth, and then, in the face of disintegrating chaos, a Puritan dictatorship with the military hero Oliver Cromwell as Lord Protector. Many sports were abolished, including cockfighting, bull- and bear-baiting, horseracing, and of course "any 'Game, Sport, of Pastime whatsoever' on the Sabbath." As with most prohibitions, these orders were not always followed, and when bear-baiting, for example, continued, the Puritan military parliamentarian Colonel Pride in 1656 ordered all the bears in the main bear garden in London to be shot to death, and the attack dogs shipped to Jamaica.[39]

Certainly a large part of the exuberance that accompanied the 1660 restoration of the monarchy in the person of the merry King Charles II was the restoration and expansion of the traditional English sporting life. Parliament was concerned, however, about controlling excessive gambling and passed the 1664 Gambling Act, limiting stakes to £100, an act that, like the restrictions on sports under Cromwell, was often ignored. After the "Glorious Revolution" of 1688 established parliamentary supremacy, dominated by the landed classes, Parliament used its power to further the interests of its own class. These interests included very much their sports, especially their field sports, which the landowners protected through such acts as the extension of the game laws. The eighteenth century was a golden age for the privileged classes to enjoy their hunting and shooting, sporting pleasures which were memorialized in the art of the period, such as the paintings of George Stubbs (1724–1806) and, in the early-nineteenth century, Henry Alken (1785–1851).

NEW SPORTING PRESS IN THE LATE-EIGHTEENTH AND EARLY-NINETEENTH CENTURIES

As a reflection of the keen interest in sports in the late-eighteenth and early-nineteenth centuries, there emerged a new sporting press. Stories about sports were now included in the regular newspapers and journals, and specialized periodicals devoted entirely to sports were founded. The first of these specialized periodicals was *The Sporting Magazine*, founded in 1792 as a shilling monthly. Other sporting journals included *Bell's Weekly Messenger* (f. 1796) and *The Weekly Dispatch* (f. 1801), best known for contributions by Pierce Egan. Even such periodicals as the staid *Times* and *Blackwood's Edinburgh Magazine* began, by the early-nineteenth century, to carry news about sports.

The new sporting press published sporting calendars, rules of the games, biographies of sports stars, and news of current sporting events. Continuing the pattern set by the *Sporting Magazine* of treating sports comprehensively, the *Annals of Sporting and Fancy Gazette*, published from 1822 to 1828, said in its first issue that it would "deal with the Amusements, the Pursuits, the Enjoyments of the MAN OF PLEASURE, in the most extensive sense of that phrase." That did not include frivolities, but rather "the SPORTS OF THE FIELD, in all their boundless and healthful variety, and RURAL AMUSE-MENTS, whatever shape or denomination they may take . . . HUNTING, SHOOTING, and angling, with the collateral and necessary information upon the best methods of training of the HORSE and the DOG." It would not only feature rural sports. "The populous *City* has its SPORTS, as well as the plain, the valley, the Country; and the stream. We shall trace life in *London*, as well as life in the Country; and it is odds but we shall bag as much game in both."[40]

In addition to the periodicals, many books on sports were also published. The upper-class literate readers of this literature, who engaged in and spectated at sporting contests, became known by the late-eighteenth century as "the Fancy." The term originally came to mean anyone attached to a particular amusement, but it increasingly referred to sports enthusiasts, and, as a marker of the importance of sports, signified the "in" set.[41] It was the Fancy, as well as the sports-loving lower classes, who would find their cozy world of traditional sports transformed by the new economic and social forces that would shape England in the nineteenth-century Victorian age.

2

The Remaking of Sporting Cultures
in Early-Victorian England

When the fresh young Queen Victoria came to the throne in 1837, succeeding her reprobate uncles George IV and William IV, she presided over a nation in transition from a rural agricultural society to an urban industrial world. The first country to industrialize, Britain in the late-eighteenth century, with its large network of domestic and international markets, needed to find a way to produce goods faster. More efficient weaving and spinning machines were developed, but the significant breakthrough came in 1769 when the Scottish engineer James Watt invented a new source of power in the form of a more efficient steam engine.

This new machine transformed not only the technique but also the organization of manufacturing, at first primarily of the exportable textile goods. Traditionally cloth had been produced in rural cottages, in what was called the "putting out" system. When the steam engine was developed and attached to more efficient spinning wheels and weaving machines, the resulting machinery was too expensive to be housed in individual cottages. Centralized work sites known as "factories" were established, and workers then left their cottages to go out to work.

There was a ready supply of workers for the new factories because of the improvements in agriculture in the eighteenth century. This "agricultural revolution," which included the enclosure of large plots of land that could be cultivated more efficiently, and also the application of scientific principles to agriculture and the breeding of farm animals, meant that fewer farm workers could feed more people. The surplus labor flocked to the new factories for work. As early as 1770, the poet and playwright Oliver Goldsmith, in his poem "The Deserted Village," lamented the decline of the traditional rural world. He idealized traditional village life as a society that included time for leisure and play, and sporting fun: "How often have I blessed the coming day, / When toil remitting lent its turn to play." Such times, he mourned, are no more: "Thy sports are fled, and all thy charms withdrawn."[1]

Rural life and sports of course continued well beyond the beginning of industrialization, into the nineteenth century and in many parts of England throughout the Victorian age. The process of industrialization was irregular and partial, affecting mainly the areas of the north, where the supplies of coal to fuel the steam machines and iron to make the machines were most abundant. Towns near these factories, such as Manchester, Birmingham, and Newcastle, mushroomed into sprawling industrial cities, while large areas of the south, where such rural sports as hunting, shooting, and cricket flourished, were largely untouched. The exception was the capital, London, in south-central England. Although not a site of large factories but with small manufacturing as well as the financial services demanded by the new industrial economy, London dramatically expanded from a population of about 650,000 in 1750 to almost 2,000,000 by the time of Victoria's accession to the throne. Despite the rapid expansion of London and the industrial northern cities, it was not until 1851 that the census showed that more people in Britain lived in urban areas (defined as cities with populations larger than 100,000 inhabitants) than in rural towns and in the countryside.

Probably the greatest impact of industrialization on the population of England, south as well as north, was from the revolution in transportation, with the invention of the railroad. In the 1820s, imaginative engineers developed the idea to use, in place of mules and horses, steam-engine-powered locomotives to pull transport carts on rails, giving birth to the railroad. Railway tracks began rapidly spreading across England and Scotland, covering 1,775 miles in 1841; 6,266 in 1851; and 9,446 in 1861, with similar increases throughout the nineteenth-century.[2]

THE DECLINE OF SPORTS IN EARLY-VICTORIAN ENGLAND

The railways and other aspects of this transportation revolution had dramatic effects on sports in Victorian England. Even before the expansion of the railways, however, sports were transformed in significant ways in the early industrial age. Urbanization meant a significant loss of green space for spontaneous games. Sports, at least for the working classes, were relegated to the streets, which became, in the words of Peter Bailey, "the new commons of the industrial poor."[3] Ball games and other working-class sports continued but in a much more curtailed way. Even if they had had more space, urban workers did not have the time for play. The hours of factory workers, unlike those of farm workers, were regimented, based on an artificial clock and calendar rather than seasonal rhythms. The hours of work were long, up to 12 or more hours a day, not just, as with agricultural workers in the planting and harvesting seasons, but throughout the year.

With scant free time, working men tended to retreat to the interior space of the public house (the "pub"), which, in that age of social dislocation, was "a centre of warmth, light and sociability . . . a haven from the filth and meanness of inadequate and congested housing."[4] There they would find recreation and escape, not only in drinking but also in such pub games as darts and snooker, which could be played even at night. Working-class women had even less opportunity for play. Young women worked the same hours in the factories as men, but they had more family responsibilities. Married women who did not have jobs outside the home found their work load increased by the need to supplement the meager family income by such domestic work as taking in laundry and boarders. The easy access that working-class women had to sports in preindustrial England was now gone. Not uncommonly, some women, usually young and unmarried, did continue to participate in sports, such as wrestling and footraces, but they were seen as anomalies, and the main appeal of such contests to spectators was "salacious."[5]

The newly wealthy industrial middle-class men—the entrepreneurs, factory owners or managers, merchants, financiers—with more control over time and resources and, through the railways, with more access to green space, nevertheless also lost the easy, spontaneous access to outdoor sports of the preindustrial age. Like their workers, they did not have the leisure time for play, confined as they were in the early-Victorian age by a strict, if self-imposed, industrial work regimen.

Women from the middle classes, who had the time and resources, did not participate in sports because of the change in their status and role in Victorian society. As traditionally female domestic work such as cloth making and beer brewing was moved from the home to the outside world of factories, middle-class women, without the economic need to earn money, remained at home. The domestic world was now seen as "woman's sphere," even as the public world of work and government was the "man's sphere." Middle-class women in the home, commonly with servants for maintenance and childcare work, took on a new role, previously associated with aristocratic women, of "lady," and were idealized as "angels in the house," guardians of those virtues lost in the outside dog-eat-dog world of industrial capitalism. Reflecting this polarization of sexual spheres, the concept of gender personalities similarly became sharply differentiated. The new Victorian sexual ideology portrayed men as competitive, aggressive, and self-focused, qualities necessary for success in the new economic world, while middle-class "ladies" were cooperative, submissive, and self-sacrificing. Participation in the physical competitive world of sports, therefore, would have been antithetical to the concept of the "true woman" in early-Victorian England. Aristocratic women, exempt from the sanctions of bourgeois ladyhood, continued their participation especially in field sports, but to a much lesser degree than they had in the pre-Victorian age.

UTILITARIAN AND EVANGELICAL CONDEMNATION OF SPORTS

Beyond the tremendous economic changes of industrialization and urbanization, probably the greatest force shaping the sporting life in early-Victorian England was in the realm of ideas. Two dominant ideologies—utilitarianism and evangelicalism—emerged in the late-eighteenth century in congruence with industrial society and shaped an ethic that we know simply as "Victorianism." Seemingly quite opposing belief systems, utilitarianism and evangelicalism interestingly reinforced each other in producing a coherent "Victorian" value system.

Utilitarianism was a product of the Age of Enlightenment, the Age of Reason. Founded by Jeremy Bentham (1748–1832), it is a philosophy of ethics based on the belief that what is useful in promoting happiness is good. The greatest good is happiness for the greatest number of people. A seemingly hedonistic philosophy, utilitarianism ironically advocated a strict moral code of self-control. Hard work rather than play, thrift rather than extravagance, reason rather than passion, self-denial rather than self-gratification, all combine to produce happiness in the distant future. Utilitarians, in early-Victorian England, were therefore hostile toward sports as a waste of time and energy that could be put to better use in work. Sports were an unnecessary distraction, that could lead to loss of self-control through gambling and drinking that often accompanied the traditional sporting life. Sports tended to release dangerous passions that subverted the utilitarian model of the useful rational person. This utilitarian code of self-control was readily embraced by the new industrial middle classes, who wanted disciplined, hardworking employees in their factories, even as they disciplined themselves for their challenging economic tasks.

These utilitarian values recast in religious terms formed the core of the Evangelical moral code. Evangelicalism was a religious movement founded in the mid-eighteenth century by the Anglican clergyman John Wesley (1703–1791). After a conversion experience, Wesley came to see the rational, easygoing Anglicanism of his time as a false way and instead insisted that people have to recognize and eliminate their sins and accept their dependence on Jesus for salvation. Feeling compelled to spread this message of sin and salvation, Wesley found that the church establishment did not accept his emotional evangelicalism, and so he was denied access to Anglican pulpits. He began preaching his "New Method" outdoors to the agricultural workers in the fields and to industrial workers in the cities. After Wesley's death, the movement officially broke with the Church of England and formed the new dissenter sect of Methodism.

Methodism was primarily a working-class religion, but the evangelical message filtered upwards, readily adopted by many of the rich and powerful who sought more from their church than just deistic rationality and moral relativism. Staying within the Church of England for social and political reasons, the wealthy classes formed an energetic and influential branch of the Church known as "Anglican evangelicalism." As with utilitarianism, evangelicalism permeated early-Victorian English society. In 1787, Evangelicals were able to easily convince the moralistic King George III to issue a "Royal Proclamation for the Encouragement of Piety and Virtue, and for the Preventing and

Punishing of Vice, Profaneness and Immorality," and in 1802 they formed the Society for the Suppression of Vice to enforce the proclamation. Getting no support from George III's heir, the notorious George IV, or from his younger brother and successor, William IV, the society found a more congenial and supportive atmosphere with the ascension of the earnest young Victoria.

Although the evangelicals saw sin where the utilitarians saw waste and uselessness, they allied together in combating gambling, drinking, sexual deviance, and other activities that many had called pleasures. Sports, if not a waste of time, were certainly conducive to sin. A distraction from religious concerns, sports focused on the body rather than the soul, on winning games rather than salvation. Sports could lead to rowdy behavior, or simply the congregation of crowds, which frightened evangelicals, utilitarians, and most people of property, whose memories of the French Revolution were still vivid. The evangelicals, like their Puritan forerunners, waged their fiercest campaign against sports that violated the sanctity of the Sabbath, and for that cause they engineered through Parliament the Lord's Day Observance Act in 1780, which banned on Sunday all entertainments, a ban which remained in effect until the late-nineteenth century.

ABOLITION OF BULL-BAITING AND COCKFIGHTING, BUT NOT RATTING

Lest they be considered only killjoys, Evangelicals were also strongly humanitarian. Working with the secular humanitarians who were inspired by Enlightenment values, they scored a major achievement with the abolition of the British slave trade in 1807, and, in 1833, the abolition of slavery in the British Empire. Much of their humanitarian energy, however, was not directed to the alleviation of suffering of humans but rather of animals. It was their campaigns against blood sports that most directly attacked the traditional sporting culture in the early-nineteenth century. In this cause, utilitarians, who extended their concept of happiness to animals, joined them. As Bentham argued, the greatest good for the greatest number should include animals. "The question is not, Can they reason? nor, Can they talk? but, Can they Suffer? Why should the law refuse its protection to any sensitive being?"[6] It was not, however, the rational arguments of utilitarians but rather the passionate emotional commitment of evangelicals to the protection of animals that fueled and spearheaded the efforts to abolish blood sports, and, of particular concern, cockfighting and bull-baiting, which Wesley's disciple George Whitfield called "the devil's entertainments."[7] (Some cynical but perhaps realistic critics, then and now, have suggested that the concern of the reformers was not so much with the welfare of the animals but rather revulsion with the pleasure the spectators got in watching the animal contests.)

In support of the crusade against bull-baiting, even such publications as *The Sporting Magazine* offered their editorial approval. Opposing what they saw as unfair contests involving tethered animals, the magazine in 1822 was uneasy about legislating morals, "but in cases of wanton cruelty to [animals], the line of mere moral demarcation is past, an act of aggression is committed, necessarily and properly within the cognizance and vengeance of the law." It did acknowledge that, in those still-anxious post-French Revolutionary days, any proposed reform was suspect. "There is even a kind of jealousy and suspicion of latent *jacobinism* in the advocacy of the rights of animals, and the relative duties of men."[8] These reforms, however, were associated with the elimination of possibly dangerous crowds at such sporting events and were clearly identified as promoted by the non-revolutionary middle classes, evangelical and/or utilitarian.

The lead that the middle classes, evangelical and utilitarian, took in opposition to blood sports has been commonly seen by historians as a means for the bourgeois to assert their role as social and moral leaders, supplanting the seemingly degenerate blood-sports-loving aristocracy. This middle-class reforming impulse was translated into greater political power when the 1832 Reform Act extended the parliamentary franchise to non-landed property owners. The campaign to abolish blood sports, however, was not just a middle-class movement, but was also strongly supported by the artisan leaders of the working classes, who felt that workers should concentrate on self-improvement rather than dissipate their energies watching or even playing sports, and especially the bloody sports involving cruelty to animals.

The first bill introduced into Parliament attacking blood sports was against bull-baiting, in 1800. The bill was unsuccessful, as were the many others introduced in the next 35 years, but it did spark a lively contentious public discussion about the morality of the animal contests. A main argument in support of the sport was the laissez-faire concern that the government not interfere with private life and individual rights, or, as the *Imperial Magazine* retorted sarcastically, "the right to inflict the most wanton cruelties upon useful and defenceless animals."[9] The arguments in support of bull-baiting also drew on tradition, which had strong appeal to many cultural romantics, who evoked wistfully the rural pleasures of the preindustrial world. Defenders appealed to a sense of Englishness. William Windham, a member of Parliament during these debates, argued that blood sports were uniquely English, and he particularly opposed the abolition of bull-baiting, because "bull dogs give character to the country," and symbolize its strengths.[10] Suggesting a linkage of two unlikely forces in support of a ban, he condemned the Methodists "who wish to banish all sports and joy from the people in order that their minds may be more prepared for the reception of their fanatical doctrines," and the revolutionary Jacobins, "who also wished to give a character of seriousness and gravity to the people, that their attention might be easier turned to their political theories."[11]

In counterattack, the arguments against bull-baiting appealed not only to moral sensibilities for the sufferings of animals, but also to the self-identified sense of English fairness. For tethered animals to be attacked by ferocious dogs was seen as an unfair contest, as not "sporting" and definitely not English. For example, *The Sporting Magazine* decried that "all those places in the country notorious for the barbarous diversion of bull-baiting, still appear to pursue the practice with an enthusiastic eagerness, more characteristic of Asiatic Turks or Tartars, than of the people so long shone upon by the glorious sun of intelligence and humanity." Ignoring (or perhaps not) aristocratic participation as gambling spectators, the writer said that bull-baiting meetings were "frequented by the most abandoned and profligate of the human race, the refuse and the off-scouring of this vast city."[12] Another way to put down the sport was to associate it, as did Hoary Frost in his mid-Victorian history of English sports, with the hated Catholic reign of the sixteenth-century Tudor Queen Mary, forever known in England as "Bloody Mary" for her fervent persecution of Protestants. Tapping into the passionate anti-Catholicism of the 1850s, Frost said that during Mary's rule, bull-baiting was "exceedingly popular; but such like cruelties were entirely consistent with that queen's reign."[13]

A leading animal rights activist, the English-educated Irish landowner Richard Martin ("Humanity Dick") (1754–1834) helped form in 1824 the Society for the Prevention of Cruelty to Animals (prefaced by the appellation "Royal" when Queen Victoria gave her support to the Society in 1840—hence the RSPCA) to work for the better protection of animals. It was not until the year after Martin's death that his goal was reached of banning bull-baiting, when in 1835 Parliament made it illegal to keep any place for the fighting or baiting of any animal, wild or domestic. This ban included not only the almost extinct bear-baiting but also the popular dog fighting. Because of the size of bulls and bears, the ban against baiting was easy to enforce, and those contests essentially disappeared in Victorian England, in contrast to the more elusive dog fighting, which continues underground to the present day. Although the national symbol of the tenacious bulldog remained, the dog itself, without a sporting function, was crossbred with pug dogs to create a domestic pet, pacifistic rather than with the temperament of its fighting ancestor.

Cockfighting, not covered by the 1835 act, was more difficult to combat. In addition to the usual arguments of tradition and individual rights, defenders argued that cockfights were "fair," in that there were two evenly matched roosters against each other. *The Sporting Magazine*, so opposed to bull-baiting and other blood sports which they felt were immoral and unjust, said cockfighting was more morally ambiguous. It therefore printed an article in strong support of cockfighting, as "one of those rural sports which our ancestors have handed down to us, and which we are legitimately entitled to enjoy . . . . The display of the courage of the noble, the gallant cock, must surely tend to keep alive the ancient John Bull Spirit, which I lament to see is sinking fast into dandyism and insignificance."[14]

Despite such patriotic arguments, cockfighting was declared illegal in 1849. To enforce this act and the other protections against cruelty to animals, the new metropolitan police forces, founded by Sir Robert Peel in London in 1829 and later in other metropolitan areas, were marshaled, alerted to violations by the ever-vigilant RSPCA. Cockfighting was, however, often hard to detect. Matches could be held secretly in the more remote country areas (to which the new railways gave access even to the poorer classes) as well as in the back streets of the cities. Cockfighting continued covertly throughout the Victorian age and well into the twentieth and probably twenty-first centuries.

There was one traditional sport of animal combat, particularly suited to urban life, which evoked hardly a whimper of protest—"ratting"—dogs pitted against rats. When the House of Lords appointed a commission to visit rat pits to determine the extent of cruelty in ratting, critics treated it as a joke.[15] Unmolested by the law, ratting continued as a popular form of gambling-sporting entertainment for the urban poor. In his 1840s pioneer survey of life of the working classes in London, published in the *Morning Chronicle* and later in book form as *London Labour and the London Poor*, the journalist Henry Mayhew gave a description of ratting in the mid-century: "Considering the immense number of rats which form an article of commerce with many of the lower orders, whose business it is to keep them for the purpose of rat matches, I thought it necessary, for the full elucidation of my subject, to visit the well-known public-house in London, where, on a certain night in the week, a pit is built up, and regular rat-killing matches take place." He observed that the sport was especially entertaining because sometimes, when the dog tried to bite the prey, the rats "curled round in his mouth and fastened on his nose, so that he had to carry them as a cat does its kittens."[16] Ratting had an advantage over other sports involving animals because of the easy availability and cheapness of rats in the slum-ridden Victorian cities. The sport was not so useful, however, in ridding the cities of the disagreeable rodent because many entrepreneurs, responding to the popularity of the rat contests, had a booming business raising rats to supply the gaming needs.

REPRESSION OF STREET SPORTS

Another traditional sport involving animals that bothered reformers was bull running, in which townspeople with sticks would chase bulls down the street for the fun of the chase. By the Victorian age, this sport survived in England only in a few areas, most notably in the Lincolnshire town of Stamford, as part of an annual early-November festival. So many money-spending visitors came to Stamford to see the running that the local authorities resisted efforts at abolition. Reformers, who saw this sport as cruelty to bulls and therefore illegal under the 1835 act protecting bulls, were nevertheless unable to get the sport abolished by direct legal action. They therefore played on its ambiguous legal status by requiring a large police force to monitor the running, the expense of which so burdened the ratepayers that they agreed to cease the sport. The Victorians, always eager to assert superiority over other countries, could now claim they were more civilized and humane than the Spanish, who have continued not just bull fighting but also bull running up to the present day.

Reformers and most people of property tended to oppose not just sports involving animals but all forms of sports played on the only accessible space available to the urban poor, the streets. It did not matter that animals were not involved. It was rather the rowdiness and perceived potential for violence that disturbed the champions of law and order. The street sports, usually spontaneous and varied from street to street, much less town to town, were considered distractions from higher spiritual and utilitarian activities. The most popular of these sports was the surviving village game of football, which involved simply kicking a ball (often just a bunch of rags tied in a ball) through a makeshift goal. Using such legal weapons as the 1835 Highway Act, which banned the game with a penalty of a fine of up to 40 shillings, the main public streets were cleared,[17] ironically turning the urban workingman even more to that site so hated by the reformers, the public house.

The most hotly fought battle over the banning of football was in the industrial midland city of Derby, where the annual Shrove Tuesday game was an entrenched part of the city tradition, but by the late 1840s, football even there was suppressed. Like cockfighting, however, it continued in the more remote and rural areas, such as in the mining communities, and also in the less-monitored back streets of the cities. Later in the century, after football was enthusiastically embraced by the elites, it blossomed again among the working classes, not as a sport imposed from above, but in continuity with the traditional games. Clearly, despite the economic changes and anti-sporting fervor of the reformers in early-Victorian England, traditional sports were not eradicated, and, as is true of most historical developments, there was continuity as well as change in the sporting life of England. Nevertheless, especially for the urban working classes and for women of all classes, there was in the early-Victorian period a significant contraction of the sporting life.

VICTORIAN HORSERACING

One sport fiercely opposed by virtuous reformers, but which was expanded rather than curtailed, was horseracing. Despite the best efforts of the Jockey Club to clean up the sport, horseracing remained dominated by gambling and therefore riddled with corruption, but it continued without restriction as a popular spectator sport throughout the nineteenth century. Reports of race fixing and other scandals did nothing to lessen its appeal. Although associated with aristocratic decadence and working-class immorality, races were also patronized by the middle classes, who were imbued with the Victorian values shaped by evangelicalism and utilitarianism, but just not on race day. Victorian horseracing, however, no longer had the support of the monarch. In 1840, the good Queen Victoria and her new German husband, Prince Albert, attended the Derby Day race. Shocked by the gambling and other corruptions, they never went again. But others did, including in the late-nineteenth century, Victoria's enthusiastically sports-loving son and heir, Bertie (in the early-twentieth century, King Edward VII), whose love of the racetrack would rival that of his great-uncle, King George IV. The broad support that horseracing received from all classes, and especially from the rich and powerful, is what allowed the sport, rife with gambling and corruption as it was, to continue unabated throughout the Victorian era.

Horseracing also grew in popularity because of the railroads, which increased the number of spectators who could attend races, and not just those in their local areas. Similarly, racehorses could now be transported to distant races, allowing them to race more often. Animal rights advocates protested that horses were ridden too hard, making racing an act of animal cruelty. Many horsemen, not bothered by issues of cruelty but rather by the viability of the sport, also warned of the dangers of over-racing, with horses entering too many races and at too young an age. Just as there was a rumbling fear throughout the nineteenth century, crescendoing in the last decades, of the degeneracy of the English human race, so also was there the fear that the prized English stock of thoroughbred horses was declining. These fears, however, were not translated into measures for change.

A new form of horseracing, the steeplechase, was developed in early-Victorian England, at first as a means for hunters to stay in condition between hunts. They would pick out a distant object on the horizon, often a church steeple, and would race across brooks, ditches, and fences towards it. This practice race became so popular, with spectators coming far and wide to watch, that it was formalized and set on a more accessible racetrack, usually four to five miles in length, with artificial bodies of water and other barriers simulating the countryside. The first steeplechase race was held in 1830, and in 1836 the premier event, the Grand Liverpool Steeplechase, later named the Grand National, was held in Aintree, outside Liverpool.

Although condemned by those concerned with the high number of injuries to horses on the treacherous course (there was less concern for the well-being of the jockeys) and never attracting the prestige of the elite flat horse races, steeplechases and especially the Grand National nevertheless became very popular with all social classes. In the face of criticisms of steeplechasing, which purists saw as a debasement of horseracing, defenders drew on familiar arguments. It was, first of all, quintessentially English in origin and spirit and was a sport in which foreigners did not participate. "There is something so manly, so English as we Englishmen are pleased to understand it, about the sport of steeplechasing. ... Chasing has just that sort of danger about it that Englishmen like to encounter, a danger which skill and courage, as a rule will surmount."[18] It was also justified as having an important military function, to keep troops fit for action. *Bell's Life* reported that cavalry officers in the Crimean War in mid-century encouraged their subordinates to steeplechase because "it excites that courage, presence of mind and skill in horsemanship without which their glorious achievements at Balaclava would never have been recorded. It also checks riotous living and its worst accessory, the use of the gambling table."[19]

Gambling was not as central to steeplechasing as it was to flat racing, but it was inevitably part of the appeal of the new sport. Even the most ardent horse lovers and supporters of horseracing recognized that horseracing, in whatever form, was popular primarily because of the betting opportunities it provided, which were all the more in demand after the abolition of such gambling venues as cockfighting and bull-baiting. The turf was, as the *Moral Reformer* said with condemnation, "a stronghold of gambling, and therefore an efficient cause of misery and wickedness. It is an amusement of almost unmingled evil."[20] Defenders of horseracing argued that track betting was a more refined form of gambling. As *Bentley's Quarterly Review* proclaimed, "if Englishmen must bet, they cannot do better than bet upon contests of thorough-bred horses on one of the beautiful English race-courses, and under an English summer sky."[21] Francis Lawley, writing in *St. Paul's Magazine*, carried these sentiments even further: "It is an undoubted necessity that Englishmen should have a national pastime, capable of affording amusement to all classes, enacted in the open air, devoid of all taint of cruelty, and conducted, as far as possible, in accordance with the rules of fair play. . . . Betting about the speed and endurance of a racehorse is unquestionably the noblest gambling in existence."[22]

Nevertheless, there was concern in Parliament that gambling had gotten out of control. Betting on horses was even more increased by the expansion of the sporting press and news about races in the mainstream sports, with regular reports on upcoming races, the odds, and the results. The telegraph, an American invention in use in England by the 1840s, also facilitated wagering on distant races. In 1845, therefore, Parliament passed a Gaming Act, which made gambling debts no longer recoverable at law, leaving debt collection in the hands of private agents. This act had the unintended consequences of the expansion of off-track betting shops, which made it easier for poor people who could not get to the track to wager. To stop this wagering, so as to protect the working classes from their presumed lack of self-control, in 1853 Parliament made off-track betting illegal. Defenders of working-class rights argued that it was unfair that the upper classes could bet in their private clubs, while working-class betting houses were outlawed. The counter-argument, going to the heart of Victorian class attitudes, was that such restrictions on public betting were necessary. For the poorer classes, betting was often "a straight avenue to penal servitude. The statute, therefore, only protects him against his own avarice and gullibility."[23] Working-class betting, of course, continued under the table, often at pubs and tobacco shops.

Despite the unsavory aspects associated with horseracing, it did produce some popular sports heroes. Fred Archer (1857–1886), son of a publican and himself later a pub owner, won the hearts of race-loving fans from all social classes. By the time he was 16, he was a champion jockey, a title he held for 13 years. His records include 2,747 wins, including many championships. Like most jockeys, he fought his hardest contests not against other mounts, but against his own weight. To lose weight for what became his last race in 1886, he dieted so rigorously that he became dangerously weak. Physical debility was compounded by mental depression, and later that year, he shot himself to death. When his death was announced, "thousands who never saw a race, including old ladies and decrepit men, mourned for the man whose name was familiar to them as that of the Prime Minister, and whose glory they had so often seen heralded in almost every paper they had taken up during the racing seasons of the previous decade."[24]

HORSEBACK RIDING AND THE SIDESADDLE

As controversial as horseracing could be, even the most militant reformer championed the simple recreative sport of horseback riding. It was even acceptable for women to ride, as long as they maintained decorum. Their modesty could be protected not only through body-covering clothing, but also through the use of the sidesaddle, so that women would not have to experience, and their viewers would not have to be offended by watching, their sitting spread-legged across a horse. The sexual fears such images evoked made the more dangerous and uncomfortable sidesaddle mandatory. The sidesaddle had been introduced in the seventeenth century, in order to protect especially royal and aristocratic women's hymens, but it was not commonly used until a second lower pommel, known as the "leaping-head," invented in about 1830, was added to the saddle for greater security for the rider. The horsewoman would put her right leg around the upper pommel, and her left leg on the leaping-head, lower on the saddle. It was a much more complicated apparatus than the simple cross-saddle. Even the late-Victorian horsewoman and enthusiast for the sidesaddle, Alice Hayes, admitted that "the great difference between men and women is that the former ride the horse; the latter, the saddle."[25]

The sidesaddle reinforced women's dependence on men in that, as Hayes advised, the rider would have to have a gentleman to put her up on the saddle, while a groom held the horse. It also made horseback riding more dangerous if a horse fell, because the rider would be trapped on it, whereas on cross-saddle the rider was usually thrown off. The rider could put pressure on only one side of the horse, and therefore could not direct it as effectively as on cross-saddle. The dangers in riding were all the greater because in the early- and mid-nineteenth century, horsewomen's clothing remained voluminous, with long skirts and riding corsets lessening mobility and increasing the chance of frightening the horse. Although horseback riding was seen as a healthy sport, sitting on a sidesaddle made the body twist to the side, causing back pain and even curvature of the spine.

The mark of respectability was given to female horseback riding by the queen herself. Victoria as a young woman loved riding, and was often seen on her horse in Rotten Road, the popular bridle path in Hyde Park, accompanied by her fatherly prime minister, Lord Melbourne, and then by her beloved husband, Albert. Other women of means also enjoyed the sport, maintaining their modesty and womanliness by following the social edict not to exert themselves too much. As the *Young Lady's Equestrian Manual* cautioned, "No lady of taste ever gallops on the road. Into this pace the lady's horse is never urged, or permitted to break, except in the field; and not above one among a thousand of our fair readers, it may be surmised, is likely to be endowed with sufficient ambition and, to attempt the following of hounds."[26]

VICTORIAN FOXHUNTING AND BIRD SHOOTING

The few mostly aristocratic women who in the early- and mid-nineteenth century did ride in fox hunts were able to do so because the new leaping-head pommel allowed them more safely to jump the fences and ditches. In so doing, they participated in a blood sport, which, along with shooting, received its share of condemnation from reformers, both evangelicals and utilitarians. The *Moral Reformer*, for example, in 1833 drew on both reforming arguments to condemn the field sports, because they were a waste of time and money, and because they do not make a man more religious. "Sportsmen are not the persons who diffuse the light of Christ, or endeavour to rectify the public morals, or to extend the empire of knowledge."[27] *The Sporting Magazine*, usually a supporter of field sports, published an article in 1823 criticizing attempts of Parliament to abolish working-class sports like cockfighting, while allowing cruel upper-class sports like foxhunting. In highly emotional language, the writer cited the horrors of the fox hunt. The fox is "driven by fear, and trusting only to her speed for her safety: but her speed avails her but little; she soon gets tired with fright and terror. . . . Now, here is a death of the most innocent and timid animal, by cruel means."[28]

Despite such protests, hunting and shooting continued without restraint throughout the Victorian age. The strongest criticisms did not come until the late-nineteenth century, in a new wave of humanitarianism. In early-Victorian England, many animal rights activists found it hard to criticize these blood sports because they themselves were often avid hunters and shooters. Even "Humanity Dick" Martin, who had spearheaded the campaign against bull-baiting and who cofounded the RSPCA, enjoyed hunting on his large Irish estates. Many members of the RSPCA were also hunters, causing some embarrassment and division in the society.

Evangelicalism did successfully inculcate a general social disapproval of hunting by clergymen, and the stock eighteenth-century figure of the "sporting parson" virtually disappeared in Victorian England. Also, hunting was rarely done on the Sabbath. Otherwise, foxes and other game were at as much risk from hunters and shooters in the Victorian age as in the eighteenth century. These sports were primarily the province of the wealthy, those represented in Parliament, who were not apt to pass laws abolishing their own pleasures. Field sports also had the stamp of royal approval. Prince Albert was an enthusiastic hunter and shooter, and his son Bertie, the Prince of Wales, followed his father's example even more avidly.

Sportsmen and their supporters did need to justify their sport on grounds other than the pure pleasure of the chase and of the victory over animals. Writers in the sporting and general magazines stressed the Englishness, the

AN HISTORICAL PARALLEL;
ELIZABETH—1580.

OR, COURT PASTIMES.
VICTORIA—1845.

manliness, and the utility of the sport. The *New Sporting Magazine* in 1859 argued that field sports "are as essentially necessary for the maintenance of our national character as sleep is to our existence. . . . There is a bold and manly character in connection with this sport which is highly in unison with the character of an Englishman."[29]

Field sports were also defended with the familiar argument of importance for military training. Early in the Crimean War, before the military unpreparedness of the English as well as the other combatants became obvious, a writer for *Fraser's Magazine* could claim that "much of our British pluck and endurance, much of that undying gameness and energy which has lately been tested so highly in the Crimea, has its origin in those early habits of sporting, which make up the principal amusement of the young Englishman." The best source of officers (including, presumably, the officers in the 600 who, following the orders of Lord Cardigan, rode to their death in the disastrous Charge of the Light Brigade) came from those who had spent their youths "in conflict with the beasts of the field." Rebutting the charge that field sports were a waste of time, the writer retorted that "the utilitarian may sneer at the sportsman. . . . We answer, 'we are not utilitarians—Heaven forbid we should ever be anything so useless! Strip life of the ideal, and you will be surprised to find how little is left. . . . All sporting is more or less ideal; nay, we go further, and aver that every sportsman is a poet, even if an unconscious one."[30]

A writer for *Bentley's Quarterly Review* expanded this argument in 1859 by scoffing utilitarians who said that it would not matter to England's destiny whether game were shot or not. Field sports, the writer asserted, were much more important than that. "He who excels in shooting game is also likely on occasion to excel in shooting men; and on the capacity of its citizens to shoot men certainly and rapidly depends the greatness and even the existence of every state." Casting the debate as a rural/urban conflict, the proponent said that "the town-bred man may learn that the results of intellectual efforts will not long suffice to secure his country against attack, and the sportsman and the soldier will thenceforward hold in his esteem a place beside the statesman, the philosopher, and the engineer."[31]

This theme of conflict of interest between the rural English countrymen, whose traditions the field sports embodied, and the market-driven, work-preoccupied, townspeople, resonated well with many Victorians who saw the new cities as the nurseries of vice. Harry Hieover, a mid-Victorian writer and sports enthusiast, condemned people who think ill of sports. "I allude to London people, to tradesmen, and their families, and other ranking in the same orders of society. They know literally nothing of sportsmen, their pursuits or habits."[32] He was wrong in his assertion that men of London knew nothing of field sports. Even as fewer women and even fewer clergymen hunted, a new group of people joined in foxhunting—urban middle-class men—who could now use the railways to reach the hunts in the early morning and return to the city in the evening. Countrymen had worried that the coming of the railways would destroy the traditional hunting areas, but instead the fast, wide-reaching transportation brought a fresh supply of eager pursuers of the prized fox.

Derisively labeled "cockney hunters" by country gentlemen, these urban middle-class hunters, aspiring to ape their social superiors and with the wealth to do so, used hunting as a means of raising their class status. They were able to join the hunts, since the riding to hounds (foxhunting), with all the attendant rituals and entertainments, had become increasingly expensive and were usually no longer held by individual landowners but rather by subscription. Anyone with sufficient cash could participate.[33] Although a subject of ridicule for their inexperience and clumsiness, and resented by those who opposed this urban invasion, these "cockney hunters," often even wealthier than their rural social betters, eventually blended in with the hunting crowd. With all wearing the distinctive red coats and white leather breeches, they formed a common front. In the late-nineteenth century, the upper and the wealthy middle classes would join together politically in the Conservative Party as a union of property rather than birth, an alliance whose ground was firmly laid in their shared "rides to hounds."

With the increase in the number of fox hunters, the number of hunts also increased, from 72 packs in 1821 to 84 by 1850.[34] The demand for foxes outgrew the supply in the wild, so foxes had to be imported from the European continent, or, more commonly, were bred for the hunt. Purists bemoaned that hunting captive foxes did not have the excitement as chasing wild animals, and certainly foxhunting could no longer be justified on the grounds that it rid the countryside of unwelcome vermin. The scientifically bred foxes were, however, faster, which meant that hunts could start in the mid-morning rather than at dawn, making it easier for the day commuters as well as for those exhausted from the social entertainments the nights before the hunt.

As with foxhunting, so also partridge and other game shooting retained its appeal as a traditional rural sport for the privileged. Colonel Hamilton, who was blind in the last 20 years of his life, took pleasure in his darkness to remember the light of the joy of the shoot in his early-Victorian youth. "What can be more enjoyable than partridge shooting, in a good breeding season, accompanied by an old sporting friend, a brace or a leash of steady dogs, and a man who marks well?" He would be so excited on the night of August 31, the eve of the opening of the partridge-shooting season, that he could not sleep.[35]

In early-Victorian England, the new method of battue shooting was developed, which was widely but unsuccessfully condemned by many sportsmen (for reasons of sport, not animal welfare). Shooters would walk in a line towards coverts, shelters for game birds that were made naturally or artificially of underbrush. Beaters would scare the birds out into the open, making them easy targets. Large numbers of birds could be shot, without great skill. The depletion of wild birds meant that, like foxes, they had to be specially bred, which made them all the easier to kill than those in the wild. Critics considered this method as little better than the massacre of birds and argued that it was un-English, having been brought over (as the name reflects) from the less-civilized France. Avid sportsman Lord Lennox lamented that battue shooting caused the sport to "sadly degenerate from the truly English manly sport of bygone days." Whereas shooting in other lands involves excitement, Lennox said sarcastically that battue shooting had no thrill to it. "In our own snug little island no mischief can accrue to the sportsman in the pursuit of this tame amusement, if he is fortunate enough to escape tripping over the multitudes of timid heads, or to avert an avalanche of feathers when a bouquet of pheasants come falling down over his devoted head."[36]

It was not sportsmen but rather the disadvantaged and their supporters who protested against another controversial aspect of hunting and shooting—the game laws—which restricted the killing of certain game only to privileged landed classes. After great rural discontent in the post-revolutionary decades that frightened men of property, the Game Law was revised in 1831. A licensing system was introduced, in which one could purchase a permit to be able to shoot the previously restricted animals. This meant that anyone who could afford a license could participate in shoots. Just as subscriptions opened the fox hunt to middle-class men of property, so also did licensing open the door of game shooting to, as the historian Sir Derek Birley said with his inimitable wit, "urban middle-class *arrivistes* seeking gentrification or escape back to nature through the wholesale slaughter of game birds."[37] The poorer rural classes were still deprived of the right to shoot even game on their own lands. They were also now without traditional entertainments like cockfighting or bull-baiting. To deflect their discontent, a writer in the *New Sporting Magazine* suggested that landlords allow greyhound coursing on their estates. It could be "an excellent safety valve to turn away the discontent of their tenants. . . . The love of field-sports is inherent in the breasts of Englishmen of all orders; and nothing is so disgusting as to see the great men of a country indulging in these diversions to an unlimited extent, while they entirely deny them to the classes under them."[38]

SPORTING JOURNALISTS: NIMROD AND SURTEES

Pleasure in the hunt and shoots were enjoyed not only in the field but also in print. With the proliferation of sporting journals and books, enthusiasts could expand their participation vicariously through the steady stream of accounts of the exploits and misfortunes of others, through fiction and factual reports. By the early-Victorian period, in the tradition of the early-nineteenth century champion of boxing, Pierce Egan, many writers emerged who supported themselves writing about sports. The first notable figure was Charles James Apperley (1778–1843), who, unlike earlier salaried journalists, was from the landed classes and was an experienced sportsman. He wrote under the pseudonym "Nimrod," the Biblical warrior in Genesis who was "a mighty hunter before the Lord." Apperley's enormous popularity as a writer on field sports made the name "Nimrod" a generic term for "hunter" in Victorian England.

As "Nimrod," Apperley was such as success because of his vivid style and even more so because, as a sportsman himself, he could write as an insider. With an education in Greek and Latin befitting his class, he would mark his status with frequent use of classical words and allusions. When he described the thrill of the chase, the camaraderie among hunters, the feelings of victory and disappointment, he wrote as a participant and not just an observer. Writing about hunts, he also made judgments on the way they were conducted. As a later Victorian commented, the arrival of the magazine each month "was awaited with mingled excitement and trepidation by members of different hunts, and especially by masters of hounds."[39] He recognized his own vanity, but, as an admirer said, "the man is yet to be who could reign as the Sun in the firmament of sport—or any other—and yet retain intact whatever of modesty Nature has bestowed upon him."[40]

Apperley resigned from *The Sporting Magazine* in 1829 to write for other periodicals and to write books about sports. He was succeeded at *The Sporting Magazine* by Robert Surtees (1805–1864), who was also from the landed classes, with a long lineage in his family of "Masters of the Hounds." After a brief stint with *The Sporting Magazine*, he cofounded in 1831 the *New Sporting Magazine*, for which he served as editor and hunting correspondent. Writing in a style completely and deliberately different from Nimrod's, whom he delighted in spoofing (calling him "Pomponius Ego"), he created satiric portraits of the pretentious and the social climbers. In what many critics consider Surtees's greatest novel, *Mr. Sponge's Sporting Tour*, Mr. Puffington, the son of a starch manufacturer, takes on a pack of hounds "because he thought it would give him consequence."[41] In periodical articles later collected in book form, Surtees creates his most delightful comic character, Mr. Jorrocks, a vulgar wealthy London grocer who wants to advance himself by participating in fox hunts. The epitome of the "cockney hunter," taking advantage of quick railway transport and subscription packs, Mr. Jorrocks develops a passion for the fox hunt: "Fox-'unting is indeed the prince of sports. The image of war without its guilt and only half its danger. . . . The *sight* of a *saddle* makes me sweat. An 'ound makes me perfectly wild. A red coat throws me into a scarlet fever."[42] "Jorrocks," like the name "Nimod," became a metaphoric figure in Victorian England, a code word for middle-class vulgarity and affectations.

One of the most eminent enthusiasts for field sports in mid-Victorian England is the novelist Anthony Trollope (1815–1882). The author of many witty social novels, Trollope said that his greatest passion was for foxhunting. His first ride to hounds in his youth "began one of the great joys of my life. I have ever since been constant to the sport, having learned to love it with an affection which I cannot myself fathom or understand." Framing this passion perhaps facetiously in the Victorian moral lexicon of duty, by which he seemed to mean a sense of compulsion, he said that

> it has been for more than thirty years a duty to me to ride to hounds; and I have performed that duty with a persistent energy. Nothing has ever been allowed to stand in the way of hunting,—neither the writing of books, nor the work of the Post Office, nor other pleasures. . . . I have written on very many subjects, and on most of them with pleasure, but on no subject with such delight as that on hunting.[43]

Hunting themes and references permeate many of Trollope's novels. He also wrote articles on hunting for *St. Paul's Magazine*, which he collected along with other sporting essays that he as editor had commissioned for that journal, in his 1868 *British Sports and Pastimes*. Hunting, he wrote, is a sport that "does more to make Englishmen what they are, and to keep them as they are." We are, he said, "to the manner born," and we accept a sport that seems an anomaly to foreigners, in which hunters ride over enclosed fields, damaging crops, "as long as hounds are running." A staunch conservative who defended the game laws in protection of his beloved sport, Trollope argued that if a man could not bear to have horsemen trample his land, he should go somewhere else to live.[44]

SPORTS IN AND ON THE WATERS: ANGLING AND YACHTING

Unlike hunting and shooting, there was very little contention about the gentler field sport of angling. A sport associated more than any other with return to nature, with Arcadian pleasures (and for many of the poorer classes, still with procurement of food), fishing escaped the condemnation of animal rights activists, who tended not to worry about the well-being of fish, just as only the most hard-headed utilitarian would complain about the waste of time. A sport of virtue, the "true angler" was, as James Bertram eulogized in his essay on fishing in Trollope's *British Sports and Pastimes*, "endowed with the gifts of patience, endurance, and observation; he is slow to anger, and full of resources; he is generally a man enjoying rude health, unselfish, careless of the pleasures that delight other men."[45]

The unpleasantness, however, of fishing in industrial England, was the pollution of the waters. Rapid industrialization and urbanization had created a grievous problem of disposal of waste, be it from factories or humans. The traditional method of disposal, simply dumping waste into the rivers, no longer worked. The rivers became "but highways for the passage of all kinds of filth, dead dogs and cats—putrid and foul,—chemical wash, and the abounding liquid refuse of towns." This significantly affected angling, for, as Bertram said, "the question of river pollution is intimately associated with the occupation of the angler. The home of the fish should be pure. . . . The future of angling is so bound up in the purification of our waters."[46]

The call to action came from sanitary reformers concerned about public health, but also from influential anglers, who formed such organizations as the Thames Angling Preservation Society. They succeeded in getting Parliament in 1861 to pass the Salmon Fishery Act, forbidding the dumping of sewage into waters containing salmon, but the act was ineffectively enforced. A stronger, more comprehensive Public Health Act of 1874 facilitated the building of sewerage treatment plants, but, despite this and subsequent efforts in the late-nineteenth century, the English waters, especially in urban areas, remained dangerously polluted. Anglers had indeed to return to nature, away from the cities, to pursue their sport.

Another water sport against which Victorian reformers could hardly lodge complaint was yachting. With seafaring and naval defense so imbedded in the history and mythology of England, yachting was seen as an appropriate and necessary endeavor, at least for the wealthy who could afford to engage in this most expensive of sports. After all, as a yachting enthusiast asserted, "If Britannia need no bulwarks or towers along the steep, it becomes more and more the duty of her sons to be prepared to defend her on the mountain wave." The author firmly denied the common notion that "yachting is an idle, otiose lounging, or what our Transatlantic friends would call 'loafing' amusement."[47]

The yachting clubs that had been formed in the early-nineteenth century continued to flourish and expand under Queen Victoria. The prestigious Royal Yacht Squadron (RYS), scornful of vulgar competition when it was founded in 1815, embraced racing by the early-Victorian era when it saw the success of the races organized by the Royal Thames Yacht Club. Headquartered at the port of Cowes on the Isle of Wight, the RYS began sponsoring races around the island, including an annual cup regatta.

English yachting received a major shock in 1853 when an American yacht defeated the English ship at the Cowes race. The faster, sleeker victor had been designed in England, but, in that tradition-bound sport, it was not adopted. An Englishman then took the idea to the United States, where it became the design for a new racing yacht, the *America*. When the *America* was sailed to England for the Great Exhibition in 1851, the RYS commodore challenged the American crew to enter their Cup championship. Queen Victoria and Prince Albert, as spectators of the race, had the trauma of seeing the *America* win the Cup. Seeking excuses for not winning, defenders of English seafaring pride claimed that the *America* had been built solely for racing, which was "a breach of gentlemanly practice" (ignoring the fact that the yacht had made the long journey cruising across the Atlantic). The English tried to win back the Cup, which had been renamed the America's Cup after the winning yacht in the first international competition, but without success. The Cup remained in American hands until Australia won it in 1983. The 1853 and subsequent defeats at the sport in which the English had assumed they were dominant was a severe blow to national pride and created rumbling anxieties, which would only increase by the end of the century, that perhaps no longer did Britannia rule the waves.

MID-VICTORIAN CRICKET

At least the English could find comfort in their unique superior game of cricket, which flourished in Victorian England. There were of course the usual naysayers, complaining that it was a distraction from higher things like religion and work, but those voices were drowned out by the loud enthusiasm especially among the elites for this game so associated with the preindustrial world of green space and leisurely pace. There was a heavy sense of tradition about the game, in that its rules had been framed in the eighteenth century and finalized (some later critics suggested fossilized), with few later revisions, by the early-nineteenth century. The general feeling in Victorian England was that it had reached perfect form. "Man might have developed a better game than cricket," extolled the Victorian author and cricketer Andrew Lang, "but certainly man never did."[48]

Cricket had also, by the time of Victoria's accession, been shorn at least ostensibly of all connection with gambling, which made it seem as pure as the distinctive whites worn by the cricketers. There was still, as a cricket writer said, "betting, of course, there is. What will not Englishmen bet about?—but it is all outside, and unconnected with the game itself." The term "it's not cricket," used in common Victorian parlance and thereafter, could authentically connote anything immoral or unfair. It was indeed a game that contributed to "manliness, self-dominion, and modesty."[49]

Many sports in Victorian England were lauded as exemplars and promoters of English virtue, but none more than cricket. This theme that began in the eighteenth century became in Victoria's reign a dominant and oft repeated refrain. To cite only several of what could be hundreds of such testimonies, James Pycroft describes cricket as "a standing panegyric on the English character; none but an orderly and sensible people would so amuse themselves. It calls into requisition all the cardinal virtues, some moralists would say."[50] Another writer details those virtues as "contentment, confidence, tact, prudence, fortitude, justice. . . . [Cricket] is directly opposed to the growth of arrogance and self-assumption."[51] As a reflection of the game's social status and moral qualities, Victoria herself encouraged her sons to play cricket, and she hired a professional coach to train them.

Part of the delight that the Victorians took in the game with its complicated rules and seemingly baroque play was its incomprehensibility to foreigners. This sense of exclusiveness and superiority of cricket was voiced in the more cosmopolitan eighteenth century but even stronger in the xenophobic Victorian age. As one commentator pridefully extolled,

> Its very associations are English. Who could, for instance, picture to the imagination the phlegmatic Dutchman, with his capacious round stern, chasing or sending the ball whizzing through the air like a cannon shot, and getting a run with the speed of a roebuck. The idea even appears beyond the pale of conception. The effeminate inhabitants of cloudless Italy, Spain, and Portugal would sooner face a solid square of British infantry than an approaching ball from the sinewy arm of a first class bowler. . . . Foreigners, as a rule, are likewise slow in attempting to unravel the mysteries of the game.[52]

In this seemingly unchanging game, the players still wore whites—in the words of the Dean of Rochester, "nothing is so manly, so becoming and work-manlike, as the plain white flannel."[53] What was added, controversially, was protective clothing for the batter and the wicket keeper, deemed necessary by the 1840s with the now prevalent faster, harder, roundarm bowling, and even more so after the legalization of overarm bowling in 1864. Older players scorned the new protections as a sign of weakness, although the counter-argument was made that it had always been the custom for gentlemen to wear gloves. Some players were concerned that the padding would be an impedi-ment, and that it would make them look ridiculous, a fear compounded by such satires as a *Punch* cartoon depicting players as dressed in medieval armor.

The ordinary urban working-class person usually did not play cricket, from lack of access to cricket fields and more so because of the lack of leisure for practice, much less the time to play three-day games. The striking exception was the continuation of the eighteenth-century practice of employing paid working-class professionals especially for the more arduous work of bowling. Such social mixing remained a source of astonishment to the continental upper classes, even though, as in the preindustrial age, the amateur "Gentlemen" and the professional "Players" did not mix socially and retained their separate dressing rooms and styles of appellation. Even so, such mixing on the playing field "might probably shock a Frenchman, but in this country the thing is far from uncommon. The amateurs meet the professionals on the field as equals

" OUT, SIR."

and playfellows, but they do not necessarily merge all differences of breeding
and education."[54]

Along with paid professional players, social class was also an issue with
umpires. To have objective umpires, it was felt that they should be free of
patronage and therefore paid for their work. This, however, created the
anomaly of lower-class men, even wearing the distinctive umpire's white coat,
judging their social betters. In one country game, when a landlord was batting,
the umpire, who was his tenant, called him out. "I'm very sorry, my Lord—
extremely sorry—wouldn't have had it happen for five pounds; but it's out,
my Lord—it's out!"[55] The landlord then muttered that "he'll never drain that

bottom field now." There was also concern that umpires, who were often former professional bowlers, were reluctant to call "no balls" when the bowler illegally "throws" rather than bowls the ball. Nevertheless, as the cricketer A. G. Steel counseled, whatever ones feels about the calls, cricketers must be respectful of the umpires and not dispute their decisions. To protest is "unsportsmanlike and ungentlemanly."[56]

Befitting the rural heritage of this gentlemanly game, in early-Victorian England cricket remained primarily centered in the southeast. The coming of the railways, however, soon spread the sport throughout the country. Teams were for the most part based on counties (unlike the later rival game for national popularity, association ["soccer"] football, which, as it became more associated with the urban working classes, had city and even factory team identification). The requirements to play on a county team were formalized in 1873, establishing strict residency requirements. Gentlemen had to live in the county for two years (which included the parental roof, "provided that it was open to a man as an occasional home,") and Players for three years (later changed to two). In addition to the county games, the school matches between Eton and Harrow, and Oxford and Cambridge, begun in the early-nineteenth century, continued as important sporting and social events. In contrast to the more prestigious county and school games, the All-England Elevens was formed in 1846, and the rival United All-England Elevens in 1852, as commercial ventures, to play matches against odds in various parts of the country.

Despite the attachment to tradition in cricket, just as in the eighteenth but more urgently in the busier nineteenth century, there were attempts to make the game shorter. Some reformers suggested ending the long tea breaks during the game. More substantially, by mid-century there was concern that batters were gaining dominance and running up huge scores, making the two-innings game last even longer. Some critics blamed the close manicuring of the pitch, which made the ball easier to hit, hence more runs scored. There were suggestions that the pitches be tended less carefully, but these came to naught. Others proposed that the bats be made narrower, or the wickets wider, suggestions which provoked intense opposition. As one advocate of the reforms commented, "We feel as if a mine had suddenly exploded beneath our feet."[57] Traditionalists were relieved when the MCC refused to accept any changes to the game that symbolized the enduring strength, character, and superiority of the Englishmen.

3

Sports in the Victorian Public Schools and Universities

By the 1840s, sports in industrialized England had experienced significant transformations as well as maintained comfortable continuities with the past. The traditional elite rural sports of cricket and foxhunting continued but with expanded social participation with the inclusion of bourgeois urban sportsmen. Many in the middle classes, however, imbued with both the utilitarian work ethic and the evangelical distrust of pleasure-seeking activities, disdained sports as a time-wasting, sin-inducing relic from the decadent aristocratic past. Women in general and especially of the middle classes were restricted from their traditional sporting activities by the new Victorian code of womanly behavior. Not from choice, the urban working-class men also experienced a severe curtailment of their sporting pleasures. Utilitarian and evangelical humanitarianism successfully made illegal such traditionally working-class blood sports as cockfighting and bull-baiting, and the lack of city space for games as well as rigid long work schedules limited the ability of the urban poor to play such popular participatory sports as football (soccer and rugby.)

SPORTS AND THE REFORM OF ENGLISH PUBLIC SCHOOLS

In this mid-Victorian climate of contraction of the traditional sporting life, there emerged a new sporting movement that would have profound impact on English social life, and that would make England's international reputation as a sporting nation and exporter of sports throughout the world. The sites of this sporting movement were the elite English public schools. These schools were "public" only in the sense that they were fee-charging boarding schools, in contrast to education by tutors in the home or religious schools that were restricted to church members. With deep roots in English history, many of the public schools were founded in the medieval and early-modern ages. The oldest is Winchester College in Hampshire, founded in 1382. (Note that the use of the term "college" for Winchester and some of the other schools describes a community of common purpose, and, in English academia, can refer to secondary as well as university-level institutions.) King Henry VI in 1440 founded the most prestigious of the schools, Eton College, near Windsor. Other historic public schools, founded in the sixteenth century, are Shrewsbury School (1552), in Shropshire in the West Midlands; Westminster School, in London (1560); Rugby School, in Warwickshire (1567); and Harrow School, outside London (1572). Charterhouse School, in Surrey, was founded under King James I in 1611.

By the early-nineteenth century, these public schools, their prestige as educators of the upper classes notwithstanding, had developed a notorious reputation as dens of iniquity. The ardent moralist John Bowdler (1746–1823), whose father Thomas Bowdler's equally moralistic zeal gave birth to the word "bowdlerization," condemned the schools as "the very seats and nurseries of vice; it may be unavoidable, or it may not, but the fact is indisputable."[1] There was no attempt to control the boys outside of the classroom, nor were there organized extracurricular activities, so the youths were free to pursue their pleasures as they would. Befitting their class background, many enjoyed hunting and shooting, but in ways that often were simply poaching. Drinking and visits to women of saleable pleasures were other popular entertainments. There was a great deal of brutality, between the boys and against animals. A student at Harrow in the early-nineteenth century later recalled that in his day, many boys kept a dog and cats, the one to kill the others.[2]

The problem of discipline became of particular concern by the 1830s with the influx into the public schools of the sons of newly wealthy industrial middle classes. These parents hoped their offspring would learn aristocratic manners, but instead the boys became inculcated with aristocratic vices. Such rowdy and often-raunchy behavior, tolerated in the Georgian world, was no longer acceptable in the new evangelical and utilitarian climate of early-Victorian England. The person most responsible for creating a completely new atmosphere and discipline in the public schools was the headmaster of Rugby School from 1828 to 1841, Thomas Arnold (1795–1842).

An ardent evangelical, Arnold brought religious commitment to his reform of Rugby. Emphasizing the formation of moral character rather than simply academic learning, he aimed at changing the wild ruffians into Christian gentlemen, and, in so doing, he transformed the concept of "gentleman" from one based on birth to that of rectitude. As an explanation and endorsement of Arnold's reforms, Thomas Hughes (1822–1896) wrote his best-selling 1857 novel *Tom Brown's School Days* based on his own days at Rugby under Arnold. In the novel, Tom Brown's father affirms Arnold's educational philosophy by reflecting on the advice he will give his son before his departure to Rugby: "Shall I tell him to mind his work, and say he's sent to school to make himself a good scholar? Well, but he isn't sent to school for that—at any rate, not for that mainly. . . . If he'll only turn out a brave, helpful, truth-telling Englishman, and a gentleman, and a Christian, that's all I want."[3]

To create Christian gentlemen, Arnold changed the boarding arrangements by bringing the boys under closer supervision of housemasters. To develop leadership skills, he made the senior students "prefects," in charge of the discipline of the younger boys. He put chapel as a central part of the school life and gave weekly sermons to inspire his students. Hughes recounted, surely through a hazy romantic filter rather than an actual portrayal of youthful response, that the boys listened keenly to these sermons, given by a man whom they felt to be "with all his heart and soul and strength, striving against whatever was mean and unmanly and unrighteous in our little world. It was . . . the warm, living voice of one who was fighting for us and by our sides, and calling on us to help him and ourselves and one another."[4]

Arnold is also credited with the most far-reaching innovation of the public-school reform movement, that of fostering organized team sports as a means of controlling unruly boys, maintaining order, and building character. Arnold in fact was not interested in sports and was especially hostile to field sports, but he tolerated games when some of his masters suggested using them as a way to instill the virtues Arnold sought to inculcate. In *Tom Brown's School Days*, Hughes helps create this public impression of Arnold's primary influence on sports in the schools by discussing at length the various games at Rugby under his headmastership. The chief prefect, Brooke, tells Tom and the other boys that "this new Doctor hasn't been here so long as some of us, and he's changing all the old customs." He advises the boys to follow Arnold's instructions. "If you will go your own way, and that way ain't the Doctor's, for it'll lead to grief. You all know that I'm not the fellow to back a master through thick and thin. If I saw him stopping [a sporting match], I'd be as ready as any fellow to stand up about it. But he don't—he encourages them."[5]

Whoever the instigator, team sports quickly became key to the new reforming mission at Rugby, and then at other schools, both the historic and also the newer public schools, enthusiastic to follow Arnold's example of moral education. Boys had long played games at their public schools, as evidenced by the Eton-Harrow cricket rivalry, first played in 1805, and the Eton-Westminster boat races. These sports, however, were without official support or endorsement, and in some cases the school officials tried to forbid the games. Now, in contrast, sports became organized and sponsored by the school administration, as a central part of the educational experience.

Sports were also valued as important in developing both leadership skills and the ability to work together as a unit, traits necessary for military strength and imperial rule. In *Tom Brown's School Days*, when his house scores a victory over another house, Brooke credits the win to their teamwork. "Why did we beat 'em? . . . It's because we've more reliance on one another, more of a house feeling, more fellowship than the School can have. Each of us knows and can depend on his next-hand man better—that's why we beat 'em to-day. We've union, they've division—there's the secret."[6] This is the context in which the quote commonly misattributed to the Duke of Wellington on the military value of sports in the public schools took on such currency. As the Victorian cricket historian Charles Box said in 1877, with words that were echoed in many other sports writings of the age, "the man who invented the game [of cricket] as surely deserves a statue to his memory as he who won Waterloo; for the grand old warrior, in the evening of his days, confessed, with an eager eye and a trembling lip, as he watched the Eton boys scoring their innings. . . . 'It was here that Waterloo was won.'"[7]

Sports were also seen as valuable for adolescent boys in draining excessive and dangerous energies that led not just to boisterousness but more ominously, to sexual excess, a great concern to moralistic Victorians. The hope of educators, parents, doctors, and moralists in general was that boys who exhausted themselves on the playing field would be too worn out to philander, or to engage in what Oscar Wilde called the same-sex "love that dares not call its name," much less to commit that most feared of sins, "solitary vice." Clearly, idle hands were the devil's workshop. Better, it was discreetly believed, for an adolescent boy to hold a cricket bat than private body parts.

Sports seemed a natural fit in the public schools because the academic curriculum was based on classical Greek and Roman culture, and the boys would have been reading, presumably in Greek or Latin, endless accounts in classical culture of physical fitness and competitive sports. Among the most sports-minded people in history, the Greeks, whose culture the Romans emulated, held as an ideal the balance of mind and body, or, in the phrase of the Roman satirist Juvenal so often quoted by Victorians, *mens sana in corpore sano* ("healthy mind in a healthy body"). The gymnasium for physical workouts and the palestra for combat sports were important buildings in a Greek city-state. Sporting contests were major events in the calendar, with the Olympic games played every four years and other inter-Greek contests on each of the other years. An individualistic society, the Greeks did not have team sports as part of their culture, but they otherwise provided a model for Victorians of a sporting life, reinforced in almost every lesson in the public-school curriculum.

A journalist writing in the *New Sporting Magazine*, drawing on the example of Greek culture to advocate for sports in the public schools, pointed out that "every one who has read Lucian or Plutarch cannot have failed to notice how those learned ancients extol the beauty and vigour of all manly pastimes, and commend the public games of those days as essential to the student in assisting his endeavours to excel in philosophical pursuits."[8] Many sports-promoting educators, however, were not so concerned about assisting "philosophical pursuits," but rather were worried that too much academic work would make boys effeminate. What better antidote to that than strenuous sports, promoting manliness in the future leaders of the British Empire?

When organized sports were first introduced into the schools in the 1840s as part of the school regimen, there was resistance from the boys themselves.

Accustomed to having their free time to do as they wished, they resented the compulsion that came from the imposition of forced activities and regulation of their leisure. Soon, however, most of the boys came enthusiastically to participate in the challenging, competitive and, yes, fun, sports of their schools. Students at Harrow formed a Harrow Philathletic Club in 1853 to promote sports and physical exercise, and other schools soon formed similar clubs. Schools were able to raise large sums of money to improve and expand their school grounds and athletic facilities—Harrow, for example, had 8 acres of playing fields in 1845 and 146 in 1900.

Clearly, in the words of Richard Holt, sports ceased to be a means of discipline and became an end in itself, as "the culture of athleticism steadily came to dominate the whole system of elite education."[9] In *Tom Brown's School Days*, Hughes gives approving testimony to the new priorities when he has the much admired Brooke exclaim that he would "sooner win two School-house matches running than get the Balliol scholarship any day," a sentiment which evoked wild cheers from the boys.[10] The star athletes became the new aristocracy of the schools, for, an old Harrovian recalled about his days at Harrow in the 1860s, "No thinking man will blame us for idolising the athlete. The cricketer in his flannels was our hero, not the student immersed in his books."[11]

ROWING IN THE PUBLIC SCHOOLS

The sports that students played and the way they played them varied from school to school, depending on the geographic layout of the campus. In schools located on rivers, rowing was the major sport in the warmer months. The image of the "eights," vigorous youth all pulling strenuously together in a rowing competition, met all the hopes of those who advocated sports as a means of promoting teamwork, self-discipline, manliness. Rowing was especially important at Eton, which was on the Thames River. The railways had by the mid-nineteenth century shifted much of the working traffic away from the upper Thames, making it more accessible to sport, of which Eton took full advantage. The cricketer Alfred Lubbock remembered that in his youth at Eton in the 1850s there was much more interest in rowing than in cricket, with marked social distinction between the prestigious "wet bobs" who rowed, and the "dry bobs" who played other sports. His house in particular was "a regular nest of wet bobs, and one heard very little talk about cricket, it would have been far from conducive to a small boy's happiness to have proclaimed himself a cricketer, or what was more commonly called a 'stinking dry bob.'"[12]

Although rowing was seen as important in developing toughness and manliness, the sport was made less dangerous by the requirement that boys had to learn to swim before going out in a boat. Lubbock, who, although primarily a cricketer did also become a "wet bob," described how boys at Eton were taught to swim. A waterman would sit in a punt,

Swimming lesson.

holding a stout rod or pole about four feet long, with a hook at the end. On to this hook are loped the ends of a sort of broad band or girth, which is passed under the arms of the pupil, who is by this means held up in the water and 'played' after the manner of a big fish. Meanwhile the water-man gives his instructions how to use your arms and hands, and kick out with your legs. When he finds the boy beginning to learn the art, he, without warning, dips the point of the pole or undoes the belt, and the pupil suddenly finds himself swimming.

Even though competitive swimming was not introduced until later in the century, passing the swimming test was, Lubbock said, "one of the most important events of a boy's education at Eton," for only in that way could he become an honored wet bob.[13]

PUBLIC-SCHOOL CRICKET

Although few called themselves cricketers at Eton and elsewhere during Lubbock's youth, that most lauded and historic English team sport soon became central to the sporting life in the public schools. The *New Sporting Magazine* would report in 1865 that "the public schools are the very nurseries where the taste for cricket is fostered and encouraged to such an extent, that most boys from those schools delight in the game all their lives."[14] Box observed that "it contains just that amount of exertion, diluted by that amount of rest, which it is desirable to give to boys in a sport extending over several hours, with just sufficient vagueness in its laws and regulations to free them from irksomeness in their observance."[15] At Rugby, the fictional Tom Brown, like his creator Thomas Hughes, became captain of his eleven. Explaining the game to one of his uninformed masters, Tom wonders rhetorically "whether I should have got most good by understanding Greek particles or cricket thoroughly." A schoolmaster, who at first did not understand the sport, comes to agree that it is a noble game. Tom replies that it is more than a game, "it's an institution." Another boy says even more extravagantly that it is "the birthright of British boys, old and young, as *habeas corpus* and trial by jury are of British men." The now cricket-enthusiastic master praises the sport for the teamwork it inculcates. "The discipline and reliance on one another which it teaches is so valuable, I think . . . it ought to be such an unselfish game. It merges the individual in the eleven; he doesn't play that he may win, but that his side may." Tom agrees that it and other team sports are much better than the old individual sports, "where the object is to come in first or to win for oneself, and not that one's side may win."[16]

Just as the gymnasia and palestras were in the Greek city-states, so did cricket fields become the center of the public-school campus. This was especially so at Harrow, without easy access to a river and therefore without rowing to compete with cricket as the major game. Interest in cricket at Harrow was intensified by the fierce rivalry with Eton. A highlight of the sporting calendar, not just at those two schools but also in the sporting world and general society, was the annual Eton-Harrow cricket match, held annually at Lord's in London in mid-July. Staying focused on the moral purpose of the sport, the headmaster of Eton in the 1850s became concerned about the dangers of sending his boys to the possibly corrupting "mysteries of London life," and for several years forbade his school to play in the match at Lord's. Old Etonians were extremely upset by this decision. As one presumably Old Boy said,

Parents cannot keep their sons from temptation. They cannot keep them from London, from the public gardens, the exhibitions, and the theatres. In all those places licentiousness walks abroad, unrestrained and unconcealed. Unhappily, it is not a part of English manners to throw a veil over temptations of this kind. They catch the eye and challenge the ear at every turn of our streets. Parents who wish to keep their sons pure must trust to something else than the absence of opportunity. . . . And the presence of schoolfellows acts, we believe, much more often as a preservative than as a seductive influence.[17]

Some Old Boys offered to act "*loco parentis*, and insure the safety of the eleven,"[18] and so the annual match was resumed, and has continued to the present day. It attracted huge crowds, who came to have a good time as much as to watch a match, much to the dismay of cricket purists. The matches were covered regularly in the fashionable as well as sporting magazines. As *Belgravia* described the 1874 match,

Where, indeed, is London society to be found on the Eton and Harrow match day, if not at Lord's cricket-ground? . . . For it is, indeed a sight well worth seeing; the ring of carriages of all sorts, and the numerous or rather innumerable spectators, render Lord's cricket-ground on the two days appropriated to this match a most brilliant scene. . . . A glorious scene it is when a sun is shining down on a large assembly of English-women and Englishmen, well born, well dressed, all watching with inter-est the progress of a really English manly game! . . . We certainly can imagine no sight more calculated to impress and astonish, if not to alarm, a foreigner; indeed, it is not improbable that he would deem the whole meeting an instance of excessive 'John Bullism'.[19]

With such attention on the game, the pressure on the players became great. Lubbock reported that some Eton and Harrow fathers gave their sons £1 a run and £5 a wicket in the match.[20] Eton was frustrated in the early 1860s that Harrow dominated the game and resorted to hiring a professional coach. A report on Eton cricket in 1864 showed that the players practiced five hours a day. Reading the report, an Eton partisan said that he and his fellow supporters "felt a little refreshed, and said to ourselves, There's a deal of dis-cipline in cricket—lots of 'head work' if they play it well—a concentration of energies—a high standard of excellence—and a self-mastery which they will carry into the graver duties of life." He was, however, keenly disappointed that, despite all these efforts, Eton still lost to Harrow. "Their cricket we regard as a discredit, not to the playing-fields, but to the school."[21]

FOOTBALL: FROM THE STREETS TO THE SCHOOLS

In the mid-nineteenth century, another team ball game was played in the public schools that came to rival cricket in importance and student enthusiasm. This sport was football, which became later, in the soccer form, arguably the most popular sport in the world today. This traditional village game, stamped out by earnest Victorians in all but the back streets and rural areas, reemerged as a gentleman's game in the Victorian public schools. Rowing and cricket could only be played during the warmer seasons, and to keep the boys occu-pied, controlled, and fit during the long winter, a cold-weather sport was needed, and the old game of football was introduced to meet that need.

When football was first played in the schools, some administrators objected that it was too violent and too plebian. Samuel Butler, the head of Shrewsbury from 1798 to 1836, condemned the sport when his boys played it casually on their own. It was a game, Butler said, "more fit for farm boys and labourers than for young gentlemen,"[22] although he later gave in and provided a football pitch on the school grounds. Notwithstanding doubts and resistance, football, fast paced and exciting, became the winter sport in most schools. In some schools, it was compulsory. "Many a would-be loafer," one commentator remarked, "has been made a man by being compelled, when a small boy, to go to football against his will. . . . What coercion there is, is only directed against the few, and those few will probably, if they are worth anything, look back upon it with feelings of gratitude."[23]

Most boys, however, enthusiastically took up the game. At Rugby, for example, football became the sport "round which the school thought of games centres."[24] When Tom Brown first entered Rugby, as Hughes wrote in 1857, his "heart beat quick as he passed the great school field ... in which several games at football were going on." Ignorant of the game, Tom was soon explained the Rugby rules for "the great science of football." Tom participated in the sport "with all his heart, and soon became well versed in all the mysteries of football by continued practice."[25] Anthony Trollope, however, in his 1868 collection *British Sports and Pastimes*, does not include an essay on football because "it has hardly as yet worked its way up to a dignity equal with that of Hunting and Shooting, or even with that of Cricket and Boat-racing."[26]

Unlike cricket, which by the eighteenth century had official rules and a governing body, there were no set guidelines for football, other than moving a ball down a rectangular field and across a goal line (or, in some forms, goal posts). Each public school played the sport differently, according to the amount of space, terrain, and geographic location of the school. It was, as one Victorian said, "a truly remarkable example of the effect of environment upon the evolution of a sport."[27] The schools could therefore only play intramural rather than inter-school matches, unless they agreed before each match on what rules to follow.

With its large playing fields, Rugby School developed a distinctive form of football, as formalized at an 1847 general meeting of the sixth form to draw up the rules at their school. It was agreed that players could carry the ball as well as kick it down the field, a way of playing adopted also at Marlborough, Cheltenham, and several other schools. Football played according to the Rugby rules was especially violent, because until 1877 "hacking," kicking the shins of one's opponents, was allowed in the schools. Enthusiasts for the game admitted that it was a rough sport but argued that hacking was useful, in that it "brought out the pluck and the manliness of boys, and induced that physical strength and endurance which in later years have stood so many of them in good stead."[28] In *Tom Brown's School Days*, Brooke denounces chronic bullying, but he advises the boys that "you'll be all the better football players for learning to stand it, and to take your own parts, and fight it through."[29] The *Saturday Review* accepted that "football is necessarily a pretty rough game all the world over; English schoolboys are not as negroes are, and a kick on the shins was generally forgotten as readily as it was given."[30]

Football at Harrow and Winchester was closer to modern soccer, in that they did not allow players to run with the ball. Kicking and dribbling with the foot was the only way to propel the football downfield. Eton developed two forms of football. The "wall game," a product of the school's more limited space, was, as the name suggests, played along the side of a wall. It was usually played only by the elite King's Scholars, those students of particular merit who paid reduced tuition and who lived in the College, the oldest house at Eton (and hence they are often just known as "Collegers"). The rest of the students, the Oppidans, could play the wall game only in their last year. Since 1845, there

The wall game was a form of football (soccer) played at Eton College, usually only by the elite "King's Scholars."

has been a big wall-game match on St. Andrew's Day, the 30th of November, between the Collegers and the Oppidans. With its limited participation, it was not as popular as the "field game," whose rules were formalized in 1847, the same year that the Rugby rules were set. Since the original playing field at Eton was quite small, this version of football was mainly a kicking game. The ball could only be caught to stop the ball, but not carried, and players could not be struck or kicked. A goal could be scored when the ball was kicked between two goal posts. Unlike those in the other schools where the numbers were changeable, only eleven players were allowed on each side.

FIVES AND ATHLETICS: OLD AND NEW SCHOOL SPORTS

Interspersed between rowing and cricket in the summer and football in the winter, the traditional game of fives was played at schools. Not meeting the character-building benefits of team sports, this game, played like modern-day handball in a walled court, did maintain physical fitness and drain excess energy. Most of the schools had at least one fives court, and some had many more. Harrow, for example, had 10. In addition to and more important than fives, a whole new category of individual sports emerged in the 1850s known as "athletics," what we call today track-and-field sports. (The word "athletics" was not used to describe sports in general until the late-nineteenth century.) More in emulation of the classical Greeks than was rowing, cricket, or football, these sports featured running contests, from short sprints to three-mile long-distance runs. Even then the premier distance was the mile, with precisely recorded times, such as the record at Rugby of 4 minutes, 39.75 seconds.

(In the early-nineteenth century, the renowned pedestrian Captain Barclay predicted that a runner would someday do a four-minute mile, but that was discounted as impossible.[31] Barclay's prediction did come true when Roger Bannister, appropriately an Englishman, ran the first sub-four-minute mile in 1954 in 3 minutes, 59.4 seconds.)

The running events developed in the schools not just from the example of the Greek contests, but more especially from the pre-Victorian boys' game of "hare and hounds," in which selected boys would race ahead, sometimes dropping paper as a trail, and other boys would then try to catch them before they reached the agreed-upon finish line, often at a distance of 10–12 miles. To control this unregulated activity, the schools reined in the running contests and put them on measured observable tracks on the school grounds. Other field contests, modeled on Greek athletics, were also added to the running events, including broad and high jumps, pole-vaulting, and contests of throwing hammers, usually of a weight of 16 pounds, approximately the same as the Greek javelin.

The human steeplechase was also introduced, which included jumping over hurdles and across bodies of water. This event, along with many of the athletics, suffered in reputation because of their association with the earlier discredited pedestrianism. Unlike their predecessor, these track-and-field sports were not ostensibly compromised by gambling, but some critics saw them as unfitting as a school sport. As with football, Trollope does not include an essay on athletics in *British Sports and Pastimes*, even though they have "undoubtedly pushed themselves into such prominent notice in late years as to give them almost a claim to be reckoned among British Sports." This role, however, he denies to them since "they have fallen somewhat short of the necessary dignity."[32] Athletics also suffered from the taint of individualism. Certainly no one could argue that Waterloo was won on a running track. Many sporting Victorians, however, would have agreed with Frederick Gale, who called athletics "manly and noble exercises."[33] As a test of physical fitness and skill, and as a venue for fierce competition, athletics became regular parts of the school sporting life.

UNIVERSITY SPORTS: OXFORD AND CAMBRIDGE

In the 1850s, when the public-school graduates went to Oxford or Cambridge, they were disappointed in the lack of organized sports at the universities. (When the word "universities" is used in the context of elite Victorian English education, the reference is to the two historic institutions of Oxford and Cambridge. The University of London was chartered in 1836, and "redbrick" universities were established in the new industrial cities in the late-nineteenth century, but these schools did not attract public-school graduates, nor did they develop a strong sporting culture in the nineteenth century.) As with the public schools in pre-Victorian times, there were the occasional inter-university sporting matches—for example, the

Oxford-Cambridge boat race, begun in 1829 but held only intermittently, as well as the Oxford-Cambridge cricket match, first played in 1827—but sports were not important in the universities. The young students, imbued with sports from their public school days, soon changed that by pressuring the universities to have more organized games, better playing facilities, and more opportunities for play. The universities responded, with some colleges developing more of a sporting culture than others. Magdalene College at Cambridge, for example, became what a critic in 1904 called "a pleasant residential sporting club for the well-to-do or more or less well-descended young men."[34] Cambridge's Jesus College and Balliol at Oxford were also among those known for their sporting life, whereas some of the other colleges had little interest in physical culture or competition. Generally, however, although not as pervasive as at the public schools, sports became an important part of the education at Oxford and Cambridge.

The spark that intensified the interest in sports at the two universities was the inter-collegiate competitions and especially the sporting rivalries between the two universities. With sportsmen at Oxford characteristically wearing dark blue, and those at Cambridge in light-blue colors, the "battle of the blues" caught the interest of people well beyond the orb of the schools. This competition was most manifest in the revived university boat race, which in 1856 became a regular, annual, and hotly contested event. Frederick Gale said of

Oxford-Cambridge boat race; the winning crew coming ashore.

the race that it was a "moral certainty that one certain day, and at a certain hour, the crews of the very pick of the manhood of Young England will be found in either boat ready to row till they drop for the honour of their University." The race had become such a national event, Gale said, that a special act of Parliament had to be passed to regulate the river traffic on the day of the race.[35]

The philosopher and sportsman Leslie Stephen extolled rowing even as he acknowledged the physical cost of the effort:

> There is a certain amount of pain connected with even a moderate degree of this exercise. There are blisters and excoriations upon various parts of your person. There is a horrid aching in the muscles to be overcome. There is the annoyance of turning out in all weathers. . . . There is the severe strain when a strong headwind makes the labour of forcing your oar through the air almost equal to that of driving it through the water.

This suffering, however, Stephen argues, is worth it, for the pleasure of the "fanatical enthusiasm" rowing arouses in the participants. "Now this is the real glory of rowing; it is a temporary fanaticism of the most intense kind; whilst it lasts it is less a mere game than a religion." Rowing creates a valuable bond among the racing crew, "perhaps the closest known, with the single and doubtful exception of marriage . . . . If rowing does nothing else, it serves as a bond of unusual strength for drawing men together at the time when their affections are, so to speak, most malleable and most cohesive." Stephen also credits the way the sport develops character and leadership abilities. To captain a university crew, for example, involves the same skills as that of a successful general. "He ought to be a refined diplomatist, to have a rapid and decisive judgment, and the power of enforcing discipline. He should have the courage to hold firmly to his own opinion, and the rarer courage to make changes when it is necessary."[36]

Another writer compared the university rower to the British sailor. "It is not alone a régime of strict bodily self-denial to which the youth who is ambitious of aquatic fame must submit. He must have tolerated without wincing, at some time or other, such volleys of vituperative exhortation as only the aquatic 'coach' can discharge." He is, however, the object of hero worship, for "after all, there is a strong strain of the old Norse pirate in the composition of the modern Englishman."[37] The training was especially intense in preparation for the university boat race and was what a surgeon called "the greatest cruelty to animals of any known game."[38] Others thought such suffering was worth it. As one enthusiast extolled, "Nothing tends more to produce manliness in the youth of the upper and middle classes in this country than the rigour and enthusiasm with which boating is pursued at both Universities."[39]

R. C. Lehmann, a late-Victorian writer for the humor magazine *Punch*, wrote with apparent seriousness about rowing, almost glorifying the arduousness of this training. Each member of the crew, he said, will have suffered much, he will have rowed many weary miles, have learnt the misery of aching limbs and blistered hands. . . . He will have laboured under broiling suns, or with snow storms and bitter winds beating against him, he will have voluntarily cut himself off from many pleasant indulgences. But on the other hand his triumphs will have been sweet, he will have trained himself to submit to discipline, to accept discomfort cheerfully, to keep a brave face in adverse circumstances; he will have learnt the necessity of unselfishness and patriotism.[40]

In his 1849 novel, *Alton Locke*, Charles Kingsley describes the race itself as "a sight such as could only be seen in England—some hundred of young men, who might, if they had chosen, have been lounging effeminately about the streets, subjecting themselves voluntarily to that intense exertion, for the mere pleasure of toil. The true English stuff came out there. . . . that grim, earnest, stubborn energy, which since the days of the old Romans, the English possess alone of all the nations of this earth."[41]

The results of the intense training tended to benefit Oxford more than Cambridge. Disgruntled Cambridge partisans attributed their losses to the large number of students at Oxford from Eton, the preeminent rowing school. Oxford also had, Cambridge claimed, better rivers, located as it was on the meeting of the Isis (as that stretch of the Thames was called) and the Cherwell, much more conducive to rowing than the river Cam. Cambridge supporters therefore raised money to improve the Cam. "If the improvement is general and substantial, we may hope that Cambridge will again be established on a permanent footing as a great school of athletic excellence in this the severest branch of the study."[42]

The university students of course played cricket, climaxed by the annual Oxford-Cambridge match at Lord's. The other new team ball sport, football, was a different matter. Since each public school played by different rules, it was almost impossible to play a game within much less between the universities. To resolve this problem within their own university, Cambridge held a meeting in 1848 to establish one set of rules by which all their students could play. The meeting, attended by representatives of the public schools, agreed on an amalgam of rules, based generally on those of Harrow, which disallowed catching or holding the ball, tripping, and hacking. Some students at Cambridge separated from the main group and played football according to the Rugby School rules. Meanwhile, the public schools, refusing to follow the Cambridge compromise, continued to play each by their own individual and distinctive rules.

Athletics—track-and-field sports—made their appearance at the universities slowly in the 1850s, then in full force in the 1860s. Oxford especially embraced athletics. It was "the *alma mater* of Athletic Sport. . . . To the historian of the future the athletic movement must be described as another of the many 'Oxford Movements.' "[43] Cambridge also took up athletic sports, and thereby added another contest to the Oxford-Cambridge rivalry. As reported in an

1866 article on "Light and Dark Blue" in *Blackwood's Edinburgh Magazine*, the author explains that "the battle-grounds on which the light and dark blue now meet are the river, the cricket-field . . . [and] to these, of late years, has been added a sort of modern Olympic festival, known as the 'Inter-University Athletics,' held alternately at Oxford and Cambridge."[44]

Although universities did not have the same mission as did the public schools to exercise moral control and foster character development, sports were certainly seen as a useful antidote to the traditional (and still current) degeneracies of the typical undergraduate. Surely it was much better that a university student

> should spend his hours of relaxation on the cricket-ground, in the racket-court, or on the river, than in galloping a wretched hack ten or twenty miles along a turnpike road to pay for a bad dinner at some roadside inn . . . or in lounging with no earthly object up and down the streets of a university town. And it is much better for him to go off to bed at a reasonable hour, thoroughly tired out with a long day's cricket, or a severe 'grind' on the river in his college eight, than to sit up to any hour of the morning at an uproarious supper-party.[45]

THE DEBATE OVER SPORTS IN THE SCHOOLS AND UNIVERSITIES

In 1857, in an article in the *Saturday Review*, the author confidently said that "We do not suppose that any one hesitates to admit the great importance of keeping up the proficiency of schoolboys in manly exercises to the highest possible pitch. It is in these sports that the character of the boy is formed."[46] In fact, there were those who did question importance of sports in the schools and universities. Despite all the exhortations about the moral benefits, by the 1860s there were naysayers who complained sports had become too pervasive in education. The ideal of *mens sana in corpore sano* had become unbalanced, and *corpore* was dominating over *mens*. There was concern that with the great emphasis placed in sports in English elite education, with English youth spending more time batting cricket balls and rowing boats than in study, academic standards were deteriorating.

In response to these and other concerns, the Royal Clarendon Commission was created in 1864 to investigate the academic standards and student life of the English public schools. The commission found that the quality of academic work had declined but it nevertheless reported positively on the effects of the sports and games: "The cricket and football fields are not merely places of amusement, they help to form some of the most valuable social qualities and manly virtues, and they hold like the classroom and the boarding house, a distinct and important place in public-school education. . . . The importance which boys themselves attach to games is somewhat greater perhaps than might reasonably be desired, but within moderate limits it is highly useful."[47]

Inter-university athletic sports.

As far as preparing boys for higher education, a university witness testified to the commission that there was a notable improvement in the moral character of the students, which he attributed to the new emphasis on sports in the public schools.[48] The witness apparently did not complain about the lack of academic preparedness, perhaps because at the universities also, the sporting culture had taken over. The *Saturday Review* in 1869 published an article harshly criticizing the dominance of sports in the universities:

> Even at schools athletics soon became a business; but at the Universities they were speedily exalted almost into a profession.... They would have discovered that the academical year is conveniently divided into terms named according to the particular pursuits to which they are principally devoted. They would have suggested that perhaps there was a classical term, and a mathematical term, and a philosophical or historical term; and they would have been told that such was by no means the case, but that rather there was a cricket term, and a rowing term, and an athletic term.[49]

Even the *Illustrated Sporting and Dramatic News* complained, in 1874, that the involvement in sports, and particularly the inter-university competitions, had been carried too far. "We are well aware that a vast amount of attention has recently been ... given to all manner of pastimes calculated to relax the mind or exercise the body ... but it is not necessary that Oxford and Cambridge establish a professoriate in every branch of recreation ready at the moment's notice to cross blades for the honour of their respective Universities." There is "bitter and increasing complaints of college authorities as to the difficulty of getting men to work up to the requirements of an ordinary pass, to say nothing of the Honours examination." However much the athletes are honored, "it will not be denied that something more is needed to fit a man for the duties of life than the honour of representing his University in one of the many tourneys she feels bound in honour to engage in."[50]

Punch voiced the same concerns, but with humor. Lampooning with many cartoons the way it felt the schools and universities had become sporting clubs rather than academic institutions, it also published satiric articles. In 1869, it suggested that "in consequence of the increasing preference now given to the study of Athletics in the University," there would soon be great changes in the two universities. "Latin will be nowhere, Leaping everything; Geometry will yield to Gymnastics; Philosophy to Fencing; PALEY to Pole-jumping; HOMER to Hurdles; Co-sines to Calisthenics; Trigonometry to Training." The examination system would deal with such subjects as "Fistiana," running, hurdles, as well as boating and cricket, and other sports. The master of the prestigious Trinity College at Cambridge would be chosen after a "stand-up pugilistic encounter in the College Quadrangle with an antagonist of his own size, age and weight." Scholarships would be awarded based on victories in sporting contests. "It must be conceded that the above arrangements are not only not improbable, but will be rendered absolutely necessary by the impossibility of Undergraduates being able to find time for [academic study]."[51]

The supporters of school athletics were able to drown out the detractors, drawing on the familiar arguments of manliness and morality. Hoary Frost maintained that sports keep education from being "toilsome and enfeebled."[52] Cricket in the universities was praised as "a game which keeps boys out of mischief. It is a training of youth for a manly life. It lays up a store of strength and health against old age. It makes individual men lifelong friends. It unites whole schools and universities." Playing such games is not a waste of time. "Cricket is consistent with study, and. . . . the cricketer makes a good schoolmaster. The truth is, that athletics are an integral part and a powerful support of all education: they make it popular."[53]

To support the argument that sports strengthened and not diminished academics, the example of Charles Burgess ("C.B.") Fry (1872–1956) was often cited. Fry excelled in school and at Oxford in a range of sports, from cricket and football to athletics, and continued into adulthood playing first-class county cricket and club football. He was "undoubtedly one of the finest all-round athletes of the century." What made him particularly remarkable to his contemporaries was not only his excellence in so many sports, but also that he "at the same time has proved himself to possess considerable intellectual ability,"[54] the winner of many prizes for outstanding academic performance. The fact that Fry, but not others, was held up so often as an example of both athletic and academic success suggests that such combinations may have been a rarity.

Headmasters and other administrators and teachers in public schools tended to give strong and sincere, if self-serving, endorsement of the role of sports in their schools. The headmaster of Clifton College, a new public school near Bristol, told the boys that in his school, "you are expected to imbibe a love for manly tastes and pursuits; something of an active, enduring, persevering spirit; something of a true contempt for effeminacy and indulgence, and torpid do-nothing idleness. The more sickly and morbid elements of character are purged out of men by the discipline of such a life as yours."[55] All of this would be achieved through sports. The physician at Rugby School, that model of sports as molders of character, advocated the removal of the "idle boy" who "does not join in games, but swaggers and lounges about, should, after failing to *make* him take part in them, be weeded out and got rid of, before he has the opportunity of corrupting others through his idleness and the evil it engenders."[56]

The physician Hely Hutchinson Almond (1832–1903), headmaster of Loretto School, outside Edinburgh and modeled on the English public schools, was the most ardent champion of a sports regimen in the schools. Making physical education and athletics central to his school program, he defended the inclusion of even rough sports like football (soccer and rugby):

Under the circumstances of the luxurious and self-indulgent habits in which boys are increasingly brought up at home, the constant panic lest they should suffer any pain, the absence of apprehension lest their moral and physical fibre should become feeble by disuse, and the tendency of the examination system to make the development of character a secondary consideration, I would not care to face the responsibility of conducting a school were there not rooted in it, as I hope, an imperishable tradition, an enthusiastic love of football.[57]

In 1896, a scathing article was published in the *New Review* criticizing the poor quality of education in the public schools, where what they teach is in fact "athletics. At least that is presumably what they teach."[58] Almond immediately responded, detailing the time spent on exercise and sports in his school—daily running, workouts in the gymnasium, compulsory outdoor games, all of up to four hours a day. "Is this amount of open air and circulation of the blood excessive? I can only say, that as a matter of duty and conscience, no power on earth could make me lessen it." He details similar programs in the other public schools, faulting only Eton for absenting boys from compulsory games when they are being punished. "That is the worst sort of punishment I know of west of Turkey." He admits that there is not enough attention paid to intellectual matters, but "our modern games are in themselves an education. They teach, as no books can do, qualities which, especially in these high-pressure times, are essential to the force and vitality of the race and are most conducive to the vigour and prosperity of the individual."[59]

The educator Edward Lyttelton (1855–1942) had been an enthusiastic champion of sports in the schools until reflection in older age caused him to question their dominance. The scion of a great aristocratic cricketing family and himself a distinguished cricketer as a student at Eton and at Cambridge, Lyttelton was assistant master at Wellington College and then at Eton in the 1880s. In 1890 he was appointed headmaster of the new public school of Haileybury College, in Hertfordshire, and, in 1905, headmaster of Eton, serving there until 1916.

As a young master, he had endorsed the encouragement of sports in schools. They were useful in developing discipline in boys, he argued, in two ways: "By interests, to obey implicitly the word of command . . . and secondly, should it so turn out, he is disciplined by being raised to a post of command, where he feels the gravity of responsible office and the difficulty of making prompt decisions and securing a willing obedience." Lyttelton also endorsed school sports on the grounds of health. He delighted in pointing out the difference between sturdy English boys and that favorite object of derision, the French youth: "Few things are more consoling to our national vanity than the contrast presented by the spectacle of English boys engaged in one of our outdoor games, and that of a troop of sallow knock-kneed French youths filing in groups of three along the high-road, for this is their corresponding and solitary recreation."[60]

Although still championing outdoor sports, Lyttelton did come to doubt that they were useful in curbing that most condemned of sins, "solitary vice." In 1883, he discreetly surveyed physicians and educators on its prevalence, the results of which revealed the startling information that about 80–90 percent of the boys indulged in the practice. Addressing a meeting of headmasters, Lyttelton admitted that the old remedy of "plenty of occupation for body and mind" was not working and that boys would have to be counseled regularly on the subject.[61]

In his memoirs written in older age, reflecting on his days as a schoolboy at Eton, Lyttelton expressed feelings of regret that so much time had been spent on sports. Cricket, he said, had been all-important in his youth, with the annual Eton-Harrow match at Lord's "the annual climax of the history of mankind." With so much emphasis on cricket, "not only were many other subjects of knowledge left in the cold and a huge amount of time and thought given to this absorbing game; but, hardly credible though it may sound, we unconsciously conceived of beauty almost entirely in terms of physical motion and physical skill." He bemoaned that "we missed out on art, poetry, music. All was cricket."[62] These words were expressed long after the end of the Victorian era. In the last half of the nineteenth century, the dominant motif was not regret but rather enthusiasm for the new sporting culture in the schools and universities, a culture that came to permeate all of Victorian society.

4

Rational Recreation and Muscular Christianity

The English public schools and universities provided a model in the mid-nineteenth century of how sports could be used to promote rather than subvert Victorian values. This was a lesson that the second generation of utilitarians and evangelicals were quick to learn. Still fervently committed to their causes of utility and godliness, they came to see that physical culture and competitive play were not necessarily a waste of time and energy or a threat to moral rectitude but that sports could be tools to help further their goal of establishing a rational, orderly, productive, and sinless society. With their championship rather than opposition, the concept of "sport" was transmuted, from that of pleasure to an activity of duty. Victorians, of course, continued to have fun playing sports, but, under the influence of the pervading social values, this pleasure was rationalized as a necessary obligation in the service of utilitarian benefits and religious work.

Utilitarians had always recognized the importance of physical exercise to maintain the body for useful work. Jeremy Bentham would "trot" regularly in his garden, a more efficient exercise using less time than the usual walking. His colleague James Mill, educating his young son John Stuart at home and teaching him to read Greek by age three, included a daily walk in his rigorous regimen. The father made sure, however, that they did not waste time, and so as they walked, he quizzed his son about his readings. John Stuart Mill remembered that "with my earliest recollections of green fields and wild flowers, is mingled that of the account I gave him daily of what I had read the day before."[1]

Mere exercise was expanded in the mid-Victorian age to include organized sports and games as useful and even necessary. With standardized rules and controlled play, sports could now be considered "rational recreation." Concerned with providing safe amusements for the working classes to keep them from the sins inherent in pub life, the defenders of rational recreation advocated opening parks and playgrounds for the urban poor, as well as encouraging them to go to museums and other instructive sites. The concept of rational recreation was not, however, just a specific program to improve working-class conditions, but it was used in a more general sense to describe the acceptance and promotion of games as well as other amusements that met the criteria of utility. Sports were commonly evaluated according to how useful they were for specific purposes. Unable to accept pleasure and playfulness for their own sake, the mid-Victorians rationalized those potentially dangerous feelings into rational recreation. As the Victorian biologist George Romanes said, "Recreation is, *or ought to be*, not a pastime entered upon for the sake of the pleasure which it affords, but an act of duty undertaken for the sake of the subsequent power which it generates, and the subsequent profit which it insures."[2] An evangelical minister, R. W. Dale, voiced the same utilitarian argument: "The object of all recreation is to increase our capacity for work, to keep the blood pure, and the brain bright, and the temper kindly and sweet."[3]

Utilitarianism, and the broader laissez-faire economic liberalism from which it was derived, espoused principles that were not only dear to the heart of industrial capitalists, but also that were integral to the very nature of organized sports. Nineteenth-century liberalism was based on the values of competition, self-help, struggle and effort, and survival of the fittest. These were the values that shaped the world of Charles Darwin, and, in his theory of evolution and natural selection, he gave them scientific legitimacy. But what better values also to describe the world of sports, in which athletes compete and struggle without assistance, through hard work, with the superior athlete or team the victor? Drawing on such congenial parallels, sports-minded Victorians, wedded to an ethic of utility, could also find specific benefits in the sporting life.

THE UTILITY OF SPORTS FOR MILITARY STRENGTH

Probably the most oft-used practical justification for sports was its military value, appropriately so since so many sports had martial origins. An argument used in the public schools, with the reiteration of the misquoted Duke of Wellington's credit of the playing fields of Eton for the victory at Waterloo, sports were seen in the larger adult social context as necessary for maintaining national defense. Sports were important, it was argued, because without them "warlike skill would not be so prominent amongst Englishmen as of old, but would dwindle into inferiority with that of other nations. Healthful recreations [add] muscular vigour to the body, rendering the people expert in warlike and manly accomplishments, and better qualified to expel our foes and defend ourselves at home."[4] This argument was particularly effective after the poor performance of the British troops in the Crimean War in 1854–1856. Britain was involved in no other European wars between the defeat of Napoleon in

1815 and the outbreak of World War I in 1914, but the maintenance of *Pax Britannica*, challenged as it was by colonial wars, and the frightening Indian "Sepoy" Revolt of 1857, as well as by wars on the continent that did not bode well for British security, required a fighting-ready citizenry. Military authorities were, therefore, quite willing to accept the convincing argument that the best way to prepare for war in times of peace was through sports.

The English, it was argued, "have always been good soldiers and sailors, and the English have always been passionately fond of manly sports. Therefore, instead of neglecting them or treating them coldly, it is the duty of every patriotic citizen to join in." Specific sports were touted as serving particular military functions. Horseracing and hunting were necessary to maintain a trained cavalry. As the Duke of Rutland said, "If we had no turf, no Newmarket, we should have no cavalry. A ride across country with a good pack of hounds is certainly no bad education for a cavalry officer, who should primarily be a good horseman before he is cunning of fence, wise in strategy, and generally accomplished in the science of war."[5] Another advocate maintained that foxhunting teaches discipline, self-dependence, and a "combination of judgment and courage removed from timidity on the one side and foolhardiness on the other,"[6] all qualities needed in successful military leaders.

Recognizing the usefulness of sports in keeping soldiers physically fit and disciplined, the Duke of Wellington, commander-in-chief of the British army, ordered in 1841 that every military barracks be provided with a cricket ground. Other sports were also fostered to maintain military readiness, but not, the *Saturday Review* pointed out, running, "for Englishman are not in the habit of running from their enemies."[7]

Tied to military utility, sports were also seen as a factor in the nurturing and maintenance of English liberty. In his 1868 book *On the Sports and Pursuits of the English, As Bearing on Their National Character*, as summarized in a review in the *New Sporting Magazine*, the Earl of Wilton argued that "a love of sports engenders a spirit of independence," and that the indifference to sports among ancient eastern nations caused their fall. The reviewer of the book praised "the noble author" for exemplifying "that where no love of sport nor of manly pastime can be found, there no spirit of freedom can be shown." In England, "the spirit of freedom" has never been quenched, "their ardour in the sports and pastimes peculiar to the land of their birth being as energetically pursed by Englishmen, as their love of liberty has been fostered and clung to."[8]

HEALTH THROUGH SPORTS

For soldiers and civilians alike, the most compelling argument for playing sports was for reasons of health. The Victorians, especially among the middle classes, were obsessively concerned about health—it was a repeated topic in letters, memoirs, and conversations. There were certainly some genuine physical reasons for anxiety. Urban life spawned many health dangers, including the frightening cholera and typhoid, which were no respecters of class.

Victoria's beloved Prince Albert, for example, died in 1861 of typhoid from faulty drains at Windsor Palace. Physical causes for illness were compounded by intense psychological pressures in that competitive age of laissez-faire industrial capitalism and of rigid moral standards, causing what we now diagnose as psychosomatic illnesses, yet which weighed as heavily on the Victorian body as did those of physical genesis. The unhealthy lifestyle of middle-class Victorian women, with the lack of physical activity and the constricting corseted dress, was intensified by the usually buried frustration that many women felt at their impotence and lack of purpose in their sheltered domestic sphere. Illness for many bourgeois women became a normal state, one which had the advantage of bringing attention to otherwise idealized but ignored self-sacrificing guardians of the hearth.

To deal with the burgeoning health concerns, the medical profession expanded dramatically in the first half of the nineteenth century. New treatments were developed, including the very popular "hydropathy" of Dr. James Gully (1808–1883) and other equally complicated cures. The simplest and most popular remedy, however, as well as for prevention of ill health, was through recreative out-of-doors sports. Stressing the connection between health and sports, the mid-Victorians focused on the physical well-being of men. (It was not until the late-nineteenth century that concerns about the health of future mothers opened sporting opportunities to women.) A recurrent theme was the ill effects of sedentary urban life, with nostalgic looks back on the idealized past in which men used their muscles in work and lived healthy outdoor lives. In his memories of earlier sporting days, C. A. Wheeler included accounts of healthy vigorous men in the early-nineteenth century, for whom outdoor exercise was an essential part of their lives. The cricketer Edward Budd, for example, could play well into his eighties and never spent any time worrying about anything. "Much of his exemption from disturbance may be attributed to his great love for, and indulgence in, Athletic out-door amusements." Wheeler delighted in describing the physical feats of the renowned pedestrian Captain Ross, who could walk two nights and a day in pouring rain over the Scottish mountain range.

> The men of the present day don't do such mad, foolish things, it may be said; still there was a ground-work of energy and pluck in the wild deeds of sportsmen of bygone days, which to a certain extent was useful. . . . In these degraded groveling, money-making times, it would do the present generation no harm, if we could bring back to life some of the old race of men, with all their madness, and reckless disregard of life and money.[9]

For maximum health, it was argued, recreation should be the opposite of one's daily life. If a man worked in an office, using brain rather than brawn, then outdoor exercise was the perfect antidote. The esteemed surgeon Dr. James Paget cited cricket as a game that allows one who has sat at a desk during the week to be able to go out and exercise muscles "wanting freer and more willing movements. . . . Recreations should exercise the powers which are the least used in the work; and this, not only for pleasure, but for utility."[10] Romanes also emphasized the duty to engage in muscular exercise for reasons of health:

> Not only does it allow time for the brain to rest when exhausted by mental work, but, by increasing the circulation all over the body, it promotes the threefold function of oxygenation, nutrition and drainage . . . . Health may be taken as implying capacity for work, as well as to a large, though to a less absolute degree, the capacity for happiness, and, as duty means our obligation to promote the general happiness, it follows that in no connection is the voice of duty more urgent than it is in the advancement of all that is conducive to health.[11]

The endorsement of doctors and scientists of the healthful benefits of a sporting life carried great weight, but no authority was as influential as the great expounder of Victorian values with the appropriately optimistic name, Samuel Smiles (1812–1904), whose 1859 *Self-Help* was a best-selling book in nineteenth-century England. In *Self-Help*, Smiles examines the lives of successful people and explains the various qualities such as hard work, energy, perseverance, and self-reliance that helped them get ahead. Among these qualities of success he stresses the importance of physical health. He quotes a letter from a soldier in India who said he got on well there, "owing, physically speaking, to a sound digestion." This oblique reference is to the chronic Victorian malady of constipation. Smiles agrees that a "sound digestion" is necessary to maintain "the capacity for continuous working in any calling" and "hence the necessity for attending to health, even as a means of intellectual labour," with physical exercise as a means of achieving good bowels and sound bodies. Concerned with mental as well as physical health, Smiles laments that the neglect of exercise leads especially among the young to emotional malaise, to "discontent, unhappiness, inaction, and reverie,—displaying itself in contempt for real life and disgust at the beaten tracks of men,—a tendency which in England has been called Byronism, and in Germany Wertherism." Smiles quotes an American doctor who said that the only remedy for this "green sickness" is physical exercise.[12]

What better stimulus to take up physical exercise than the fear of becoming like the Germans, or even like the discredited Romantic poet Lord Byron (forgetting that Byron himself was a sportsman)? Sports enthusiasts used the argument of the healthfulness of sports as a reason for English superiority over what they considered the less fit continental countries. Romanes scorned countries such as Germany that did not play team sports. "I know from experience that it is hopeless to persuade German students, as a class, to adopt what they consider childish toys—the bats and balls of cricket. All I can say is, so much the worse for the Continental universities."[13] Even if they did not pick up a ball or bat, the Germans did develop in the nineteenth century a distinctive form of gymnastic exercise known as *turnen*, to strengthen their youth in the age of increasing militarism, exercises which the English tended to dismiss as boring and too mechanical. Most English sportsmen extolled their own sporting traditions and attributed to the healthfulness of their sports the very power of the British Empire. As the cricket historian Charles Box boastfully claimed, "Much less than any other nation do the English need to be taught the art of preserving health. They are admitted to be the strongest of races—proof enough that they are the healthiest. Their rural and aquatic sports, athletic games, tastes for country life ... nourish in them that muscular pith and animal impetuosity which crush down all obstacles."[14]

In addition to the traditional sports, new sports were developed particularly for reasons of health (or at least the new sporting pleasures were justified by claims of health). The most frequently prescribed exercise for those who were not fit enough or so inclined towards team sports was swimming, or, to use Victorian terminology, bathing. By mid-century, water exercise was recognized as useful for health, and, in the interest of promoting beneficial rational recreation and sanitary facilities for the working classes, Parliament passed a Baths and Washhouses Act in 1846 (a linkage which accounts for the English use of the word "bathing" to describe swimming as well as washing). Towns and cities began building baths, both indoors and outdoors.

Even more healthful and invigorating than bathing in pools was, according to Victorian health experts, swimming in the sea. Facilitated by the easier and quicker transportation that railroads provided, sea bathing became a very popular medicinal duty in mid- and late-Victorian England. As an enthusiast extolled, "The mere mention of the sea sends a thrill of delight through the hearts of all true swimmers."[15] Sea bathing was a sport that the working classes as well as propertied classes could enjoy, and one in which even proper ladies could participate, with their modesty protected by the full-body bathing costumes and by the development of "bathing machines." These contraptions were like little cabins on wheels, which women could enter from the back, and which were then wheeled into the sea, often by horses. Women could then exit straight into the water without their bodies being exposed.

To get the full health benefit, one should actually exercise in the water, and so there was a push to teach swimming, useful for "promoting great muscular strength [and] tranquilizing of the nervous system. ... It is easy to conceive of what utility swimming must be."[16] The ability to swim also had the easily defended utilitarian value of personal safety. As the 1868 edition of *Every Boy's Book: A Complete Encyclopedia of Sports and Amusements* pointed out, "The English, above all other persons, should be good swimmers, exposed as they are by their insular situation, and commercial pursuits, and disposition to visit other lands, so frequently to perils by sea."[17] A swimmer could also save someone else's life, especially important because so many people did not know how to swim, which was, a sports advocate declared, "a national disgrace. ... We should lay down the axiom that every man and *woman* in this country should be able to do so."[18] To facilitate this goal, Victorian ingenuity came up with all kinds of devices to teach swimming. In addition to the pole holding up novice swimmers used at Eton, patents were taken out for a "device consisting of gaiters with flaps buckled to the leg," an apparatus with "light steel bands or straps fastened round the ankles, to which is attached a wing or fin," and a wire "drawn tightly along the bath, some twelve feet above the water, so the top of which travelled a grooved pulley made with a hollow-rimmed wheel."[19]

SPORTS AND SOCIAL PURITY

Just as sports were used to control the sexuality of young adolescent boys in school, so they were seen as a means to maintain purity and moral rectitude in adults. The Victorian sexual code, based on gendered spheres and personalities, implicitly accepted a double standard of morality, recognizing the sexual needs of men and denying such desires to women. Even respectable men could quietly go to prostitutes, and indeed in Victorian England prostitution was a booming occupation for poor women. For respectable women, absolute chastity before and outside of marriage was strictly required. Nevertheless, despite the greater tacit latitude for men, the code of respectability was in support of as much male self-control as possible, which could be achieved through participation in vigorous, exhausting sports.

It is athletic sport, a late-Victorian said proudly, that has kept the youth from unsavory amusements and that has therefore "made the nation stronger, manlier, cleaner and more sober than it was before the pursuit of athletics became a national characteristic."[20] Hoary Frost, in his 1856 survey of "National Sports, Ancient and Modern," took a longer perspective. He argued, with exaggeration, that all English monarchs, from William the Conqueror to Victoria, have encouraged "manly sports and recreations of the people" to foster moral behavior: "It is right to diffuse amongst the people a relish for such recreations, which, it may be truly said, divert thousands from the apparently voluptuous, but ultimately degrading sensual indulgences to which most men are exposed; and which, but for the encouragement given to good old English sports, would lure the best of men within the meshes of iniquity."[21] All writers, he said, "agree in the importance of encouraging national sports as entirely consonant with the habits of Englishmen.... They are often a safeguard against the vicious allurements of large towns, and the dissipations of youth." The Greek city-states and the Roman Empire fell, Frost warned, when they gave up sports. "Let the State, therefore, watch over and encourage the national sports of Old England; for such are of more importance than the majority of legislators are disposed to imagine."[22]

Extending the primarily middle-class moral code to the working classes, the clergyman James Pycroft claimed that "drinking, gambling, cudgel-playing insensibly disappear before a manly recreation, which draws the labourer from the dark haunts of vice and misery to the open common." Rev. Pycroft, an avid cricketer, was certainly in agreement with the general consensus that the best "manly recreation" to inculcate the Victorian moral values was cricket.

Not only a game of rules and orderly play, it is also one in which there is no touching, and the players all wear pure white.[23] Refuting the arguments of those who say that cricket was a waste of time and energy, W. J. Ford replied,

> Political economy and its votaries ... tell us that such labour as is expended on hitting, or on bowling, or on stopping, or on catching a mere ball, is unproductive labour, and consequently labour lost, while they show no limit to their contempt for those who, not being actually players themselves, squander—so they call it—valuable time in watching other people waste time that is equally valuable. ... We may fairly ask ... what would [they] do with themselves if there were no cricket to watch. He would be a poor philosopher indeed who would find fault with the open-air stage of Lord's or the Oval, and would yet allow the music-hall and the theatre to stifle their nightly victims. The strictest of Puritans could hardly find fault with bat and ball as being the inculcators of evil principles; rather like the study of the ingenuous arts, do they 'soften our characters and forbid them to be savage.'[24]

Ranking the cricket field as "infinitely more than the hunting-field ... the true national civiliser," an author in *All the Year Round* defended sports in general as neutralizing "the temptations which, before they were established and recognised amongst us, existed for a very pernicious variety of idleness." Athleticism "has done more than any other invention of this century has done towards stamping out that physical and moral malady which, in the pages of this journal, was once powerfully described by the author of David Copperfield as 'dry rot in men.'"[25]

SPORTS AS A MARKER OF MANLINESS

Even as Victorians wanted to make men good, they did not want to make them weak. There was a rumbling fear that in the industrial age men were becoming soft, or, that most feared of qualities, effeminate. Machines were taking the place of muscles in doing work, and women could now do the same physical work as men, blurring the differences between the sexes. It was definitely not appropriate, as in many other cultures, for a man to prove his virility by the number of his sexual conquests. For Victorians, therefore, sports, so often described as "manly," took on particular importance as a means of engendering and displaying masculinity. An ethic that reinforced the sanction on female participation in sporting activities, it legitimated in that utilitarian world the importance given to sports for men.

Men who spent their days in offices or factories could display their manly muscles if not in their work then in their play. Frederick Gale could proudly claim in 1885 that sports had made even lower-middle-class workers into true manly men. Employees, who had "from overwork and constant late hours in cities and large towns, degenerated into effeminate Englishmen, who were designated by the opprobrious name of 'Counter-Skippers,'" have now been converted into "fine, manly young fellows of pluck and sinew. And when a lady goes into a shop to make a purchase now, very likely the attendant, who serves her, will, on Saturday afternoon, be the champion of the cricket field, the best oarsman in his crew on the river . . . or the quickest runner across country in any other athletic sport."[26] Physical exercise and sports could even increase manliness in a biological and not just social sense. A former boxer reportedly was concerned that he had no children. His boxing coach advised him to work out, "and you'll soon have a family, never fear." He and his wife then had twins.[27]

MOUNTAINEERING AND VICTORIAN VALUES

Along with cricket and other established sports, a new sport was developed in mid-century that supported and embodied Victorian values—that of mountaineering. Throughout history people had climbed mountains, but now it became for the English an organized, systematic, and extremely popular sport. The strenuous effort of climbing up mountains required hard work, discipline, and struggle, even as it also served to work off excess dangerous energies and anxieties. In a world of tremendous change, and with the pressures of strict moral control and constant improvement, the escape and effort of mountaineering became a welcome relief.

For many Victorians, the pressures of life were compounded by religious doubts, the seeds of which were sowed in the Enlightenment. In the nineteenth century, developments in the science of geology, which challenged the Biblical account of the creation of the earth, nurtured these doubts. Religious faith was most sorely tested by the theories of Charles Darwin, as set forth in his *Origin of Species* in 1859 and *Descent of Man* in 1871, in which evolution and natural selection replace divine providence with mere chance as the creator of the human species. Some Victorians, like Thomas Carlyle (1795–1881), drowned out what Carlyle called the "Everlasting No" of religious doubt with the "Everlasting Yea" of work. For Carlyle, that work was writing. Others found relief through the work of athletic sports, including for many, the challenge of climbing mountains—vigorously, strenuously, and therapeutically.

Mountaineering first became popular as a sport in the mid-1850s, when railroads and steamships made the Alps easily accessible to English sportsmen and some sportswomen. There were mountains in England, and also in Scotland, but none had the extraordinary challenge of the Alps of Switzerland and its neighboring countries. Until the late-nineteenth century, mountaineering was essentially synonymous with alpine climbing. The person most responsible for popularizing the sport in England was the journalist Albert Smith, who climbed the summit of Mont Blanc in 1851 and then returned to England to lecture and write about his adventures. In 1857 he and like-minded colleagues formed the Alpine Club. With only a few members at its founding, the Alpine Club grew rapidly and soon had "hundreds of high-spirited Britons, well educated, well mannered, with high tastes and sympathies, blest with abundant vigour, but moderate means, [who] find it impossible to gratify the national longing for sport within the old-established boundaries, or in the time-honoured ways."[28]

The secularist philosopher Leslie Stephen (1832–1904), a grandson of a first-generation Anglican evangelical and the father of the Bloomsbury novelist Virginia Woolf, made the arduous journey from clergyman to agnostic, and in so doing, found in alpine climbing the psychological relief he needed. Stephen epitomized the meaning of mountaineering to earnest Victorians, when he described his determination to conquer a mountain:

> Why not break the mountaineer's code of commandments? . . . Why not sit down in the first bit of shade, to smoke my pipe and admire the beauties of nature? . . . I struggled, however, against the meshes of false reasoning which seemed to be winding themselves tangibly round my legs, and toiled slowly upwards. I raised my feet slowly and sleepily; I groaned at the round, smooth, slippery pebbles, and lamented the absence of water. At length I reached a little patch of snow, and managed to slake my parched lips and once more to toil more actively upwards.[29]

Stephen had been a weakling as a boy, but at Cambridge, he got caught up in the cult of athletics and excelled as a rower and a runner. After graduation, he became a fellow and also a priest (until he lost his faith) at Trinity Hall, Cambridge, where he ran a mile in 5 minutes 4 seconds at the university's athletics games in 1860, and he walked on a hot day from Cambridge to London, a distance of 52 miles, in 12 hours.[30] It was the new sport of mountaineering, however, which soon completely absorbed his energies and passion. He first went to the Alps when he was 25 and fell in love with the mountains. He enthusiastically joined the Alpine Club in 1858 and served as its president from 1865 to 1868. When Alpine Club members, with their difficult and sometimes dangerous ascents, were accused of being mentally unbalanced, Stephen readily assented, and with humor said that yes, the club had become "a byword for a set of harmless lunatics."[31]

For Stephen, troubled by the stresses of religious doubt and the other pressures of Victorian life, alpine climbing brought soundness rather than lunacy of mind. The Alps were for him, as one of his old mountaineering companions said, like a cathedral, a substitute for the religion he had lost. Mountaineering was a sport that Stephen insisted was "to be put beside rowing, cricket, and other time-honoured sports of Englishmen." For him, "to breathe the pure air of the Alps after eleven months in London streets is an escape from a close prison."[32]

The 1860s have been called the "golden age" of mountaineering, with members of the Alpine Club and many other adventurers in large numbers eagerly tackling the challenges of the Alps. Even mainstream periodicals were full of articles praising the sport, which provided not only sublimity of spirit but also represented human (namely, the British, and especially the English) conquest over nature. As G. C. Swayne said proudly,

> It is to be esteemed a national honour, that most of those peaks hitherto considered inaccessible, and many of those passes hitherto considered impassable, have yielded to the courage and perseverance of those islanders. ... While France, ... still pants for that military fame of which the world has heard so much before, Great Britain strives for newer and bloodless laurels, and seeks, according to the Creator's sanction, to assert the supremacy of Man less over his brother than over material Nature.[33]

With so many sporting Victorians climbing in the Alps, the positivist philosopher and mountaineer Frederic Harrison (1831–1923) complained that "men (to say nothing of women) have come back from the mountains as gushing over with their adventures as children from a fair." The true Alps, Harrison insisted, are not a well-trod path and have not been tamed, but represent wildness, remoteness, and challenge. Alpine climbing is better than other English sports, for "no serious man could place these mere exercises of muscle beside the mounting into the supermundane world of ice, the inexhaustible visions and meditations amidst those unearthly solitudes." Cricket and other outdoor sports are useful as counterbalances to the ill effects of sedentary urban life, but no sport, Harrison argued, offers the refreshment and renewal as does mountaineering. "The dull mechanic round of life grates so hardly on the free spirit, that to live it must escape sometimes from its cage, and soar up exulting to the gates of heaven. We live for the most part in a very iron mask of forms. Our daily ways are at bottom so joyless, so trite, so compulsory, that we must be free and simple sometimes, or we break."[34]

Claiming their sport to be the purest and most morally uplifting, mountaineers also justified their sporting addiction on the utilitarian argument of its usefulness to science. Few alpine climbers were actually geologists or botanists, but some were, and they combined their scientific curiosity with their love of alpine climbing. Most notably, the physicist John Tyndall (1820–1893) made a trip to the Alps in 1856 with fellow scientist Thomas Henry Huxley to study the structure of glacier ice, which resulted in Tyndall's classic *The Glaciers of the Alps* (1860). Tyndall fell in love with the mountains, and, becoming a skilled climber, joined the Alpine Club, making yearly trips to the Alps. Like so many other Victorian intellectuals, Tyndall had been plagued with religious doubts and experienced a religious crisis on his path towards agnosticism. Alpine climbing must have provided for him as for others a solace of the spirit, but, in his book *Mountaineering in 1861*, he rationalized the pleasure he took in climbing in terms of the key Victorian virtues of duty and struggle. What motivated him to keep climbing, he said, even when the way was tough, was that he "thought of Englishmen in battle, of the qualities which had made them famous, it was mainly the quality of not knowing when to yield; of fighting for duty even after they had ceased to be animated by hope. Such thoughts had a dynamic value, and helped to lift me over the rocks."[35]

As with most other Victorian sports, alpine climbing became highly competitive, with mountaineers competing to be the first up each peak. The art and social critic John Ruskin (1819–1900) enjoyed walking in the Alps but complained that the alpine climbers "had made race courses of the cathedrals of the earth."[36] It was this competition which some critics thought caused the death of four experienced British climbers in 1865 on their ascent of the Matterhorn. *All the Year Round* blamed such accidents on the intense competition among climbers to be the first to reach mountain peaks: "There has been too much nonsense got up on the renown to be won by scrambling high, rather high, higher, highest among Peaks and Passes—which yield, in nine cases out of ten, no new aspect of Nature—simply because nobody has ever been up there before."[37] The periodical qualified its criticism by insisting that it was not condemning the sport itself.

> No living creature could dream that any one permitted to speak in these pages could use a paragraph, a word, a syllable, a letter, in disparagement of earnestness, bravery—free use of the limbs, readiness in emergency to be enhanced by training (though such has been proved to present itself as an instinct to those who believe in DUTY—under circumstances the most trying, not merely of thew and sinew, but also of imagination and nerve.[38]

It could also understand why men need to leave the often-dreary Victorian world of work to head for the mountains. There, a usually office-bound sedentary man could prove to himself that he is "neither effete nor effeminate." There is, however, "a limit which sense and sanity prescribe."[39] In a follow-up article the next month, *All the Year Round* was more condemning of alpine climbing, with all its dangers. Turning the argument of manliness from physical muscles to upright behavior, it agreed that mountaineering was a manly exercise, in that "it is not womanly." It was not, however, "manly to expose a parent, a brother, or a wife, to the chance of quite uncalled-for sorrow." No one will say that Englishmen are afraid to face danger, but the risk must be one of redeeming purpose and not reckless imprudence.[40]

Despite, or perhaps because of, climbing accidents, Victorians continued eagerly to test their mettle by conquering Alpine peaks, and, later in the century, mountains further and even more challenging. After all, as W. T. Mainprise said in *Cassell's Family Magazine* in 1886, "There is the desire, innate in a powerful and dominant race, to meet difficulties, to grapple with them fairly and to overcome them." Once again justifying the sport in terms of Victorian values, he argued that "There is the indomitable disinclination to being beaten, no matter what obstacles may stand in the way. The fact that difficulties exist is only a spur to the energetic mind and body: that dangers must threaten is only an additional incentive. This is the true spirit of mountaineering—the idea of doing work for its own sake, and for the sake of the reward which it brings with it in the consciousness of conquest."[41]

MUSCULAR CHRISTIANITY

Religious support for the sporting life, in congruence with utilitarian arguments for the use of sports to uphold Victorian values, was strengthened all the more with the development in the mid-1850s of a new approach to religion known as "muscular Christianity." This new religious physicality was based on the view that goodness and virtue are not signs of weakness, and that on the contrary, religious faith and physical strength are in harmony with each other. Rather than denying the importance of the body as the source of sinfulness, muscular Christians saw a strong healthy body as a fitting temple for the soul.

The "muscular Christian" movement came as a reaction to the perceived feminization of religion in Victorian England. The doctrine of two gendered spheres assigned to women the role of guardians of moral standards and religious values, even as the men of the families struggled competitively in the amoral dog-eat-dog world of laissez-faire industrial capitalism. Reflecting this division of labor, church congregations became increasingly female. The clergy remained male, but the tendency was to associate them in their "womanish" world with effeminate behavior. After all, Anglican and some nonconformist clergymen wore skirts as the dress of their religious vestments, they preached the unmanly if Christian message of turning the other cheek, and glorified the womanly virtue of self-sacrifice instead of the self-assertion demanded of competitive successful Victorian men. Some religious critics even viewed religious faith itself as effeminate, with its dependence on a higher authority rather than the sturdy independence and self-reliance of secularism.

Church officials were concerned not only about the feminization of religion, but even more so about the increasing secularization of the larger society. Rather than begrudging female attendance, they probably wished more women would attend, since congregations, Anglican and non-conformists alike, were diminishing by mid-century. The census of 1851, which included a survey of church attendance, revealed the figure that was shocking to many Victorians, that only half of the population attended church services, at least on the day the census was taken. Faithful Victorians grappled with the problem of how to attract people (especially men) back to Christ and to the churches. The muscular Christian movement paved the way, linking religion with manliness and toughness, and legitimated and incorporated that which so many men loved to do—playing sports. It was a "new religion," a critic said, "that enjoins its disciples above all things to fear God, and run a mile in four minutes and a half."[42]

The term "muscular Christianity" was apparently first used in the 1857 *Saturday Review* review of the clergyman-sportsman Charles Kingsley's novel *Two Years Ago*. The reviewer, T. C. Sandars, wrote, "We all know by this time what is the task that Mr. Kingsley has made specially his own—it is that of spreading the knowledge and fostering the love of a muscular Christianity. His ideal is a man who fears God and can walk a thousand miles in a thousand hours." Sandars endorsed this philosophy as a useful counter to the "tendency to speak of religious men as effeminate, and to connect coarseness with field sports, we may think a man who labours to show that the good may be bold, and the bold good."[43]

Anointed by Sandars as the leader of the new muscular Christianity, Kingsley disavowed the name, but certainly upheld its principles in his own life and writings. As a student at Magdalene College, Cambridge, racked with spiritual conflicts and depression, he, like so many of his contemporaries, sought refuge in vigorous exercise. A colleague said of him that "with all his spiritual struggles, his physical strength did not fail." As Leslie Stephen had done, Kingsley impressed colleagues by walking in one day the 52 miles from Cambridge to London "without much fatigue: and for years after this a walk of five-and-twenty miles was a refreshment to him."[44] The social commentator W. R. Greg described Kingsley as "endowed by nature with a vigorous and exuberant organization, [who] is a sportsman, a fox-hunter, an athlete, and would probably have been a gladiator if he had not been a Christian. He revels in the description of every species of athletic exercise and desperate strife."[45] (Although Kingsley gave up foxhunting after he resolved his religious doubts and became a clergyman, he continued his otherwise active sporting life.)

A novelist as well as clergyman, Kingsley, like fellow sportsman Trollope, incorporated sports and muscular endeavors in his many writings. He also, in his work as a country vicar, preached physical exercise and health. In a letter to his good friend Thomas Hughes, who was also considered a leader of muscular Christianity, Kingsley denounced the "Pietists of all ages [who] never made a greater mistake . . . than in fancying that by keeping down manly θυμός [spiritedness] . . . they could keep down sensuality."[46] Rather than suppress our animal spirits and physical energy, we should cultivate them. "The body is the temple of the Living God. There has always seemed to me something impious in the neglect of personal health, strength and beauty, which the religious, and sometimes clergymen of this day affect. . . . I should be ashamed of being weak. I could not do half the little good I do here, if it were not for that strength and activity which some consider coarse and degrading."[47]

A keen advocate of the principles of muscular Christianity, Kingsley hated the label because he feared it suggested that only the physically strong could be true Christians. He considered it "calumny" to say that he preached its message. "I find talk which pains me bitterly, about muscular Christianity! Now—I am called by noodles and sneerers the head of that school. . . . I consider the term as silly and offensive."[48] Nevertheless, because he preached "the divineness of the whole manhood," he conceded that he was content "to be called a Muscular Christian, or any other impertinent name." For him, it meant simply a "healthy and manful Christianity, one which does not exalt the feminine virtues to the exclusion of the masculine."[49]

Despite Kingsley's discomfort with the name, the ideas of muscular Christianity spread rapidly in the fertile environment of mid-Victorian England. Repeatedly the message went out that one could be both manly (as shown by participation in muscular sports) and a Christian. As expressed in the *Universal Review* in 1859, "that a man should be manly is certainly important; that he can be manly without losing anything of the purity and gentleness of a Christian and a gentleman is surely not to be doubted. If the phrase 'muscular Christianity,' now so common, mean anything, it ought to mean this."[50]

Also offering religious endorsement to the Christian athletic life, the evangelical clergyman R. W. Dale rejected the "fussy concern" of the earlier religious enthusiasts over such things as harmless amusements and sports, a concern which he said would "produce an effeminate moral delicacy, instead of a heroic vigour." It is important "to remind sincerely religious persons that they have no right to condemn as morally wrong amusements which are simply distasteful to the higher instincts of their own nature." The weak should not give laws to the strong. "Weakness is a bad thing ... I may think it right, for the sake of my own moral vigour and for the sake of the moral vigour of those who are in danger of becoming morbidly scrupulous, to live the bolder and freer life, which my own conscience approves."[51] He insisted that he did not glorify muscles, but at the same time, the body, "with its instincts and wants, is not to be treated as the enemy of the soul, but as its friend—a friend of inferior rank, but still a friend."[52]

Kingsley had complained, in trying to distance himself from the movement, that "when muscular Christianity is spoken of either Tom Hughes or I rise to most folks' minds."[53] Certainly in *Tom Brown's School Days*, Hughes presents a model of the Christian athlete. In the less-popular sequel, *Tom Brown at Oxford*, he carefully distinguishes between mere "musclemen" and muscular Christians. "The only point in common between the two being, that both hold it to be a good thing to have strong and well-exercised bodies. ... Here all likeness ends, for the muscleman seems to have no belief whatever as to the purposes for which his body has been given him." The muscular Christian believes that "a man's body is given him to be trained and brought into subjection, and then used for the protection of the weak, and advancement of all righteous causes and the subduing of the earth, which God has given to the children of men. He does not hold that mere strength or activity are in themselves worthy of any respect of worship. ... For mere power, whether of body or intellect, he has (I hope, and believe) no reverence whatever."[54]

In his 1880 *Manliness of Christ*, Hughes promotes the mission of muscular Christianity by emphatically refuting the idea that Christianity makes ones weak. He does complain that Christianity does tend to appeal "to men's fears—to that in them which is timid and shrinking, rather than to that which is courageous and outspoken." This is not, he argues, the message of Christ. At the same time, Christian manliness is displayed not in athletic prowess, but in moral courage and self-sacrifice for the welfare of others. The best example of the truly manly man, Hughes concludes, is not an athlete, but rather Christ in his agony on the cross.[55]

CHRISTIAN SOCIALISM AND THE WORKING MEN'S COLLEGE

Although trying to tone down the exaltation of athletic sports as agents of spiritual as well as physical strength, Hughes showed in his life and work how important they were for a good life. He did this especially through the work that he and Kingsley and others did for working-class men as Christian Socialists, a label that, unlike muscular Christianity, Kingsley and Hughes welcomed. Interpreting Christianity as including concern for the poor and for the basic social and economic rights of all men (like so many others at that and other times, women were not factored in their concept of equality), Christian socialists supported the working-class Chartist movement, organized in the 1840s for universal manhood suffrage. When that movement fizzled by the beginning of the 1850s, they focused on efforts to better the lives of the working classes. Kingsley did that primarily through his ministry, and Hughes concentrated his energies on assisting in the Working Men's College, founded by Christian Socialists in 1854.

The college was a night school intended to help working-class men improve themselves so they could achieve through economic and social advancement what they could not through political protest. It included classes on basic literary skills as well as art and literature classes taught by some of the leading cultural and intellectual luminaries of the time. Hughes felt that the best way he could help was to teach physical fitness. He was concerned about how unhealthy the men looked: "Many of them were strong big men . . . but there was scarcely one amongst them who seemed to have the free use of his arms and legs. Round shoulders, narrow chests, stiff limbs were, I submitted, as bad as defective grammar or arithmetic, quite as easily cured, and as much our business if we were to educate the whole man."[56] Through Hughes's influence, physical recreation, including a cricket club, was integrated into the college program, and the college built a fully equipped gymnasium. As his contribution, Hughes taught the sport that he considered among the most important for a truly manly man—boxing.

PRIZE-FIGHTING AND RECREATIONAL BOXING

The boxing that Hughes taught was not the commercialized, violent, bareknuckled prize-fighting that had been discredited by the time Victoria came to the throne, and which continued only in illegal underground venues. The last significant prize-fight in England was that in 1860 between Tom Sayers and an American fighter, John Heenan. Billed as the "championship of the world," the match, although supposedly secret, aroused tremendous popular interest. The date of this illegal match was commonly known—even the *Saturday Review,* in anticipation of the match, could "venture to speak of the great event fixed for the 16th of April without any danger of not being understood."[57] The location, however, was not revealed. When the word spread that a special train would be leaving Waterloo Station at 4 a.m. on the designated day, crowds of eager spectators, including many aristocrats and members of Parliament, were so huge that two trains with 63 carriages were required. Police were stationed at various points along the track to keep the trains from stopping, but the match site was near an unguarded stretch of the route, so the enthusiastic spectators were able to disembark successfully to watch the historic fight.

As eagerly expected, the match was a long bloody contest, lasting over two hours. The fight ended before a final knockout when the police arrived and brought it to a close. Along with the crowds if not the fighters, the *Saturday Review* lamented this seemingly premature ending, expressing the fear that the Americans would think that the English police stopped the match because Heenan was winning. Nevertheless, even with its inconclusive end, "never in the annuals of pugilism were skill, coolness, judgment, variety of resource, pluck, and bottom displayed in such a wonderful degree as by Sayers in this splendid battle. Wherever manly courage and manly sentiments prevail, his name will be held in honors."[58]

Opponents of prize-fighting vehemently disagreed with the verdict of the *Saturday Review*. In an open letter to "the noblemen and gentlemen who attended the fight," the evangelical clergyman Baptist Wriothesley Noel, from an aristocratic family himself, strongly protested such brutality:

> Two hours those brave men were bleeding, staggering, grinning horrible their ghastly smiles, and dealing their deadly blows, till one was within five minutes of being blind, and the other within ten minutes of being powerless, like a child in the grasp of a giant. . . . Two hours you watched with shouts of delight the horrible sufferings of Heenan, and the rapid transformation of his manly face into something too hideous for most men to look upon.[59]

Noel refuted the idea that spectating at such matches made working-class men manlier. "You say that you wish to make the people manly. . . . If you wish them to be manly, improve the ventilation of their workshops and cottages; raise their wages by encouraging emigration; teach them self-respect by a good education; then with good food, temperance, and a sense of duty, you may make them the bravest and manliest nation in the world."[60] The authorities agreed, not with the idea of improving working-class lives but with closing down such contests in the future. The wish of the *Saturday Review* that Sayers be honored, however, was fulfilled. When he died in 1865, his funeral was like a state occasion. "Publicans and shopkeepers along the route closed, some private houses lowered their window blinds. Huge crowds lined the streets. Crepe flags were displayed, Union Jacks were flown at half-mast and a large sign read 'Peace to England's Champion.'"[61] In 2002 the English Heritage had a blue plaque, the marker to honor great figures in English history and the buildings they inhabited, installed on the north-London house in which Sayers was born.

Crushed by the police authorities, nostalgia for prize-fighting nevertheless remained. Even Gale, writing in 1885, credited the sport in that it "brought out many manly qualities and developed the pluck of an Englishman."[62] George Bernard Shaw made a prize-fighter the eponymous main character in his 1899 novel, *Cashel Byron's Profession*. Probably more to attack other more current medical practices and blood sports than to defend prize-fighting, Shaw nevertheless has Cashel Byron argue that prize-fighting is much better than vivisection, war, and respectable blood sports:

> Baking dogs in ovens to see how long a dog could live red hot! ... Why, it's just sickening. ... And *he's* to be received and made much of, while I am kicked out! ... Plenty of your friends go pigeon-shooting. ... *There's* a humane and manly way of spending a Saturday afternoon! ... Do you think foxes like to be hunted, or that the people that hunt them have such fine feelings that they can afford to call prize-fighters names?[63]

Despite such justifications, bare-knuckled prize-fighting could hardly be called either rational recreation or muscular Christianity. The pugilism that Hughes and others championed was quite different and fell easily within the rubric of a useful and Christian sport. Boxing was not to be done for money—that only led to corruption and degradation. Nor was it to be bare-fisted. Despite objections that protection made man effeminate, gloves were commonly used in recreational boxing. Boxing was seen as excellent exercise and served the valuable utilitarian purpose of self-defense. Lord William Lennox, echoing sentiments expressed during the French wars in the late-eighteenth and early-nineteenth centuries, but now with a Victorian spin on them, praised boxing as "a national sport," one that "when it is carried on upon honourable and humane principles, it is an antidote to the knife and stiletto. It is one so purely English, so manly, and praiseworthy, that I trust it will ever exist in the breasts of my countrymen."[64] Henry Hieover credited boxing with creating "a manliness of bearing and conduct. ... [The pugilist] has neither the treachery of the Spaniard or the wiliness of the Italian; if you offend him, he knocks you down."[65] *Cassell's Complete Book of Sports and Pastimes* was able to put boxing in the context of chivalric muscular Christianity: "The boxer can constantly protect the weak without actual violence, by just keeping a big bully at bay while the victim escapes. ... I do not know any spectacle more degrading than that of a fellow ill-using a woman or child, and men looking on without daring to interpose."[66]

With gloved boxing as a recreational sport and a means of manly self-defense differentiated from the condemned prize-fighting, boxing clubs for gentlemen sportsmen flourished by the 1860s. One of the leading promoters was John Graham Chambers, who was a founder in 1866 of the Amateur

Athletic Club. Concerned with the respectability and safety of boxing, he formulated a new list of regulations, revising earlier looser rules. Thinking that an aristocratic title would give respectability and prestige to his rules, he persuaded his friend and fellow avid boxer, John Douglas, the ninth Marquess of Queensberry, to publish them under his name. Queensberry, an avid steeplechase rider and hunter who was also considered one of the best amateur boxers of his day, readily agreed. These 12 regulations, known forever after as the Marquess of Queensberry boxing rules, were published in 1867 and became the accepted rules for the sport to the present day. The regulations include the size of the boxing ring as 24 feet (which, a first-time spectator at a match in *Cashel Byron* was surprised to see, was actually a square); a ten-count for a knockdown; rounds of three minutes in duration with a one-minute break between each round; and the mandatory use of boxing gloves. Considered a victory for humanitarianism, in recent years the use of gloves has been called into the question as more dangerous than bare-fisted boxing, in that boxers no longer have to protect their hands, they can fight more often, and can jab more repeatedly with harder blows at the head of the opponent, causing greater brain damage. In late Victorian England, however, gloved amateur boxing was viewed as a civilized, useful, and certainly very popular sport.

FOUNDING OF THE YOUNG MEN'S CHRISTIAN ASSOCIATION

Boxing and other sports were fostered in working-men colleges, sporting clubs, and other sporting associations, but no organization had as large an impact on the spread of sports in England and later throughout the world than that most muscular Christian of institutions, the Young Men's Christian Association. Founded in London in 1844 by the evangelical George Williams (1821–1905) and a group of like-minded lower-middle-class young men who gathered for prayer and mutual support, the YMCA had as its mission to arouse men "to a sense of their obligation and responsibility as Christians in diffusing religious knowledge to those around them either through the medium of prayer meetings or any other meetings they think proper." Reflecting the utilitarian as well as evangelical concerns of the day, they included in their buildings such benign and useful attractions as libraries, "to keep young men off the 'broad path' of city pleasures that led to destruction."[67] Before long, again reflecting the spirit of the age, an attraction more appealing to the general populace was added, in the form of a gymnasium.

As YMCAs spread throughout England and then globally, gymnasiums and other sporting facilities became essential to their mission. In 1894, on the fiftieth anniversary of the founding of the YMCA, George Williams received the "Freedom of the City of London" honor (similar to the key to a city), and he was knighted by Queen Victoria. There was, however, at least one dissenting voice in the enthusiasm for the athletic direction of the YMCA. The last surviving member of the founding group wrote to a friend in 1909 that he was saddened by the athletic emphasis of the YMCA. "It was born of the spirit, and now it appears to be yielding to the flesh."[68] This member was correct in noting the changing function of the organization. Today, when people say they are going to the Y, the assumption is that it is not to pray.

Just as the YMCA used sports as a way of furthering their mission, so did other religious organizations. Evoking the rhetoric of muscular Christianity, Anglican and nonconformist churches alike began sponsoring sports teams and clubs as means of recruiting new members and strengthening the loyalty of the existing believers. Sports and religion were perceived as so integrally connected that the Christian message could be presented in terms of sports metaphors. The Rev. Thomas Waugh, for example, entitled his late-nineteenth century book of religious teachings *The Cricket Field of a Christian Life*, in which he describes a Christian team batting against Satan's immoral rule-violating bowlers.[69]

5

The Sporting Revolution

By the 1870s, sports had permeated all levels of English society with more and more people across class lines, and by the 1890s, across gender lines, playing and watching, as well as reading and talking about an increasing array of sporting contests. Public-school and university graduates continued playing games in their adult lives. Earnest rational-recreation reformers and muscular Christians remained active in making sporting opportunities more available to the general populace. Soldiers who played sports as part of their military training continued to play as civilians. Working-class men (but few working-class women), whose sporting culture had been so restricted in early-industrial England, now had more leisure and means to play. Along with the traditional field sports and cricket and the sports of the public schools—especially football, in all its various forms—many new sports were developed that expanded the possibilities of participation and competition. This "great athletic revival," the late-Victorian sportsman N. L. Jackson said, "will be noted by historians as one of the distinguishing features of the nineteenth century."[1]

Observing a trend in 1860 that would soon explode in the next decades into a sporting revolution, the *Saturday Review* commented,

> There used to be a wide gulf between the sporting and the non-sporting world, and between those who led an athletic and those who led a sedentary life. . . . Now, those who are accustomed to exert their brains, and who carry off the highest intellectual honours, not only partake of a great variety of out-of-doors amusement, but talk without any affectation as if cricket, rifle-shooting, and boating were the primary subjects of their thoughts, and the centre of all their interests.[2]

Although sports continued to be justified in terms of utility and morality, less attempt was made to rationalize the pleasures of play. A cultural shift was taking place in the late-nineteenth century, away from a distrust of play and leisure towards an acceptance of having fun, with no higher purpose. Just as, by the 1880s, art was no longer seen as having to serve a utilitarian or moral purpose but was justified simply for its beauty and the pleasure it gives—in the words of the Aesthetic philosopher Walter Pater (1839–1894), "art for art's sake"[3]—so also one could now more openly enjoy sports for sports' sake, sports for the sake of fun and not necessarily improvement. A sportsman in 1882 expressed well this new attitude when asked what he saw in football. He replied that it was like an old lady who when asked why she had a drink of gin and water at night said that "Some folks takes it 'cause it does 'em good; but I takes it 'cause I likes it."[4]

Just as Queen Victoria, when she came to the throne in 1837, represented the new moralism in sports, so in the last part of the century her hedonistic sports-loving heir, Albert ("Bertie"), the Prince of Wales (later King Edward VII), in the tradition of his great-uncle King George IV at the beginning of the century, represented this new free acceptance of pleasure for its own sake. An avid sportsman, he hunted enthusiastically until he got too fat to foxhunt, and shifted to shooting. He was a yachtsman, and again, until weight became a problem, a cricketer. A patron of the turf, he was also a regular spectator at important sporting matches, lending royal authority and prestige to the contests.

SPORTS AS BIG BUSINESS

Utilitarians certainly could no longer argue that sports were a distraction from the business of producing wealth, since one of the major Victorian manufacturing industries became the production of sporting equipment and paraphernalia. By the end of the century, sports were such big business that sporting advocates could extol its contribution to the national wealth. As one sportsman pointed out in 1894,

> The number of persons who in these islands devote at least a portion of their time to sport is enormous, while the sum of money spent annually in this direction would, were we able to arrive at it, cause us no slight degree of astonishment. ... The money spent during the same period would be sufficient to defray the stipends of the whole of the Ministry, all the judges, and, besides leaving a handsome balance, to found as well a considerable number of bishoprics.[5]

The equipment that was produced was transformed for some sports by such technological innovations as the American Charles Goodyear's 1838 invention of vulcanized rubber, which was harder, more durable, and less sticky, revolutionizing the manufacture of game balls, padding, and other sporting supplies.

Without this technology, the new sports such as tennis and cycling that emerged in the late-nineteenth century could never have developed as they did. Tradition-bound cricket, on the other hand, refused to use the new rubber technology and stayed with the traditional leather balls.

SPORTING CLUBS FOR THE MIDDLE CLASSES

Sporting enthusiasts eager to play their games in their adulthood organized into sporting clubs, usually based on a particular sport. The fees charged and a vigilant selection process carefully controlled membership for especially the upper-middle classes. The names of the clubs were often references to the member's former public school or universities, indicating their elite membership. These clubs enjoyed playing games among themselves, and more importantly, competing against other clubs. Alfred Lubbock, for example, described how when he left Eton, he worked in his father's bank in London and played cricket for recreation. He helped found and organize the Eton Ramblers, an "old boy" cricket club, to play matches in the summer within easy reach of London, often against such other old-boy cricket teams as the Harrow Wanderers.[6]

The other club sport that rivaled cricket in popularity was football. The difficulty, however, with organizing football matches was that there were so many different versions of the game. Football would never be a "national game," many enthusiasts lamented, because for many players, coming from the public schools, "to touch the ball with the hands is in some eyes a heresy, and in others an uncommon virtue. Some schools advocate running with the ball, while others consider such licence as antagonistic to the proper principles and well-being of the game."[7] This was a problem that Cambridge University had confronted when it tried to draw up a consistent set of rules for its intermural play in 1848, but few others outside the university followed their rules. For clubs to play football matches against each other, they had to agree before each match what rules they would use, an awkward practice not conducive to skillful play. Even casual pickup games were difficult. One sportsman remembered that in his youth, when he was at a country-house for the Christmas holidays, the guests all decided to play a game of football. Because they all played by different rules, "it very soon appeared probable that our match, which had held out such a charming prospect, would not be played at all."[8]

FORMATION OF THE FOOTBALL ASSOCIATION (FA) AND THE RUGBY FOOTBALL UNION (RFU)

In an attempt to come up with one consistent set of rules for football, representatives from the mostly southern football clubs gathered in October 1863 in London at the Freemason's Tavern (appropriately a public house, reflecting the traditional connection between pubs and sports). Forming themselves into a Football Association (FA), these representatives, many of whom were public school "old boys," engaged in heated debates in the following months. The particular points of contention were the questions of whether a player could pick up the ball with his hands and whether the player could then run with the ball, as was the custom at Rugby and several other schools. There was also fierce disagreement over whether "hacking"—kicking the opposing player in the shins—should be allowed. In defense of hacking, a representative of Blackheath, a club composed mainly of Old Rugbeans, argued that, "If you do away with it, you will do away with all the courage and pluck of the game, and I will be bound to bring over a lot of Frenchmen who would beat you with a week's practice."[9]

The followers of the Rugby style of playing were not pleased with the final rules that the new Football Association promulgated in December 1863. With the majority voting for a game that was played with the feet and not the hands, the FA decreed that "no player shall run with the ball," "neither tripping nor hacking shall be allowed, and no player shall use his hands to hold or push his adversary, a player shall not be allowed to throw the ball or pass it to another with his hands," and that "no player shall be allowed to take the ball from the ground with his hands under any pretence whatever while it is in play."[10] In protest over these rules, followers of the Rugby style of play refused to join the FA.

In the first several years after the FA was formed, only ten football clubs, and no public schools, joined. Other than the Old Rugbean defections, clubs refused because there was no offsides rule that would forbid an offensive player without the ball from positioning himself between the goal and three

Association Football—"dribbling."

(later two) opponents. To be offsides was, in Eton parlance, "sneaking."[11] A defender of an offsides rule argued that "there is undoubtedly no rule of more importance than this. . . . For a player to place himself nearer to his opponent's goal than the ball, and to wait for it to be kicked to him, is not anywhere recognised but as being decidedly unfair."[12] With sports as a moral educator, the sense of fair play encoded in the offsides rule could extend to conduct off the field. In the words of an 1883 poem simply entitled "Off-side":

> And if you act up to your old football rule
> When you're launched on the world's busy tide,
> You'll find a much greater honour to lose,
> Than to win by the game of 'off-side'.[13]

When the FA did adopt the offsides rules in 1866, many more clubs joined, bringing the membership to 30 by 1868. The hopes that a compromise could be finally reached with the followers of the Rugby style of football was, however, not realized. In 1871, 21 clubs formed their own Rugby Football Union (RFU), allowing use of hands as well as feet, although they did abolish hacking. Eventually all late-Victorian football clubs adopted either the association or the rugby rules. The game as played according to the FA rules was nicknamed "socker," or more commonly, "soccer," short for "Association," the name of the game used in the United States, and the game according to the RFU rules was styled "rugger."[14] Both were called "football." It was not until the twentieth century that the word "football" came to be identified primarily with

ASSOCIATION V. RUGBY.

She plaintively—to famous Rugby half-back. "WOULD IT GET YOU VERY MUCH OUT OF PRACTICE IF WE WERE TO DANCE 'SOCKER' A LITTLE?"

association football (not to be confused with the American football game). The game according to the RFU rules was simply called "rugby."

Football in both forms quickly became popular national sports. The game became even more interesting when "soccer" football developed in the early 1870s as a passing as well as dribbling game, while rugby continued to attract fans because of its rougher style of playing. Football soon came to be seen as a rival to cricket as "the" national game, even though the two sports complemented each other well, one being a fast-moving winter and the other a leisurely summer game. Football enthusiasts, however, tended to be defensive about their sport, which did not have the gentlemanly traditions of cricket. Like new nations trying to establish their place in the world, or new royal dynasties asserting a long lineage as their claim to power, footballers insisted that their sport dated back to earliest times, that it had "a history to which the history of cricket is but of yesterday."[15] Football "may fairly claim to be not only the oldest and the most characteristic, but the most essentially popular sport of England."[16]

Critics of football denounced the game, with its bodily contact and frequent collisions, as too dangerous, even after hacking was abolished. Defenders denied that football was any more dangerous than other outdoor sports, and insisted that the roughness of the game was a virtue. It was an essential part of the English character to handle pain and roughness: "What is true of the game is that it does give a scope to that delight in 'rough and tumble' which in a greater or less degree is part of every young Englishman's nature, and bred in his very bone. There is no gainsaying the fact that, while the typical Englishman is more humane than most foreigners, he does find pleasure more than any foreigner in mere animal roughness."[17]

Frederick Gale (who sometimes signed his works as "The Old Buffer") warned that if all danger were to be removed from football and other sports, sporting life itself would cease. "Are we to have feather-beds placed on either side of a fence in the hunting-field? Is shooting to be stopped because some wretched Cockney pulls his gun at full-cock through a hedge, and 'pots' himself or a friend because he does not know the first rudiments of handling a gun?"[18] When protective shin pads were introduced for footballers, the same complaints were heard as when pads were first used in cricket. As the *Saturday Review* lamented, "That our boys should descend to such a depth of effeminacy is terrible indeed!"[19] As had been frequently argued in earlier defenses of rough sports, football was defended as a means of making men more manly and more vigorous, which was so necessary in an industrial sedentary urban world. Probably the most effective argument was that of military preparedness. In that age of *Pax Britannica*, most Englishmen did not ever experience war, but they could importantly do so in its surrogate form, on the football field. "The joy of battle, which has now and again and yet again burned like a fire in the nation's heart, smoulders through these long days of peace; and it may well be that ... great football matches are helping to keep it alive for England's next great war."[20]

In 1871–1872, the Football Association established the FA Cup champion-ship competition, which generated such excitement that participation in the game and club membership in the association increased dramatically in that decade. The FA Cup remains to this day the most watched national sporting competition in England. The Rugby Football Union was more reluctant to introduce such competitions, but the clubs playing in Yorkshire under the RFU rules organized for their area the Yorkshire Challenge Cup in 1877, with 16 teams competing, a competition which, like the FA Cup, is still very popular today.

WORKING-CLASS LEISURE AND INCOME

Much more than cricket, organized football by the 1870s attracted a large new group of participants—working-class men. The early football clubs, and certainly the membership of the FA, were mainly middle class and primarily based in the south. In late-Victorian England, however, working-class men (but not working-class women) had more opportunity for participation in sports and were an important part of the "sporting revolution." From mid-century on, working men had greater leisure time. The Factory Acts of 1833 and 1847, which restricted the hours that women and children could work, gave *de facto* to male workers the same protection, and the acts were later extended for all factory workers limiting work to eight hours a day. Few women were able to benefit from the restrictions, in that the time they had off was usually spent on the house work that was so arduous in the pre-twentieth century. Moreover, most working women were not employed in fac-tories but were in either domestic service or needlework in sweatshops or at home, and they never had the benefit of government protection. The sporting revolution in working-class lives was indeed gendered.

The most important increase in leisure time that dramatically affected men's ability to enjoy sports was the introduction, beginning in the 1850s in textile mills and soon extending to most businesses and factories, of the Saturday early closing. Allowing workers a half-day on Saturday was a benefit of the prosperity of mid- and late-Victorian England, since factories and businesses could still make a profit if open only five and a half days. This half day allowed for daytime hours for sporting activities that previously could be played only with difficulty in the workday evenings. Sports that could fit into this discrete amount of time—most notably football—were therefore especially popular among the working-class men. A Saturday half day did not, however, accom-modate the leisurely three-day cricket match, which usually started on a Monday or on a Thursday, working days for all but the leisured classes.

The Saturday time off was also important because, even with the increasing secularism by the mid-nineteenth century, Sunday remained sacrosanct, with no recreational activities allowed. A movement begun by the Puritans in the sixteenth and seventeenth centuries and resurrected by the evangelicals in the late-eighteenth and early-nineteenth centuries, Sabbatarianism was still a strong political force in the 1870s. Through such organizations as the Lord's Day Observance Society, formed in 1831 to defend and implement the 1780 Lord's Day Observance Act, Sunday remained what Charles Dickens had bemoaned in 1836 was "a day of general gloom and austerity. . . . The day which his Maker had intended as a blessing, man has converted into a curse . . . depriving him of every comfort and enjoyment."[21] In 1855, the National Sunday League was established, lobbying for the Sunday opening of museums. Even when some "improving" amusements were reluctantly allowed, sports, or at least those played in public view, remained off limits until the end of the century. The fun-loving Prince of Wales did pioneer the "weekend," a two-day time of holiday, including Sundays, but this greater freedom did not percolate down to the working classes. The Saturday half day therefore remained a curb on their sporting life.

Even though workers could not use Sundays for organized play, they along with the urban middle classes did gain some Mondays in the form of bank holidays. In 1871, Parliament passed the Bank Holidays Act, declaring four Mondays in the year as holidays: Easter Monday; Whit Monday (the day after the seventh Sunday after Easter—today regularized and secularized as the last Monday in May); the first Monday of August (later changed to the last Monday in August); and Boxing Day, the day after Christmas (the day that the landlords traditionally gave boxes of food to their tenants and servants). Spearheaded in Parliament by Sir John Lubbock (1834–1913), the brother of the cricket-playing Alfred Lubbock, these holidays, which grateful workers called "St. Lubbock's Days," were the first secular holidays in English history, supplementing the remaining traditional religious holidays of Christmas and Good Friday. Despite the name, these new holidays were not only for banks but were so designated to indicate that bills would not come due on those days. Lubbock said he chose the misleading name because "if we had called them National Holidays or General Holidays . . . it would perhaps call too much attention to the proposed change." Critics complained that workers would just use those days to get drunk and be unruly and even violent, but Lubbock insisted that "people in fact quarrel and break the law not when they are happy and enjoying themselves, but when they are suffering and miserable."[22] These holidays did indeed become occasions for recreation, with sports so quickly filling up the new leisure time that many people think that Boxing Day was so named because it is a day when boxing matches and other games take place.

In addition to more leisure, working-class men also had more money that they could spend on sports. After the decline of the standard of living for the working classes in the early-industrial age and the "hungry forties" in early-Victorian England, there was from the 1850s to the end of the century a long period of prosperity for the working as well as propertied classes. Although there was still in London and the other large cities a large subclass of desperately poor people who were barely subsisting, waged laborers especially in the skilled crafts but also in the factory work enjoyed higher wages, and had therefore more discretionary income.

When working-class men used their leisure and money to gather to play and watch sports, their congregation did not create the fear of mob action as it had in the French Revolutionary period and the turbulent decades thereafter. There was by the 1850s a sense of social peace, fueled by the prosperity of the age. The mid-Victorian social harmony did not last into the late-nineteenth century, when social tensions became heated again. The riots before the 1867 Reform Act, granting the vote to urban working-class men, were a harbinger of future conflict. By the end of the century, social and political agitation led to violence (mainly on the part of the reacting authorities) in such demonstrations as that in Trafalgar Square in November 1887, forever known as "Bloody Sunday" (in which only three people were actually killed). The Dock Strike of 1889 and the beginnings of the "New Unionism," composed of unskilled workers who used strikes as the primary bargaining tool, also increased class conflict.

These conflicts were not, however, manifest in working-class participation in sporting events. The propertied classes did not fear, nor had reason to fear, for workers to gather to play or watch sports, for whatever violence there was usually took place only on the playing field. Although in other countries sporting clubs were often subterfuges for revolutionary action, that was not so in England. The spectators, however enthusiastic for their team and sometimes vocal in a way that bothered the more respectable middle classes, tended to be well behaved at the games. The hooliganism of especially football fans, which has so dismayed the British authorities and embarrassed the FA, did not develop until after World War II. Just as in the revolutionary days early in the century when the authorities and people of property argued for sports for the working classes to deflect them from revolt, so also now the powers that be were probably relieved to see workers out kicking at a football rather than at them.

WORKING-CLASS FOOTBALL CLUBS

Late-Victorian working-class men played a variety of sports, but unquestionably the most popular organized team sport was football, in both soccer and rugby forms. Football is a game that can be played in the limited time available on the Saturday half days. It is exciting with its fast pace and constant movement up and down the field. Unlike cricket with its almost incomprehensible baroque rules, football is an uncomplicated game. It has few rules, even fewer for soccer than rugby, and is easy to understand, clearly a factor in the later spread of especially soccer football throughout the world.

Probably the major reason that workers took so avidly to football in whatever form in the late-nineteenth century was that it was their traditional game. Despite the best efforts of the early-Victorian defenders of law and order to stamp it out, football had continued throughout the nineteenth century as a backstreet working-class game. Only such continuity could explain the very rapid spread of football among the working classes. Sports historians are convinced now that football was not just a sport that developed in the public schools among the privileged and was then passed down to the working classes, but that it also had an unbroken continuing tradition among the working classes, a game which was then adapted to the rules of the FA and the RFU.

Following the middle-class model, working-class men tended to organize their recreational activities and especially football into sports clubs. Churches sponsored some of these clubs as part of the muscular Christianity movement. Public houses sponsored others, continuing the long tradition of pubs as patrons of working-class sports. The increasingly vigilant temperance workers were concerned about this public-house association with the sports clubs and continued to oppose sports as promoters of drink. Most commentators, however, accepted the argument that participation in sports kept men sober.

Football-playing workers also organized clubs based on where they lived, with their teams named after their streets or districts, or, most commonly, after their town or city. This pattern of organization and nomenclature based on locale helped create for workers a new loyalty to what had been an impersonal urban setting. In so doing, they created a new sense of urban community among not only the players, but also the supporters who, in cheering their team were also cheering their city. Workers who had tended to live more isolated provincial lives were also brought, through their regional and even national sporting competitions, more in contact with the outside world.

Factories and other workplaces also sponsored sports clubs for their workers. Employers used these clubs as a way of forging bonds with workers who might otherwise see the boss as the enemy. The clubs also helped businesses and factories recruit skilled workers who were attracted by the sporting opportunities that employment there would bring. Some clubs named after a factory were founded not by employers but by workers themselves, who used the factory name to identify their club. Some of the major football teams in England today have such factory/business origins. West Ham United, originally known as the Thames Ironworks, was established by the employer in 1895 as a workplace recreational society, with the intent to foster better industrial relations, and Manchester United was formed originally just outside Manchester in 1878 as the Newton Heath Lancashire and Yorkshire Railway Football Club. Arsenal was formed in 1886 by workers at the Woolwich Arsenal in the London area, without any help from the management.

Although there were a few interclass teams, most football clubs maintained strict class segregation. The regulating FA board also remained firmly middle and upper class and, despite the growth of football in the north, was located in London, as were most of the other sports governing organizations, such as the Rugby Football Union, the Marylebone Cricket Club, and the Jockey Club. Even with the maintenance of segregated teams, there was concern among some of the so-called respectable classes that people from the lower orders were invading the gentlemanly world of organized sports. With class prejudice as strong in Victorian England as race was in American history, there was constant fear of infiltration. The secretary of a Yorkshire rugby club, therefore, felt it was necessary, in writing to arrange a match with another team, to give assurance that "as our club is pretty nearly free from the working-class element, you have nothing to fear about a rough or noisy game."[23]

FA CUP COMPETITIONS

Although not on the same teams, working- and middle/upper-class men did play against each other in the FA Cup competitions. Through the 1870s, the southern gentlemanly teams composed of public-school and university graduates, with the Old Carthusians, the Old Etonians, and the Royal Engineers dominating the games.[24] Such dominance was taken for granted, for it was assumed that those "who had not enjoyed the advantages of a public school or college training, could not hold his own with the young athlete who had been tutored in Greek and Latin, as well as football, at Eton, Harrow, Charterhouse, or Westminster, and afterwards perhaps been able to continue his education in these branches of learning and sport at Oxford or Cambridge."[25] Such facile class assumptions received a severe shock in 1883, when the Blackburn Olympic, a northern working-class team from industrial Lancashire that was sponsored by an iron foundry firm, defeated the Old Etonians in the FA Cup final held at the Kennington Oval in London. As a reflection of the new civic pride that teams engendered, the city of Blackburn was overjoyed. The town band came out to greet the returning heroes, and people danced in the streets. The *Blackburn Times* heralded the result as "the meeting and vanquishing . . . of a Club composed of sons of some of the families of the upper class in the Kingdom" by "Lancashire Lads of the manual working-class, sons of small tradesmen, artisans, and operatives."[26]

The next year, another Blackburn team won the Cup. This time it was the Blackburn Rovers, a more middle-class team founded in 1874 by the sons of local businessmen, but nevertheless still tainted in the eyes of traditionalists because of its northern industrial location and non-public-school players. The town of Blackburn was once again jubilant. A local newspaper reported that the streets

> quickly became filled with thousands of persons all anxious to get a glimpse of the members of the club which had brought such honour to the town. . . . The procession then began to move. . . . Then followed the carriage containing the team, all standing, in the centre being Jimmy Brown, the captain, holding the cup on high so that everybody could see it. . . . Along the route they frequently sang "Our Jack's come home to-day."[27]

The Blackburn Rovers followed up by winning the Cup again in the next two years, clearly establishing the dominance of the north in the FA. Such an ominous development caused great alarm. The sportsman C. W. Alcock warned that "the abnormal development of football among the operative classes in the midland and more northern districts, particularly in Lancashire, was of itself an element of danger which one would have thought would not have altogether escaped the attention of those who directed the Association."[28] But what could be done? One of the strong appeals of sport for Victorians was that contests embodied the values of unrestricted competition and survival of the fittest. May the best man win, even if he be a northerner and, even worse, from working classes.

THE SPORTING REVOLUTION IN THE PRESS, LITERATURE, AND SCHOLARSHIP

With increased leisure time and higher wages, the working classes were able to participate in the late-Victorian sporting revolution as players and as spectators. With the higher literacy of the age, they were also able to participate as readers on sports. Widespread working-class literacy was a new development in the 1870s. England had earlier lagged behind most other western European countries in providing state support for education, leaving the task to voluntary and private agencies. After the 1867 Reform Act extended the vote to working-class men, however, there was a concern that these new voters be able to read about the issues on which they would have influence through their suffrage. In 1870, therefore, Parliament passed an Education Act that created elected school boards to oversee the building of elementary schools in areas where the voluntary schools were not sufficient and made elementary education compulsory for all children ages 5 to 12. This act and its subsequent extensions dramatically increased the literacy of the working classes.

The Education Act provided for physical education in the schools, but only in the form of military drills (for girls as well as boys). It was assumed that children of workers did not need the games and sports so prominent in the public school and increasingly also in most private-school curricula. Moreover, most state schools did not have the space for the large playing fields that were the hallmark of the public schools. Drills could be conducted in limited space and even in the classroom, which, although lacking in fun, did have the conscious benefit of preparing boys for future military service.

Even though the state schools did not include sports in their physical education programs, they did significantly expand the sporting life of the working classes by giving them the ability to read. The sporting revolution took place not only on the playing fields but also in print. The genre of sporting newspapers and reporting about sports in mainstream publications, which had begun early in the century with such publications, expanded exponentially by the 1870s. Newspapers, magazines, and books were now much cheaper, thanks to both political and technological factors. Parliament abolished the newspaper stamp duty in 1855 and the excise duty on paper in 1861. The steam-powered rotary press was developed in the 1840s, allowing faster printing. The technique of manufacturing paper from cheap wood pulp allowed the printing of cheaper "pulp" newspapers and books.

Previously dominated by the London press, sporting periodicals proliferated throughout the provinces, covering the sports of interest in their particular towns and regions as well as national sporting competitions. There were specialized publications for individual sports and prominent sporting sections in the general periodicals. The publications were geared towards class interests, with some clearly aimed at the privileged classes, especially those publications specializing in field sports and cricket, while others, usually the cheaper "penny press," were aimed at the new working-class reading public, with football of major interest.

These sporting publications became even more interesting when the techniques of reproducing pictures, usually in the form of engravings, improved by mid-century. Sporting illustrations became all the more frequent and interesting with the invention of the camera. Sports photographs were introduced into publications in the 1880s, although they were usually indoor studio pictures. By the late-1890s, photography, with faster shutter speed and better lenses, had so improved that outdoor action photographs could be taken and included in the publications. These late-century photographs could catch sports in action, which not only made the contests more vivid and alive to readers, but also increased the pressures on the referees and umpires, with their decisions now reviewed by this end-of-the-century form of instant replay. This was all the more so when, at the end of the Victorian era, the technology of making motion films was developed. Some of the earliest films that were made were of sporting events, mostly of horse and boat races.[29]

Along with periodicals, there was an outpouring of books, mainly aimed at the middle classes, dealing with all aspects of sport. Sporting novels became popular, not just as a minor theme as in the novels of Trollope, but as the central focus of the story. Children's literature, in the tradition of *Tom Brown's School Days*, also had sports as a recurrent theme. Late-Victorian scholars took investigations of sport seriously, with historians exploring the origins and history of the various games, mostly with the intent of showing the English origins of the major sports and to illustrate the manliness of each game. The newly developed field of anthropology examined such aspects of "primitive" life as marriage and sex, of prurient curiosity to repressed Victorians, but there was also great interest in the sports of the various peoples.

One of the most important and certainly comprehensive sporting publications was the massive multivolume *Badminton Library of Sports and Pastimes*, founded and edited by Henry Somerset, the eighth Duke of Beaufort. The series was named after Badminton House, Beaufort's ducal home in Gloucestershire, and dedicated to that avid sportsman, the Prince of Wales. The first volume, published in 1885, was appropriately on the oldest of aristocratic sports: hunting. Subsequent volumes survey angling, horseracing, shooting, cricket, mountaineering, skating, swimming, yachting, archery, and many other sports, including the new sports developed in the late-nineteenth century. In 1888, a combined volume was published on "Athletics and

Football," suggesting the still relative unimportance of each of the sports, at least in the view of the Badminton editors, but a separate revised single volume on "Athletics" was published in 1898 and on "Football" in 1899. There was also a volume on a questionable "sport"—dancing. The editor Alfred Watson explained that he was at first reluctant to include such a topic, "fearing the obvious criticism that it was 'not a sport,' though it is the oldest and most universal of all pastimes." After he heard Mrs. Lilly Grove give a paper on dancing, he was convinced it should be included. She edited the volume, published in 1895, and was the only female editor in the series.[30] The only volume in the Badminton series not focused on a particular sport or sports (if one considers dancing a sport) was the literary volume, The Poetry of Sport (1896), with selections of poems on the sporting life from Chaucer and Shakespeare to the Victorian period.

SPORTING COMPETITIONS AND RECORDS

As charming as sports poems could be, and as diverse as the literature on sports was, the sports-reading public was much more interested in the current competitions which characterized most of the sporting activity in late-Victorian England. Despite the gentlemanly ethic that the play itself and not victory was what was important, sports of all varieties centered on competitions, with prizes and glory for the victors. By the late 1880s, leagues were formed for football and other sports, with a fixed number of teams in each league and a set schedule of games at home and away, arousing even more popular enthusiasm for the games.

Blossoming along with the competitions was an avid interest in sporting records. The sporting press fed this interest by constantly reporting on which player or team scored the most runs or goals, covered distance the fastest, climbed the most or highest mountains, or other sporting feats. Records had always been part of sports, as evidenced in the profit-driven motivation of early-Victorian pedestrians to walk further and faster than others, and in the statistics kept on which horse won the most races in the fastest times. In the atmosphere of this late-Victorian sporting world, however, record-keeping became obsessive and record-breaking a primary goal. The pressures to set a record as well as to defeat opponents led to more concern about training and practice, techniques of playing, and improvement of equipment. Despite constant urging from idealistic traditionalists that one should play the game for fun, or health, or other improving benefits, the pressures to excel and to break records grew stronger. As a critic said in 1893, "The air is so heavily charged with the spirit of 'competition'. . . . Still, it might be worth remembering that 'recreation' and the real enjoyment of play are often wholly forgotten or ignored in the voracious effort to 'break a record.'"[31] Such pleas, however, fell on deaf ears, for, as another commentator admitted, "Although every sportsman should set his face against an undue reverence for records as a complete standard of athletic ability, these same records are exceedingly interesting."[32]

THE GRACE OF CRICKET

The venerable sport of cricket kept pace in the late-Victorian sporting revolution with its upstart rival, football. Despite its large time demands and complicated rules, cricket spread not among the urban working classes but widely among the middle classes. Along with school, university, and elite county teams, there was a proliferation of club teams throughout England. Adding to the interest was the establishment in 1873 of the County Cricket Championship, founded the year after the Football Association established its very

Dr. W. G. Grace.

LORD'S IN DANGER.   THE M. C. C. GO OUT TO MEET THE ENEMY.

[" Sir EDWARD WATKIN proposes to construct a Railway passing through Lord's Cricket Ground."]

In this *Punch* cartoon, the aging and portly W. G. Grace is satirized as leading a charge to protect the Lord's cricket field, with a roller used to prepare the cricket field attached to his horse instead of artillery.

popular FA Cup Championship. Again following the football example, cricket clubs in the various regions formed leagues, with the Birmingham League as the first, founded in 1888, the same year as the English Football League was established. In the 1890s, the MCC created the designation of "first-class cricket" for matches of two innings, usually played over three days, between teams that the MCC ranked of high skill.

One of the most important reasons for the tremendous popular interest in what was an essentially elite sport was the dominance of the game in the late-nineteenth century of an extraordinary, flamboyant, and highly skilled cricketer, William Gilbert Grace (1848–1915). Many sports stars emerged in this sporting revolutionary age, their fame augmented by the press, whose illustrations and photographs of the players helped fans know the stars, even though vicariously. No sporting figure, however, reached the almost mythical stature and dominating presence or was more recognizable than that of Grace—or, as he was affectionately and familiarly known, "W. G."

Grace was born in Gloucestershire into an avid cricket-playing family. His father was a doctor, as W. G. himself became, but both were clearly more passionate about playing cricket than healing the sick. W. G.'s mother was also an ardent player, unusual for middle-class women in mid-Victorian England, except perhaps in villages like the one in which the Grace family lived. Grace's four brothers were also outstanding cricketers, who might have achieved even more fame if not overshadowed by their extraordinary brother. Unlike most first-class cricketers at that time, Grace did not learn the game in a public school but was rather taught by his father and especially his mother. He recalled his childhood, even as young as age six, as one filled with cricket. "It was as natural for me and every one at home to walk out to the [cricket] ground, as it is for every boy in England to go into his nursery."[33]

Grace broke all cricket records, and some of the records he set still stand today. He was able to do so not only because of his amazing talent as both a batter and a bowler but also because of his incredible longevity as a cricketer. He first started playing club cricket in 1862 at age 14 and then first-class cricket two years later. Playing mainly on his home Gloucestershire county team but also on such teams as the All-England Elevens, Grace was in his peak years in the 1870s and 1880s, but he continued playing first-class cricket until almost age 60. In his nearly 45-year career, as a batter he made close to 100,000 runs, and as a bowler he had taken almost 7,500 wickets. He was to Victorian cricket what Babe Ruth, Ty Cobb, and Lou Gehrig combined were to early-twentieth-century American baseball.

What made Grace such a star was not only his record-breaking play but also his distinctive appearance and personality. He was a huge man, with ever-widening girth, and an enormous black beard—hardly the conventional image of the gentlemanly cricketer. His fearsome appearance often intimidated new and even experienced players. Although he wielded the bat with ferocious power, terrifying bowlers and fielders, a contemporary suggested that his skill as a bowler was due to the incongruous gentleness of his bowls. "The batsman, seeing an enormous man rushing up to the wickets, with both elbows out, great black beard blowing on each side of him, and a huge yellow cap on the top of a dark swarthy face, expects something more than the gentle lobbed-up ball that does come; he cannot believe that this baby-looking bowling is really the great man's and gets flustered and loses his wicket."[34] Sir Charles Tennyson, grandson of the Victorian poet laureate, Alfred, Lord Tennyson, relished remembering seeing Grace play in two matches in the late-1890s, when Grace was over 50 years old, and "so portly that his bat looked like a match-stick in his hands and he could only lumber across the pitch at a little over walking pace." Nevertheless, "He defied the cream of Britain's professional bowling, for the best part of a steaming summer afternoon, on Lord's cricket ground, while great batsman, twenty or thirty years his juniors, foundered helplessly or ignominiously failed."[35]

Compounding the effect of his appearance, Grace had flamboyant and decidedly ungentlemanly behavior on the field. He would roar at opponents and would try to distract them from their play. He challenged the decisions of umpires—definitely "not cricket." Umpires were often reluctant to call him out, not because of his belligerence, but to keep from infuriating fans, who flocked to matches in dramatically higher numbers and paying higher entrance fees if he were playing.[36]

Although his appearance and behavior were not particularly gentlemanly, Grace was adamant about his status as an amateur Gentleman cricketer. Accepting the two-tiered division in cricket of amateurs and professionals, Grace disliked the concept of players being paid for what they should do simply for love. He himself, however, profited handsomely from cricket. He was one of the first sports stars to make money through product endorsements, most notably in the 1890s for Colman's Mustard. He was paid for periodical articles and books on cricket that were published under his name but that were "ghosted"—sometimes with distinguished cricketers as the actual authors. Some bold critics accused him of being a "shamateur" (a term coined in the late-nineteenth century), but such criticisms did not diminish the overwhelming popular adulation of W. G.

Shamateur and ungentlemanly though he was, just about every commentator on cricket acknowledged that Grace as a player was simply the best. Gale described him as "the eighth wonder of the world."[37] Robert Lyttelton, as avid a sportsman as his brother Edward (see Chapter 3), voiced the general consensus of cricketers when he said with confidence, "If ever prophecy were safe, it is that his like as a cricketer will never be seen again,"[38] as did the great Anglicized Indian cricketer for Sussex County, Ranjitsinhji, proclaiming Grace as "the finest player born or unborn."[39]

HORSERACING, BOATING, AND ATHLETICS IN THE SPORTING REVOLUTION

Notwithstanding the crowds at football and cricket matches, the most popular spectator (and gambling) sport, historically and still in the late-nineteenth century, was horseracing. In addition to the traditional competitions, the number of horse races expanded significantly in the late-nineteenth century. The races became all the more exciting when the invention of starting gates in the late-1890s made the beginning of the race more exact, and the use of photography gave more accurate photo finishes.

Another sport with a long history of competitions that became all the more exciting to athletes and spectators was boat racing. The most important of the boat races, other than the ever-popular Oxford-Cambridge race, was the Henley Royal Regatta. First held in 1839 with only a few (and mainly university) boating clubs, by late-Victorian times the Regatta had become a major sporting as well as social event, with up to eight different challenge cups, based on various criteria including the number of rowers. In the various cup challenges, public-school teams competed against university college teams, college teams against each other, and carefully selected non-academic rowing clubs from London and elsewhere against the elite schools and colleges. Held the first week of July on the Thames River, starting at the riverside town of Henley, the distance of the race—one mile and 550 yards—has never changed.

"Athletics," developed as a modern sport in the public schools in mid-century, and including foot races, broad and high jumping, throwing the hammer, hurdling, and other sports that we call "field sports," continued to be avidly played and contested among the graduates of the schools and universities into their adult lives. In 1866, some university graduates formed the Amateur Athletic Club, to sponsor athletic competitions. Other athletics clubs were formed, whose members were amateur but not necessarily of public school background. To serve as a governing body over all the clubs, with consistent rules and policies and to supervise national championships, the Amateur Athletic Association was formed in 1880. In these athletic contests, one competed to win and also, more than any other sport, to set records. The foot races especially produced a storehouse of records, with times over the various distances measured and compared in split seconds.

SWIMMING FOR SPEED AND DISTANCE

Although swimming is a physical activity that has existed from earlier days, it only became an organized competitive sport in late-Victorian England. There had been earlier individual swimming feats, most notably the dramatic swims of Lord Byron in 1810 across the Hellespont (Straits of Dardanelles). In early- and mid-Victorian England, however, swimming was taught primarily as a means of survival in water, as, for example, with the requirement that Eton rowers learn to swim. When swimming in the form of "bathing" became popular for health in the mid-century, competition was not a factor. Swim racing did not emerge as a recognized sport until the 1860s.

English swimmers through most of the century used mainly the sidestroke and breaststroke. A new stroke, the overhand, was first introduced in 1844, when nine members of the Ojibbeway Native-American tribe made a visit to England, to demonstrate their customs and culture, including dancing before the Queen. Known to be expert swimmers, three Ojibbeway men put on a demonstration race. Observers rejected their overhand style of swimming as barbaric: "They lash the water violently with their arms, like the sails of a windmill, and beat downwards with their feet, blowing with force, and forming grotesque antics."[40] The overhand stroke was for the rest of the century known scornfully as the "Indian" style.

As swimming became more popular in the 1860s, swimming clubs were formed, with the inevitable races between the clubs. To better organize the competitions, the London Swimming Association was established, which was expanded and renamed in 1874 as the Swimming Association of Great Britain. In 1880, when pressures towards the professionalization of sports was intensifying, the association added the word "Amateur" at the beginning of its name. Swimming competitions were also introduced into that breeding ground of modern sports, the public schools.

As swim races in both pools and rivers became more hotly contested and important in the sporting life of late-Victorian England, there was interest in developing more efficient and faster strokes. There was still skepticism and scorn, however, when a young Englishman, John Trudgen (1852–1902), reintroduced the "Indian" style of overhand swimming. As a boy Trudgen had gone with his parents in 1863 to Argentina, where his father worked for an engineering firm. While there, Trudgen learned from the South American Indians the overhand stroke, which he combined with the breaststroke "frog" kick. When he returned to England and attempted to train English swimmers in this faster stroke, he, like the Ojibbeway swimmers, was met with derision. An 1873 sports reporter mocked the "Trudgen stroke" as one "with both arms entirely out of the water, in action peculiar to Indians. . . . I question, indeed, if the swimming world ever saw a more peculiar stroke sustained throughout a 100 yards race . . . both arms are thrown partly sideways, but very slovenly, and the head kept completely above water."[41]

However ungainly the appearance, this overhand style was clearly effective for speed, and soon caught on as the stroke of choice in "freestyle" races. Many, however, still regarded it with contempt. These overhand strokes, a sportsman said in his 1899 memoirs, "have completely demoralized Londoners as swimmers." The endeavors "to imitate Trudgeon [sic] have degenerated Londoners to the level of mediocrity."[42] The Trudgen stroke became even faster when Fred Cavill, a champion English swimmer, emigrated to Australia in 1879 and there witnessed South Sea Islanders using the flutter kick. As a teacher of swimming, he combined that kick with the Trudgen overhand stroke but with side breathing, creating what is still considered the fastest swimming stroke. With the stroke giving the appearance of crawling through water, it is sometimes called the "Australian crawl." Despite concerns that it was ungentlemanly to splash so much in the water and certainly to "crawl," this style was quickly and widely adopted in England by the turn of the century.

The most publicized swimming contest in late-Victorian England was not swimmer against swimmer but rather swimmer against the elements and the limits of human endurance. In 1875, Captain Matthew Webb (1848–1883), a member of the merchant navy, announced that he was going to attempt to do what no one else in history had been able to do—swim the English Channel. The idea of an Englishman swimming the Channel fired the public imagination. The waterway, 21 miles at its narrowest point, had served historically as a barrier for England against invasion. There were plans and debates in the 1860s and 1870s to build a tunnel under the Channel, but the idea was rejected as dangerous to national defense, a rejection overlain with strong Francophobia. If a Frenchman had announced that he was going to swim "La Manche" over to England, there definitely would not have been the enthusiasm that greeted Captain Webb's decision to breach the French seacoast by swimming.

Webb's first attempt in early August 1875 failed, but his second one, later that month, was successful. Coated in oil, he had no aid except a support boat that followed him along and gave him cod-liver oil, beef tea, brandy, coffee, and ale. English passengers on a passing ship cheered him on by singing "Rule Britannia."[43] What should have been a 21-mile swim was actually over 40 miles because of the tides. Using mainly the breaststroke, he completed the swim, according to the precise Victorian time-keeping, in 21 hours,

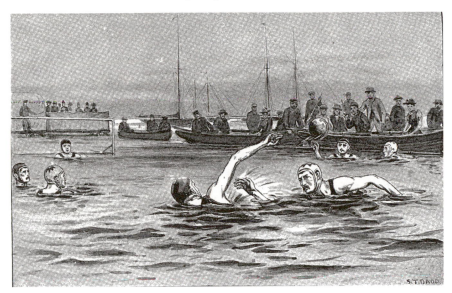

Water polo.

44 minutes, and 55 seconds,[44] the first documented successful swim across the Channel. Webb returned to England a hero. A future swimming challenge had a less felicitous ending. In 1883, concerned to earn money for his family, Webb went to the United States to make the very dangerous swim across the rapids at Niagara Falls. He drowned in the attempt.

As exciting as swimming competitions and long-distance feats could be, late-Victorians swimmers, accustomed as many of them were from childhood to team ball games, sought to create such a sport in the water. Various types of games were played informally, with no rules or organization, until in 1870 the London Swimming Association appointed a committee to draw up a code of rules for a water ball game. The game they devised, with six swimmers and a goalkeeper on each side, was called by various names: football in the water, water handball, and aquatic handball. They finally settled on the name used by a new equestrian sport brought from India, polo, which was a South Asian word for "ball." This new aquatic sport followed the typical pattern of Victorian sports by founding in 1888 the London Water Polo League, which sponsored the first water polo championship in that year.

ANGLING IN THE AGE OF COMPETITION

One would think that the traditional English field sports of hunting, shooting, and fishing, carried out in the often remote rural countryside and removed from the success-oriented pressures of modern industrial urban life would focus on the pleasures of the sport itself, without competition between sportsmen over who could capture the most foxes, shoot the largest number of birds, or catch the biggest fish. Field sports, however, just as most of the other sports in late-Victorian England, became consumed with competition, records, and victory.

Competition was perhaps most incongruent in the gentle individualistic sport of angling, but it became a dominant feature of especially the working-class angling clubs that proliferated in the last half of the nineteenth century. These clubs, often sponsored by pubs, organized cheap railway excursions to fishing sites, established competitions, and offered prizes for the biggest and most fish caught. Some of these clubs were named after that revered seventeenth-century father of angling, Izaak Walton—such as the Walworth Waltonians or the Isaac Walton Angling Society, although Walton would have been appalled by the organized clubs and the competitions. Fishing joined the ranks of other bureaucratized sports when angling associations were formed, beginning with the Angling Association of Sheffield in 1869.

The middle classes formed their own separate clubs. There was competition between the classes, not over prizes but over fishing sites. One middle-class fisherman, for example, complained in the *Field and Fishing Gazette* that he was driven from his peaceful fishing site by rowdy members of a working-class angling society.[45] The leisured upper classes did not have to suffer such indignities. They tended to fish further afield, in more remote areas and for game fish like salmon and trout, in contrast to the "coarse fishing" of the working classes— freshwater fish like carp, pike, and perch. The gentlemen anglers continued to eulogize the Waltonian solitary pleasures of fishing, and especially of more skilled fly-fishing. They nevertheless found themselves spending a great deal of money for their sport, in the purchase of the expensive fishing rods which had became one of the many sporting big businesses, as well as on travel to remote fishing streams in search of surviving game fish. Even more expensive was the new sport of sea fishing, organized in 1893 into the British Sea Anglers' Society.

SHOOTING AS MANY BIRDS AS POSSIBLE

With faster guns and stocked coverts, shooting also became a highly competitive sport, with careful records kept on the amount of game shot. More and more sportsmen were shooting in the late-nineteenth century, as evidenced by the increased number of applications for licenses. Many huntsmen turned to shooting as they grew too old or heavy to ride to hounds, as, for example, the Prince of Wales. There was also the ever-increasing supply of new middle-class shooters eager to join the ranks of country gentlemen, at least for a day.

As England moved towards greater democracy in late-nineteenth century, there were renewed demands that hunting and shooting also be democratized by the elimination of the remaining game law. This early-Victorian law still prevented farmers from shooting even rabbits and hares on their land to better protect their crops, unless they first purchased a costly license. Defending the game laws as a right of property, one sportsman complained about the proposal "to vest in the tenant-farmer a right . . . to be inalienably installed in

WHAT WE ARE COMING TO.

Swell Keeper. "There, My Lords! I have any Number of Birds for you, and you 'll find them quite Tame!"

Critics thought that the shooting of domestically raised game birds was too easy and was therefore no longer a sport.

possession of the sporting on his farm, and whereby any contract between himself and his landlord on the subject of the reservation of game is to be null and void."[46] Despite such opposition, a new Ground Game Law was passed in 1880 under the liberal William Gladstone even before agricultural workers gained the vote in 1884, which allowed tenants to kill animals on the ground, but not winged game, a distinction of rights that still exists today.

Without competition from unlicensed farmers for bird game, shooting enthusiasts were able also to enjoy or at least achieve more success in their sport because of the introduction in the 1850s of the new breech-loading guns, which could be loaded at a much faster pace than the old muzzle-loaders. These new weapons not only allowed the Prussians to easily defeat the Austrians and French in their wars of German unification in 1866 and 1870–71, they also enabled competitive English shooters to kill more birds faster. The kills were made all the easier by the continued use of the controversial "battue," with shooters walking in a line towards a covert, stocked with often specially raised partridges or pheasants. Shooters kept game books, recording the number of birds killed, as, in the words of Raymond Carr, "an index of the sport enjoyed."[47]

This almost obsessive record-keeping and competition among shooters was decried by traditionalists who thought that the pure pleasure of the sport itself was lost. Others complained that the pressure to shoot the largest number of birds caused sportsmen to lie or exaggerate, especially those from the "*parvenu* class."[48] Some critics argued that the records were meaningless, because battue shooting of tame birds made it too easy to get large numbers. A defender of the practice suggested that the opposition to battue shooting was due to the French name, which connotes effeminacy. He insisted that this form of shooting required a great deal of skill.[49] Many sportsmen must have agreed with him, because the number of shooters only expanded with the spread of the battue system.

THE NEW HUMANITARIANS VS. FOX HUNTERS

There was some humanitarian concern about the mass destruction of inno-cent birds, but most of the newly revived sentiments against blood sports focused on that most hallowed of English field sports, the fox hunt. Following the pattern of other sports, the number of foxhunting packs increased in late-Victorian England, withstanding such mockeries as Oscar Wilde's famous denunciation of the popular idea of health as "the English country gentleman galloping after a fox—the unspeakable in full pursuit of the uneatable."[50] Fox-hunting also became more organized and bureaucratized, with the formation of the Association of the Masters of Foxhounds in 1880. The sport, which had become more challenging in the eighteenth century with the erection of fences in the fields, became now even more so with the use by the 1880s of the newly developed barbed wire for fencing instead of wood or stone. Some landowners would, for a fee, take down the barbed wire in the fall and put it back up in the spring, but the amount of remaining wire fencing created real dangers to the hunters. Humanitarians, however, despite their name, were not concerned with the lives of human hunters but rather with the well-being of the poor beleaguered fox.

In the early-Victorian humanitarian campaign against blood sports, the con-cern was with bulls, bears, and cocks, with the often foxhunting reformers ignoring their own prey. In the late-nineteenth century, there was a renewal of humanitarian activism, with foxhunting now coming under particular opposition. Just as in the earlier campaign against blood sports the underlying concern seemed to be the unholy pleasure of the participants, so in the humanitarian debate against foxhunting, a subtext was opposition to the life-style and privileges of the landed classes.

The historian Edward Freeman launched the debate when he published in *Fortnightly Review* in 1869 a denunciation of what he called the immorality of field sports, and foxhunting in particular. The essence of the "sport," he argued, is "the needless fright, weariness, and suffering of a living creature." What is the hunter, he asked, but a butcher "who takes up the trade out of sheer love of slaughter?"[51] That most passionate of hunters, Anthony Trollope, answered Freeman. He voiced the oft-repeated argument that fox-hunting creates a strong sense of community among all classes, bringing city and country men together, an argument which Freeman answered by saying that "if that was a rationale, then it must clearly be justifiable to bring about railway collisions on purpose on the chance of the estranged ones coming together that way." Trollope also argued, echoing the earlier defenses of cock-fighting, that the fox was "so precious" to sportsmen that "the word vulpicide has been created to denounce the most hated crime." Moreover, it is the nature of foxes to hunt and be hunted. In the wild, they suffer "the double agony of hunger and of bloody destruction," and therefore "the soft-hearted, rose-leafed, velvet life which Mr. Freeman would desire for animals is not in accordance with Nature." Freeman responded by converting red-toothed Nature back into God, and argued that "once [we] admit the principle that we may inflict suffering for our amusement on the ground that such suffering is in accordance with the will of God, and it is hard to see where we are to stop."[52]

Many other hunting enthusiasts joined in the debate with humanitarians to defend their sport. The arguments are familiar. The appeal to manliness was always effective, with such images as that of a "shy, nervous youth, who has been brought up at his mother's apron-strings, [who] may be converted, by the influence of field-sports, into an open, manly character, losing all his silliness while retaining all his modesty."[53] As had been done in the defense of other blood sports earlier in the century, appeals were made to tradition, with foxhunting called "the 'Roast-beef-of-Old-England' sport."[54] Foxhunting was also argued to be important as a healthy release from the pressures of work. A gentleman, for example, burdened with the cares of work, goes hunting. "Where are all these [cares] now? Ask of the winds! They are vanished. His whole system is steeped in delight; there is not space in it for the absorption of another sensation. Talk of opium? of hatchis? they cannot supply such voluptuous entrancement as a run like this!"[55]

To defend their sport from attack, hunting supporters formed in 1884 the National Sports Protection Defence Association, changed the next year to the Field Sports Protection and Encouragement Association. In response, Henry Salt (1851–1939), a leading opponent of foxhunting, organized the Humanitarian League in 1891. The League had a broad agenda for progressive social reform, and within it an Animals' Defence section was established, that included opposition not just to foxhunting and other blood sports (a term which Salt coined), but also to zoos, circuses, and definitely vivisection.

The Field Sports Protection and Encouragement Association and other pro-hunting forces had little work to do, for the opponents of foxhunting had minimal political strength. Those who wielded power in Parliament included, along with foxhunting aristocrats and gentry, the wealthy middle classes who no longer had to take railways out to the countryside to hunt but who used their wealth to buy landed estates and enjoy the life and sporting pleasures of the leisured gentleman. Allied together in defense of their sport, they successfully crushed all attempts at abolition. Denunciations of foxhunting continued throughout the twentieth century, but it was not abolished until 2005. Unlike in Victorian England, lovers of the hunt today no longer have the power to protect their sporting pleasures.

6

The New Sporting Woman

The expansion of sports in late-nineteenth-century England was indeed revolutionary because it dramatically increased the number of participants and spectators, in an increasing number of diverse sports. Sports clubs, governing organizations, competitions and leagues, sporting journalism and literature, and sporting businesses all proliferated. Old sports were organized, bureaucratized, and standardized, even as new sports were developed to further challenge and enrich the sporting experience. With more leisure and higher wages, working-class men could join actively and enthusiastically in a sporting life that, since the early-nineteenth century, had been largely the province of the affluent classes. Equally as revolutionary, a whole new social group entered the sporting fray—middle-class women—whose participation both reflected and caused larger social changes in women's lives.

By the 1860s, women began to challenge the restrictive ideology of the passive submissive lady who stays protected in her domestic sphere. Organizing to demand greater legal rights, women achieved easier though not equal access to divorce with the 1857 Matrimonial Causes Act. The Women's Property Acts of 1870 and 1882 gave married women control over their own assets and income. Women first organized to win the right to vote in the 1860s, and, although they did not achieve the parliamentary vote until 1918 for women over 30 and equal suffrage in 1928, in the late-nineteenth century they did win the right to vote in such contests as municipal and school-board elections. Mid- and late-Victorian women also organized and campaigned for better female education and greater employment opportunities, and for many other causes that affected the lives of women.

This movement for what the Victorians called "the emancipation of women" peaked in the 1880s and 1890s, with the emergence of the "New Woman," who demanded not just legal, political, educational, and employment rights, but also physical freedom from the stifling inactivity of Victorian ladyhood. Women demanded the right to exercise their bodies, to play outdoors, and, most controversially, to compete in sports, even as their brothers, husbands, and sons did.

Those concerned about the chronic ill health of conventional middle-class ladies welcomed the new sporting woman. The biologist George Romanes, who had so strongly endorsed men's sports for reasons of health, did so also for girls and women. He complained that the girl is "shut up in a very prison-house of decorum; every healthful amusement is denied her as 'unladylike.'" He said he could not draw "too dreadful a picture of the consequences" of such lack of physical activity. Arguing that exercise should be as much a duty for women as paying calls, he acknowledged that there would be opposition from those who believed that, "by encouraging active outdoor games among schoolgirls, we should rub off the bloom, so to speak, of refinement."[1]

Opposition there indeed was, not so much to girls and women getting exercise, but to doing so through sports. The sporting woman, a term some considered oxymoronic, challenged Victorian sexual ideology in fundamental ways. Sports were seen as a way of maintaining and displaying manliness, so what did it mean for women also to play? The concept of femininity was the opposite of the active, strong, competitive athlete. A true woman was essentially frail, sheltered in her sphere, under male protection. She was cooperative, while man, her complementary opposite, was competitive. A woman should not sweat, nor exert herself, and certainly not in public. As T. Pilkington White argued, "If there be one unwritten axiom that the universal custom of civilised communities has stereotyped into recognition, it is that the gentler sex must on all occasions consult appearances in a special manner not demanded of men. . . . If she be very woman, it would seem not possible that she could under any circumstances consent to exhibit herself in an ungainly manner before the world, least of all before men."[2]

Although some women defied or ignored concerns about traditional femininity, many sporting women maintained at least the semblance of womanly behavior and appearance as they played, not the best method of achieving athletic excellence. By the end of the century, however, the sporting woman was such a familiar sight that, even competing and sweating, she received grudging acceptance by all but the most diehard of conservatives, and in so doing, transformed the concept of women's physical capacities.

Women's participation in outdoor physical activities also caused a revolutionary reform in clothing, at least on the sporting field. Long before the Rational Dress Society was formed in 1881, "to promote the adoption, according to individual taste and convenience, of a style of dress based on consideration of health, comfort, and beauty,"[3] women's rights advocates and health reformers had been demanding change in the constrictive dress of the Victorian lady, with her tight-laced corsets and heavy long skirts. It was difficult, however, to counter the ridicule and scorn that clothing experiments evoked. When the comfortable American "bloomer," for example, with its pantaloons and over-blouse, was introduced in England in the 1850s, it was greeted with such derision that reformers, both in England and the United States, decided it was not worth wearing. Participation in sports, however, necessitated a modification in women's clothing, not as a cause but as a practicality. Although women in pants, however disguised, were seen as aping men, even ardent defenders of traditional values and female behavior came to recognize that if women were to engage in physical activities outdoors (and many wished they would not), then their modesty, much less their safety, was better protected in some kind of utilitarian sporting dress that often included a modified form of trousers.

CROQUET

The first organized competitive sport that Victorian women played provoked the least challenge to conventional mores. This sport was the lawn game of croquet, brought from France via Ireland to England in the 1850s. Adapted from the traditional French game of *maille* (mallet), and named probably for the French word "croc" for "hook," croquet quickly became very popular, especially among the suburban middle classes, as a sport that women could play in conventional dress, and without sweating, touching, or running. It was also a game that women and men could play together. Not requiring much exercise, croquet became notorious as an occasion not so much for sport as for flirting, difficult to do otherwise in properly chaperoned Victorian society.

Despite the frivolous play, croquet did also become a serious competitive sport. Enthusiasts urged the codification of consistent rules, "so that, instead of the existing anarchy and confusion, there should be one recognized code, occupying the same position in the croquet world as the laws of the Marylebone Club do in the cricket world or the decisions of the Jockey Club in the racing world."[4] An All-England Croquet Club was formed in 1868, open to women as well as men, which issued rules for the game. In 1870, the club bought grounds at Wimbledon, a village southwest of London and now part of the greater metropolis, where it held championship matches for men.

As intense as the All-England Croquet Club championships could be, and as popular for women and men in the mid-nineteenth century, by the early 1870s croquet had faded as a sport for any but garden-party play. It did enjoy a brief revival in the 1890s and was taken seriously enough as a sport to be included, for the only time, in the second modern Olympics in Paris in 1900. Englishmen, however, tended to consider it too tame and effeminate, as reflected in its French name. Trollope did not include it in his *British Sports and Pastimes* because he viewed it as "too delicate, too pretty, too refined to be dealt with by men who profess that, in speaking of British Sports, they have intended to speak of things rough and violent."[5] H. G. Wells (1866–1946), in his one of his later novels, *The Croquet Player*, voiced sentiments that he would have learned in his late-Victorian youth, when he describes his title character as "a trifle effeminate and ridiculous" and "what the Americans call a sissy" because croquet is his game.[6] A significant problem of the game for men, according to one commentator explaining the "psychology of croquet," was that women could play it equally as well as men, and men do not like such physical equality and potential challenge.[7] Probably the major reason, however, for the decline in interest in croquet was the spectacular rise of the new suburban sport which was more vigorous and fast moving, yet nevertheless acceptable for women—lawn tennis.

LAWN TENNIS

Unlike most sports that evolved through time, lawn tennis was specifically created in the early 1870s as a game for suburban play. Sharing the name and claiming descent from the medieval court game, it was not similar to indoor "royal" or "real" tennis, which was much closer to Victorian fives or modern-day racquetball. This new game did, however, use the old French royal tennis form of scoring, with the strange terminology of "love," meaning "zero," probably from "*oeuf*" (egg); "*deuce*" from "*deux*" (two), for the two points by which one had to win; and the 15, 30, 40 presumably from the clock in the royal tennis court wall.[8]

A retired army officer, Major Walter Wingfield, is credited with creating the game of lawn tennis, for which he received a patent in 1874. It was a game, he said, that could be "played in the open air in any weather by people of any age and both sexes." Dependent on the new technologies of the nineteenth century, the game not only used vulcanized rubber for the ball, but also the necessary use of the recently invented lawn mower and the roller to make the ground suitable for play. Wingfield named his game *Sphairistike*, Greek for "ball-game," an unfortunate name that understandably was not popular. Not liking its easier nickname, "sticky," he quickly renamed the sport simply "lawn tennis." An entrepreneur, he successfully marketed tennis kits, with rackets made of wood and gut strings, balls, and nets. His original nets were high, and got progressively lower to facilitate play, until in 1882 the height was finalized at three feet six inches, as it still is today.

A game intended to be played on private grounds, it was, as Wingfield had announced, considered appropriate for women as well as men, even though it did involve physical exertion and some strength. Girls and women at first were advised to play cooperatively, hitting the ball to their opponent, rather than the more male way of a competitive contest. That advice was not long followed, as women more and more got into the competitive spirit of the sport. There were proposals to make a women's version of the game, with a smaller court, but, as a defender of women's tennis was glad to say, "these subversive efforts ended in failure."[9] Although young girls could play in shorter, calf-length skirts, women were expected to keep even their ankles covered. A ladies' magazine advertised an outfit, hardly designed for serious play, as a tennis costume: "A cream merino bodice with long sleeves edged with embroidery; skirt with deep kilting, over it an old-gold silk blouse-tunic with short wide sleeves and square neck." Such elaborate outfits were soon replaced by more utilitarian "rational" tennis costumes, howbeit still with skirts.[10]

Since tennis was a game which women could play, it was never considered a "manly" sport, but, as Richard Holt said, "From a gender viewpoint, tennis was the first truly national game."[11] Unlike croquet, women and men could not play tennis on equal terms, since physical strength was a factor in success and men could assert their physical dominance on the court. It quickly became a widely and frequently played game for both men and women, especially among the middle classes. As evidence of its popularity, in 1877 the All-England Croquet Club added "Lawn Tennis" to its official name. In 1882 the name "croquet" was dropped from the name altogether, although later it was restored, but with "lawn tennis" given priority in the title.

What transformed the essentially garden-party game into a serious competitive sport was the establishment of a national championship. Just as the Football Association Cup Championship intensified interest in football, so did the founding in 1877 of the All-England Croquet and Lawn Tennis Club tennis championship for men, held at their grounds in Wimbledon, and known ever since simply by the name of the town. Even more interest and also controversy was created with the establishment in 1884 of a women's championship. Even though women's matches were limited to three sets in contrast to the five sets for men, in this and other tennis championships women were able to compete fully as trained and skilled athletes, in the full glare of public view. Despite criticisms for their appearance "as competitors for prizes in the full blaze of publicity at such places as Wimbledon . . . to be scrutinised, bet on, and applauded by crowds of strangers,"[12] women continued to compete, and with ever-increasing athletic skill. In so doing, even wearing modest skirted dress, they challenged not only their opponents, but also, fundamentally, the basic precepts of Victorian gender ideology.

The first female star athlete emerged from the Wimbledon competitions—Charlotte "Lottie" Dod (1871–1960). Dod was born into an affluent and athletic family, with her older brother, for example, winning a gold medal for archery in the 1908 Olympic Games. In childhood she played sports equally with her brothers, and she had the private financial means to continue a sporting life throughout her adulthood, without concern for propriety or social expectations. Learning the new game of tennis as a child, she entered her first big competition in 1885, at age 13, where her victory earned her the label from the press of the "Little Wonder." In 1887, at age 15, she entered and won the championship at Wimbledon, a feat she repeated many times. She became so popular that she developed a following among young girls, who would avidly attend tournaments in which she was competing and cheer her victories enthusiastically. Dod retired from competitive tennis at a young age, to concentrate on other sports. She excelled in archery, hockey, golf, and mountaineering. Despite her achievements in those sports, her fame remained as a tennis champion, and appropriately, in her old age in 1960, she was listening to Wimbledon on the radio as she died.[13]

Just as the women's tennis championships dispelled myths about women's physical limitations, so it did also for another group, twins. The twin Renshaw brothers dominated Wimbledon in the 1880s, as did the Baddeley twin brothers in the 1890s, refuting the commonplace medical assumption that twins were physically weaker than other people. Along with the serious championships in which women and men, twins and all, competed, tennis continued as a popular casual suburban game. In typical Victorian fashion, tennis clubs were formed throughout the country, affiliated with the regulating Lawn Tennis Association, founded in 1888. By the end of Victoria's reign, there were 300 clubs as members of the association.[14]

BADMINTON AND TABLE TENNIS

Two other games similar to tennis that were also created in the late-nineteenth century—badminton and table tennis—were similarly considered appropriate for even conventional women to play. Badminton was derived from the traditional children's game of "battledore and shuttlecock," in which children use a paddle ("battledore") to keep a small-feathered shuttlecock in the air as long as possible. There are diverse accounts of how this children's game became a modern sport, named after Badminton House, the residence of that great patron of sports, the eighth Duke of Beaufort. British soldiers in India first played it seriously in the 1860s, and they devised a set of rules. The game was brought back to England in the 1870s and quickly became popular as a sport that could be played indoors in inclement weather, required little space, and was gentle enough for women to play without raising social anxiety. Even in the opinion of one of the strongest critics of women's physical sports, badminton was "a wholly unobjectionable and becoming amusement for the fair sex." Badminton clubs were formed throughout England, and that hallmark of modern sport, a regulating organization, the Badminton Association, was established in 1895, with an All England Championship first held in 1899.[15]

Table tennis emerged in the 1880s, with the first games apparently improvised using "cigar-box lids for bats, corks for balls, and a row of books for a net."[16] In 1884, a noted sporting goods store advertised a "Miniature Indoor Lawn Tennis." The game was significantly improved when the technology was brought over from the United States for the manufacture of the lighter celluloid balls, which created a "ping-pong" sound when hit. Sir Charles Tennyson remembered that when he was a student at Cambridge, at the turn of the century, "one could not walk through the narrow streets of the old town without one's ears being continuously assailed by the monotonous 'ping pong, ping pong' of the celluloid ball colliding with the vellum bat in countless students' lodgings."[17] Clubs, regulating associations, and competitions were soon established.

ARCHERY, ICE SKATING, AND SWIMMING

Archery had long been a sport of aristocratic women, but middle-class women also began playing in the 1860s. Despite its military roots, it was considered an acceptable sport for women because it did not involve that triad of prohibitions—sweating, running, or touching—and could be played in ordinary, respectable female dress. Archery never achieved large participation in late-Victorian England, but there were the inevitable clubs, associations, and competitions. Most clubs, such as the Royal Company of Archers, the Royal Toxophilite [a lover of archery] Society, and the Woodmen of Arden, were for men only, but some mixed clubs were formed, with men paying higher subscription fees. In the competitions, women archers shot over shorter distances, with different bows and targets, than did men.

Ice skating was popular among young women. A sport that required balance and skill as well as providing freedom of movement, ice skating allowed women and men to relate together physically in ways that otherwise would not be acceptable in respectable society. The journalist T. H. S. Escott took some amusement in observing the reaction of English mothers to the adventures of their ice-skating daughters: "Not without a shock to her sense of maternal propriety did the English Matron of old fashioned ideas see, or hear of, her daughter being twirled in the arms of some youth just introduced, or perhaps without even the preliminary of that easy form."[18]

Ice skating was fine in the cold winters, but in the summer swimming was the physical recreation of choice. Maintaining decorum with the use of bathing machines, women had been "bathing" since the mid-nineteenth century, but in late-Victorian England they began swimming in earnest, for speed and endurance, including in competitions. They took particular pleasure in the challenges and thrills of open-sea swimming. One female swimmer, Constance Everett-Green, extolled "the joys of really deep-sea swimming. . . . That is the real way to enjoy yourself. The buoyancy of the deep water is in itself a wonderful exhilaration. . . . How different from the heat and horror of the bathing machine and the turmoil of the beach!" The problem with serious swimming was what women should wear. The full-bodied bathing costume might protect modesty but hardly safety or comfort when vigorously swimming. Everett-Green advocated simple pantaloons, with a high-body blouse and short sleeves. "The lower limbs of the bather are only seen as she enters and quits the water. . . . So as the skirt only fulfils its purpose when the bather walks or dives into the water . . . I do not think it worth her while in a general way to wear one." If, however, a woman swims with men, Everett-Green conceded, she should wear a skirt.[19]

HORSEBACK RIDING AND HUNTING

Horseback riding was another aristocratic pleasure that in the late-nineteenth century more and more middle-class women began to enjoy, following of course the social requirement of using a sidesaddle. Although perched on one side of the horse, women riders were made safer by improvements in the acceptable riding habit. A safety skirt was developed, which would come off in case of emergency, with trousers underneath to protect modesty even in a crisis. The horsewoman Alice Hayes objected to this kind of skirt: "I consider this a very unsanitary arrangement, for it is obvious that the undergarment must be kept clean." Usually the groom cleaned his mistress's hunting boots and skirt, "but a combination garment should not be cleaned by a male servant." Hayes instead devised her own safety skirt that did not include trousers. However, she acknowledged that any kind of skirt that improves safety is better than the cumbersome clothing of earlier days.[20] Other commentators also welcomed such dress changes, but the new sporting horsewoman was warned that she is "still open to the reproach that she attempts to dress as much like a man as possible."[21]

The only times women dared defy convention by riding cross-saddle was when they ventured far from England. The intrepid traveler Isabella Bird Bishop (1831–1904) was bold in her explorations but conventional in her dress and values. Nevertheless, when she went to Hawaii in the early 1870s and saw women there riding astride, she adopted that style, in Hawaii and on her future travels in the Americas and Asia, as "the easiest, the safest, the most enjoyable pursuit imaginable."[22] Ethel ("Mrs. Alec") Tweedie (ca. 1861–1940) describes her decision to ride astride. Like Bishop in Hawaii, when Tweedie was travelling in Iceland and saw women riding "like men," she became convinced that it was safer and less tiring than riding sidesaddle. She first tried it when riding with her brother and other men on the rough Icelandic roads. The journey was so difficult that she felt it was impossible to try to ride "ladywise on a man's saddle." She determined that either she must turn back, or "mount as a man. Necessity gives courage in emergencies." Keeping her brother back with her, she told the others in the party to ride ahead. She had her brother shorten the stirrups and hold the saddle. After several attempts, she

> succeeded in landing myself man fashion on the animal's back. The position felt very odd at first, and I was also somewhat uncomfortable at my attitude, but . . . arranging my dress so that it fell in folds on either side, I decided to give the experiment a fair trial, and in a very short time got quite accustomed to the position, and trotted along merrily. . . . The amusement of our party when I overtook them, and boldly trotted past, was intense; but I felt so comfortable in my altered seat that their derisive and chaffing remarks failed to disturb me.[23]

The debate over riding cross-saddle was carried back to England when *The Illustrated Sporting and Dramatic News* published articles in 1880 on "Ladies on Horseback," by the noted Irish horsewoman, Nannie Power O'Donoghue, which were then republished in one volume. O'Donoghue's argument in support of the sidesaddle for women provoked a lively correspondence on the issue. One correspondent confessed that she, as Bishop and Tweedie had done, rode astride when abroad, "far beyond conventional bondage, and it is incomparably better." She argued that with appropriate dress, "there is nothing to hurt the extremely proper feelings of the most modest." No woman, she insisted, "would ever be twisted and packed on to a side saddle again if she could help it, after once enjoying the ease and freedom, as well as complete control of her horse which a man's seat gives."[24] O'Donoghue answered sternly that the man's saddle might be more comfortable, just as were many other aspects of men's clothing and lives, "which ladies may envy the sterner sex, without at the same time advocating the propriety of encroaching upon their privileges." Women should accept the reality that "men have their costume, their avocations, their sayings and doings, their varied callings in the world, and women have theirs. Each should be separate and distinct from the other. A manly woman, or a womanly man, is, in the eyes of all rightly-judging persons, a most objectionable creature."[25]

No matter how bold, even riding cross-saddle, women did not race horses, at least in public competition. Women did, however, become all the more eager spectators and gamblers at the races, much to the dismay of men who saw the turf as a male province. They also, to male chagrin, participated more in hunts. A favorite sport of aristocratic women in the eighteenth century and

HUNTING LADIES AGAIN.
Fiora (who has been riding down her dearest Friend all the Morning), "AH! WON'T THOSE BRAMBLES SCRATCH YOUR FACE NICELY FOR THE BALL TO-NIGHT, MISS ETHEL!"

earlier, by the mid-nineteenth century few women, even from the aristocracy, rode to hounds. In the last part of the century, however, upper-class women rejoined the chase, now in the company of more affluent middle-class women. Male hunters were vociferous in their complaints. They protested that women talk too much during the hunt; that if women hunters ran into trouble, men had to stop their own chase to help them; and that they want equality but did not do their fair share by, for example, keeping a gate open to men behind them at the start of the hunt.[26] On that last point, Hayes, a defender of the hunting woman, acknowledged that "the intense annoyance entailed by a gate being dropped into its intricate fastenings through want of ability or of consideration on the part of the fair Amazon immediately preceding him, has brought into the mouth of many a chivalrous sportsman a muttered anathema of the feminine taste for hunting that scarce any other provocation would have availed to rouse."[27] Some hunts responded by refusing to allow women to join the chase.

Not only foxes but also birds and other game fell prey to the new sporting woman. Lady Boynton, with the rank if not the gender to entitle her to speak on shooting, observed the changes that had taken place in recent years.

A few years ago a 'shooting-lady' was almost as much a *rara avis* [rare bird] as the Great Auk; if here and there one member of the sex, more venturesome than her fellows, were bold enough to take to the gun in

"ONE TOUCH OF NATURE."
(*George has promised his Ethel the first shot, for luck! A covey rises!*) *Ethel* (*at the critical moment*), "OH, GEORGE! *PERHAPS THEY TOO HAVE LOVED!*"

preference to the knitting needle, she was looked upon as most eccentric and fast, and underwent much adverse criticism. Now, however . . . ladies who shoot, and who shoot well, too, are springing up on all sides.

Despite harsh criticisms of the shooting woman from many fronts, Lady Boynton defended her. "That a woman who is fond of sport need lose nothing in grace, charm, or refinement, we have ample evidence to show. She does not necessarily become masculine either in manner or conversation."[28]

CYCLING

As revolutionary as such sports as tennis were on women's lives, no physical activity had as much impact as the new sport of cycling. Developed in France, a form of the bicycle had been around since early in the century. The earliest was the wooden "hobby horse," propelled by one's feet. In the late 1860s, an improved "velocipede," or, a term coined in 1867, a "bicycle," was developed. Appropriately nicknamed the "boneshaker," it had somewhat equal-sized wheels, made of solid rubber tires, and was heavy and inefficient as a means of locomotion. Next came the "ordinary," popular in the 1870s and 1880s,

The tricycle, developed in the 1860s, was considered especially appropriate for women.

which looked odd with its very large front wheel and small rear wheel, but it was more rideable than earlier versions.

Although men took to the ordinary, women were advised to use another new cycling form, the tricycle. It gave greater stability and safety to the presumed weaker sex, while at the same time provided them the sporting pleasure of pedaling down the open road. As one tricycling woman enthusiast proclaimed, "All worrying cares, all fretting petty details of daily life, seem to fall from one like an ugly shadow when one mounts one's iron steed. Who can keep a wrinkled brow or a heavy heart as one darts swiftly and smoothly through the sweet keen air; or glides down some long descent with an exhilarating rush which is more skin to flying than any known motion?" She assured her readers that there was nothing "fast or unwomanly" about riding the tricycle.[29] Not all social commentators agreed. White, critiquing the "modern mannish maiden," was appalled to see women on tricycles, "bodies bent well forward, knees up and down anyhow—struggling along with purple faces and hair awry." Such as sight may make one inclined "to put the three-wheeled abomination incontinently out of court."[30]

The opposition to the tricycle was nothing compared to that of the "safety bicycle," which emerged in the late 1880s and quickly became the cycle of choice for women as well as men. Instead of tires of solid rubber, this bicycle had lighter, air-inflated pneumatic tires, a process developed in the late 1880s by the Scottish veterinarian and inventor, John Dunlop. It had a chain-driven rear wheel, allowing the tires to be of equal size. Enormously popular in the

Bicycle versus pony at Hammersmith.

1890s, the mass production of safety bicycles became a major English industry, and they were priced within reach of even the lower-middle classes. If purchased used, they were accessible to the working classes. As many advocates pointed out, a bicycle as a means of transportation was certainly cheaper than a horse, and it did not require a groom or stable. (Along with its spoofs of the cycling craze, *Punch* portrayed a poignant cartoon of a now redundant horse looking sadly at a bicycle.[31]) Bicycles were even used for some military purposes in place of horses. Although of French origin, nationalistic cycling enthusiasts claimed that the bicycle was a truly English invention, which was "till recently an almost exclusive *habitat* in these islands. England was for many years the only country where cycling flourished, and whatever machines were found across the Channel bore tokens of their English origin."[32]

Useful for transportation, the bicycle in the 1890s received the most attention as a vehicle of sport. Cycling periodicals emerged, as did cycling poems and songs. It indeed became, as one skeptic said, an epidemic: "Truly, if we were a professedly Pagan people, the next step would be the setting up of temples and the dedication of altars to this new-found Divinity of the Wheel, to whom we offer such incessant incense."[33] The Cyclists Touring Club, founded in 1878 with 142 members, had 60,000 by 1899. In 1878, the National Cyclists' Union, the "Jockey Club of Cycling,"[34] was formed, to promote the interests of cycling and to establish championship races. As with the other sports, records were kept which cyclists strove to break. Racing times got faster and faster, typically over distances from one to fifty miles, with some sporting traditionalists arguing this was due not to "increased pluck and endurance of the cyclists themselves," but to improvements in the bicycle and the track over which it was raced.[35]

Clearly the most controversial part of this cycling craze was the presence of female bicyclists. Debates over the propriety as well as ability of women to bicycle were heated throughout the 1890s. Eliza Lynn Linton (1822–1898) was one of the fiercest critics of the new woman, and especially the new sporting woman. She was convinced that bicycling would be too hard for the weaker sex. It "seems to be such a doubtful kind of amusement—such a queer cross between the treadmill and the tight-rope—demanding such a constant strain of attention to keep your balance, with such a monotonous and restricted action of the limbs as to render it a work of penance rather than a pleasure."[36] Like others, Linton was concerned that cycling would destroy the passive quietude that was the essence of Victorian femininity, and that most important quality, modesty. "The modern bicycling craze," Linton warned, "is not only far beyond a girl's strength but it tends to destroy the sweet simplicity of her girlish nature. Besides, how dreadful it would be if by some accident she were to fall off into the arms of a strange man."[37]

If a young woman did fall into the arms of a strange man, there probably would not be a chaperone to rush to her protection. A Chaperon Cyclists' Association was formed, with married women, widows, and "spinsters over thirty" with their own cycles, to accompany young ladies on their rides.[38]

"With a proper teacher of their own sex, and with suitable dresses for the preliminary practice, ladies can obtain such a command over the velocipedes in one week's practice, of an hour daily, that they can ride side-saddle-wise with the utmost ease."—*New York Sun*.

OH! THEN, THIS IS WHAT WE MAY EXPECT TO SEE THIS SEASON.

They were not successful in maintaining surveillance, and the association faded by the end of the century. Girls and women not only lost their chaperones, they also lost their skirts. There was no way to get around the necessity of women riding cycles astride, despite what were probably only spoofs proposing a cycle sidesaddle. When riding astride, the conventional skirt with crinolines, which could blow up in the wind, was hardly modest. A more rational cycling costume was devised, the notorious but popular knickerbockers, with baggy trousers and a long over-blouse. Despite the safety and modesty of the new costume, the outcry against women in pants was intense. Linton was disgusted to see women walking about "in cut-away coats and knickerbockers ... their whole being a compound of masculinity and insurgency welded into a kind of aggressive, not alluring, *dévergondage* [shamefulness]."[39] Lady Jeune approved of women's cycling, but argued that it could be done in a skirt. "There is no doubt to some minds a pleasure and excitement in donning the dress of our masters. ... No woman looks well in male attire."[40]

The concern about appearance was a major detriment to many otherwise aspiring sporting girls and women. A good way to keep women in the assigned sphere was to mock the way they looked when they left. This was especially so for bicycling. Many critics described the sporting woman as unattractive. Sweating, straining men were also not appealing to look at, "but be it remembered, *pace* the new woman, there is a difference in the sexes. How a man looks is of small matter: how a woman looks is a matter of the greatest consequence."[41] Nevertheless, despite these attempts to intimidate girls and women into returning to their lives of immobility, the cycling female became a familiar sight on the public roads and was an important physical and also psychological catalyst for emancipation from the constraints of Victorian ladyhood.

On the cycle, a young woman, especially dressed in the liberating knickerbockers, could feel for the first time a sense of freedom:

There is a new dawn, a dawn of emancipation, and it is brought about by the cycle. Free to wheel, free to spin out into the glorious country, unhampered by chaperon or even more dispiriting male admirer, the young girl of to-day can feel the real independence of herself, and while she is building up her better constitution she is developing her better mind. ... How little and cramped seems the life before the cycle came into it![42]

The novelist and biologist Grant Allen (1848–1899) asked if "when man first set woman on two wheels with a pair of pedals, did he know, I wonder, that they had rent the veil of the harem in twain, I doubt it. But so it was. A woman on a bicycle has all the world before her where to choose; she can go where she will, no man hindering."[43] She even entered bicycle races, although with great opposition, including that of the National Cyclists' Union. A supporter of cycling for women but a strong opponent of female racing mockingly said that women who race "are in exactly the same position to the lady cyclist as the circus rider is to the horse-woman taking her morning canter in Row" (the Hyde Park Rotten Row riding path).[44] Similarly, cycling received medical endorsement as a healthy sport for women, but not racing or efforts to break records. "Both are physiological crimes."[45]

Not only women but also men of lesser means in constricting jobs found new freedom in the bicycle. Wells, in his 1896 novel *The Wheels of Chance*, describes a lower-middle-class store clerk, Hoopdriver, who takes a cycling holiday and rescues a bicycling young woman from a compromising situation. When the holiday is over, Hoopdriver returns to his boring work life "with a difference, with wonderful memories and still more wonderful desires and ambitions."[46]

GIRLS' SCHOOLS AND WOMEN'S UNIVERSITY COLLEGES

Just as boys' public schools and university colleges were the matrix in which, in mid-Victorian England, modern organized team sports were developed for boys and men, so also were the new girls' schools and colleges in the late-nineteenth century the cultivators of women's physical education and participation in team sports. As much resistance as there was to women playing such individual sports, there was so much more opposition to competitive team sports for women. The schools and colleges provided the private space, removed from public scrutiny, where girls and young women could safely develop their skills and compete without restrictions except those imposed by the relatively autonomous school authorities.

These institutions were able to play such a key role in the development of the female sporting life, especially for middle-class women, because of the tremendous expansion and reform of women's education in late-Victorian England. In the first decades of Victoria's reign, female education was aimed at inculcating and supporting the ideals of ladyhood. Training girls in the social graces, teaching them to be pleasing to men, this "finishing" education indeed finished the intellectual and physical development of many girls. There were certainly highly educated early-Victorian women from the middle and upper classes, but their education usually came not from schools but from having a free rein in their father's libraries.

By the mid-nineteenth century, the social reality of middle-class women who did not have a male protector and therefore who could not live sheltered in the domestic sphere emerged as an urgent public concern. Some middle-class women who had to support themselves did so through writing. For most single women, however, the only work they were qualified to do and could do without losing their class status was as governesses. The work of a governess was so uncertain, and most women so poorly trained to teach anything but good manners, that even social conservatives supported better education for women. The Queen's College in London was therefore founded in 1848 to train women to work professionally as governesses and as schoolteachers. In 1850 the North London Collegiate School for Ladies and in 1853 the

Cheltenham Ladies College were opened, with curricula that rivalled that of boys' schools. In the next decades, there was a proliferation of new girls' schools, both day and boarding, with curricula of varying rigor but all aimed at preparing girls intellectually, and importantly physically, for full productive lives, in their expected roles as wives and mothers, but also with the ability to support oneself if fate so decreed. Working-class girls could at least receive the rudiments of an education in the new state schools that were established by the Education Act of 1870.

Girls who were intellectually stimulated by their secondary education increasingly demanded the right to a higher education. To meet this need, and withstanding great opposition, women's colleges were established at Cambridge University—Girton College in 1869 and Newnham College in 1871. Oxford, more conservative on women's as well as other issues, eventually followed the Cambridge example in 1879 with the founding of Lady Margaret Hall and Somerville College. At these colleges and in the girls' schools, physical education was considered an important part of the curriculum. The ideal of *mens sana in corpore sano*, which justified sports in boys' schools, was arguably important for girls also, especially with their history of poor health as a result of inactivity. Physical fitness was important for boys as future soldiers and as leaders of government and business, but it was equally important for girls as future mothers. The argument of healthy motherhood and racial progress became more and more compelling with the development of the evolutionary theories of Charles Darwin and the concept of survival of the fittest, interpreted in a national and racial sense by the late-nineteenth century.

Gymnastics

In the 1850s and 1860s, physical education in the girls' schools consisted mostly of gymnastics, exercises which did not involve competition or great exertion and which therefore did not challenge the norms of femininity. The leading figure in gymnastics education was a Swedish woman, Madame Bergman-Osterberg, who was appointed superintendent of physical education for girls in the state schools in 1879. The Swedish style of gymnastics she taught was a more flexible and graceful floor exercise than the rigid German *turnen* methods, which used vaulting horses, rings, and bars. It was indeed welcome change from the military drill the girls had been taught in the state schools. Bergman-Osterberg left that position in 1885 to found the Hampstead Physical Training College and Gymnasium (later moved to Dartford, Kent, and known then as the Dartford College of Physical Education) to train physical education teachers for the expanding number of schools for middle- and upper-class girls.

A fervent proponent of physical fitness for girls and women and a dress reformer who abhorred such constricting apparatuses as the corset, Bergman-Osterberg nevertheless made conservative and therefore socially acceptable arguments in favor of her programs. She accepted that women are naturally weaker than men and therefore all the more needed physical training. She saw a woman's main role in life in terms of motherhood and felt that it was important to strengthen girls to fulfill their maternal role and to improve the Anglo-Saxon race: "I try to train my girls to help raise their own sex, and so to accelerate the progress of the race, for, unless the women are strong, healthy, pure, and true, how can the race progress?"[47] Like so many other female education reformers, she had strict rules on the dress and behavior of her students, to deflect the argument that strong fit women were mannish.

Tennis, Boating, and Hockey

As girls grew more self-confident and self-assertive with their challenging education, just as the critics of women's education had warned they would, they also demanded the right to play as boys did. In the interests of health as well as female development, organized sporting programs more interesting to most girls than gymnastics were introduced in the schools, although often limited by the lack of space for playing fields. It was in the new women's colleges that organized and especially team sports took the deepest root and flourished. The first sports in the colleges were the noncontroversial individual games of croquet and badminton, and most popularly, tennis. Competitive tennis teams were soon organized, with Newnham College first challenging Girton to a match in 1878, an intercollegiate competition that became in 1882 an annual event of great importance in the college calendars. The Oxford colleges also began an intercollegiate tennis rivalry, and in 1883 the first inter-university match was held between representatives of the women's colleges at Cambridge and Oxford. The collegiate women also cycled, for pleasure as well as transportation, although with restrictions on where they could go. Newnham College, for example, did not permit female students to cycle to lectures until 1910.[48]

That most popular of university male team sports, rowing, was also considered acceptable for collegiate women, although with the softer name of "boating." Even though named "boating," for successful performance the sport required great muscular strength and endurance, close team cooperation, and a competitive drive, qualities that alarmed the guardians of traditional femininity. Rowing could, however, be done more privately, away from the public glare. At Oxford, for example, women's rowing was only permitted on the Cherwell River when men were not around, and not at all on the Isis River, more popular with male crews.[49]

Unlike the men's schools and universities, athletics in the form of track-and-field events were not offered regularly to girls and women. The prohibition against women running was too strong. As T. Pilkington White advised, "The sex should avoid any pursuit of diversion which necessarily involves violent running. ... To run, nature most surely did not construct her."[50]

This prejudice lasted well into the twentieth century. The Olympic Games, revived in 1896, did not allow women's running events until 1928, and then only for short distances. Women were not allowed to run the marathon in the Olympics until 1984.

Interestingly, field hockey became the most popular women's team sport, even though it requires running up and down the field and necessitates the wearing of knickerbocker-type clothing rather than skirts. It did not involve touching and did not have the association with men or manliness that other nineteenth-century team sports had, and was therefore more acceptable for female play. Hockey had been a traditional village game, which, like football before the mid-century, had almost faded from the sporting consciousness until, with the enthusiasm for all sports in late-Victorian England, it was revived as a men's sport in the 1870s. It was modernized and regulated in the 1880s, with the establishment of men's clubs and the creation in 1886 of a national governing organization, the Hockey Association. Hockey never became a major male sport, however, because women took it so avidly, and it soon came to be seen, in men's eyes, as an effeminate game.

Hockey was played in the girls' schools and even more enthusiastically as the premier sport at the women's colleges. Intercollegiate and inter-university matches were hotly contested and attracted great interest. When the women graduated, they wanted to continue playing the game they so enjoyed in college, so, as men had done for their sports, the women formed Old-Girl clubs and their own association, the Ladies' Hockey Association. This association was refused admission to the (male) Hockey Association, and so women's hockey remained under female leadership. In 1885 they dropped the word "Ladies" from the association name, calling it instead the All England Women's Hockey Association.[51]

CRICKET AS A MAN'S GAME

By the turn of the century, women also played another team sport which, like hockey, did not meet with great resistance because it had not been integral to the Victorian male sporting life—the North American native game of lacrosse. (See Chapter 8 for a discussion of lacrosse in England.) The two most popular team sports for men, however, cricket and association football, women played only marginally, and with intense criticisms when the games were played off the school grounds and in public view. Cricket was the iconic traditional sport of England, one that did not welcome change, much less the change of the gender of the players. Although played in pristine whites and seen by foreigners as a somewhat effete game, Victorians viewed cricket as the essence of manliness as well as virtue and fair play and considered it all that represented the best of the (male) English character. Ignoring the fact that women in preindustrial England and into the nineteenth century (including W. G. Grace's mother in mid-century) had regularly played cricket, male cricketers and critics of the new sporting woman did not take kindly to the female invasion of the sport and held them off with pronouncements of female unfitness and with ridicule.

Opponents argued that women were not physiologically constructed to play cricket. Despite being trained in the sport by his cricket-playing mother, W. G. Grace believed that women were not "constitutionally adapted to the sport."[52] There were fears that if women played, their shoulders would become dislocated with bowling, they would not be able to handle the strain of hitting and fielding, and that they might develop a malignancy if a ball hit them in the breast.[53] More damning, women cricketers were portrayed as ridiculous, lumbering between the wickets dressed in pads. If at all concerned about their appearance, girls and women would not be attracted to a sport which, in the words of that redoubtable critic of the new woman, Linton, made them lose all femininity. "The prettiest woman in the world loses her beauty when at these violent exercises. Hot and damp, mopping her flushed and streaming face with her handkerchief, she has lost that sense of repose, that delicate self-restraint, which belongs to the ideal woman."[54] J. Hamilton Fletcher, who had in earlier years strongly supported outdoor athletic sports for women, in 1896 drew the line at cricket. Cricket, he said unequivocally, "is not a game which will ever be taken seriously by ladies."[55]

In 1887, some mainly aristocratic women in Yorkshire formed their own cricket club, the White Heather Club. Their rank and private play allowed them to escape public condemnation, but another women's cricket club did not fare so well. In 1890, a group of male entrepreneurs, hoping to capitalize on the spectacle of women playing cricket, organized a short-lived professional touring team, the "Original English Lady Cricketers." The players were advertised as "elegantly and appropriately attired," with "every effort" made "to keep the organisation select and refined." However respectable in intent, the players felt the need to protect their reputations by playing under assumed names. Once the novelty wore off, spectators stopped coming to the games, and, overwhelmed by mockery and poor attendance, the team dissolved.[56]

THE BRITISH LADIES FOOTBALL CLUB

Women's attempts to play football (soccer) in the late-nineteenth century also failed. Football did not have the cultural baggage of tradition and iconic status as did cricket, but, as an aggressive and sometimes rough sport it was considered completely inappropriate and dangerous for girls and women. Instead, women's desire to play a fast-moving competitive team sport was channeled into the more acceptable field hockey. In 1895, however, an enterprising sportswoman with the wonderfully appropriate name of Nettie Honeyball, decided to organize a women's football team, the British Ladies Football Club, and with an overtly feminist agenda. Defending her plan, Honeyball argued that women were as good as men. "We ladies have too long borne the degradation of presumed inferiority to the other sex. If men can play

The first match of the British Ladies Football Club, in March 1895, attracted a large crowd of mostly skeptical spectators.

football, so can women."[57] When questioned about the presence of married women, she scoffed that husbands had nothing to do with it.[58]

Honeyball invited the distinguished sportswoman and writer, Lady Florence Dixie (1855–1905), to be the president of the club. From an old distinguished aristocratic sporting family, Dixie was the daughter of the eighth Marquess of Queensberry. Her older brother was John Douglas, the ninth Marquess, who gave his name to the 1867 rules of gentlemanly boxing. More notoriously, he also had accused Oscar Wilde in 1895 (the same year that Douglas's sister was president of the women's football club) of sexually violating his son, Lord Alfred Douglas, which led to Wilde's conviction and imprisonment for homosexuality.

As a member of aristocratic family, Dixie had been a skilled hunter and shooter, until she became repulsed by the "horrors" of blood sports.[59] She was also a strong advocate of women's rights. In her 1890 utopian novel, *Gloriana, or the Revolution of 1900*, Dixie describes a coming society of complete sexual equality, including equality in athletic ability, for if girls had the same physical opportunities as boys, "the girl would prove herself every inch his equal in physical strength."[60] With this conviction, she readily accepted the presidency of the new women's football club. Defending the sport, she pointed out that in association football a player must be "light and swift of foot, agile, wiry, and in good condition; and are not these physical requisites just the very characteristics of good health most to be desired for women?"[61]

The general public did not agree. When the highly publicized first game of the club was played in March 1895, with the team divided into "north" and "south" to play against each other, there were reportedly 10,000 curious spectators, who, according to the reports in the hostile press, left out of disgust with the poor play and ridiculous appearance of the players. Reported widely in the press, the game was treated almost universally as a joke, or as a misguided and disastrous attempt of women to invade the male territory. When Eliza Lynn Linton saw a picture of the players in a newspaper, she indignantly wrote the editor that "these boy-girls—these worse than hoydenish football players—sin against the laws of modesty in force at the present day, and we look in a perplexed disgust at the exhibition they make of themselves."[62] The British Ladies Football Club continued to play on tour that season throughout England, but then, like the English Lady Cricketers team, it dissolved.

DEBATE OVER THE NEW SPORTING WOMAN

If not for the female cricketer or footballer, the new sporting woman otherwise had strong and enthusiastic support from women's rights advocates, and also more broadly from those who believed in the domestic role of women but who wanted women in their duties to be healthy and fit. The opposition, however, was strident and vociferous. In addition to the fears that specific sports evoked, there were often repeated concerns about the loss of femininity, the blurring of sex differences, the immodest exposure of women's bodies, and the female invasion of the male sphere. As women defied opposition and continued to play and compete, opponents drew on the strongest argument of all, that sports would ruin a woman's reproductive capacity.

Dr. Arabella Kenealy (1859–1938) was an influential exponent of this argument. Herself a new woman who defied social expectations by qualifying as a doctor, she was concerned with women's health and was a member of the Rational Dress Society. She increasingly pitted herself, however, against the women's emancipation movement and especially against the new sporting woman. Drawing on the theory of conservation of energy, she argued that if girls and women expended energy in sports anytime during their fertile years, that energy was taken from the potential or actual work of reproduction. She gave an example of two contrasting pregnant women who came to her office. One was an active healthy sportswoman who continued an active life throughout her pregnancy. Her child was puny and ill. The other woman was a true womanly woman, passive in life and inert during pregnancy who had a robust healthy child.[63]

In subsequent writings, in addition to the dubious biological theories, Kenealy drew on familiar social arguments. She condemned the female athlete as selfish, neglecting her womanly duties, by, for example, going off cycling rather than putting flowers on her sister's bonnet. Her greatest selfishness, however, was in sacrificing "the birthright of the babies," by expending on muscles "the laboriously evolved potentiality of the race."[64] When a defender of women's sports retorted, "Who has decided that it is not woman's province to be muscular?"[65] Kenealy's lame response was that the sporting woman is "deficient in a quality for which I can find no better term than atmosphere— a species of aura, magnetic charm. . . . Without it woman is as incomplete as is a flower without perfume."[66] As evidenced by the number of girls and women who hopped on their bicycles, picked up a tennis racket, and wielded the hockey stick, many new sporting women were content to have vigor and fun rather than perfume.

7

The Professionalization of Sports in Late-Victorian England

Opposition to sports in late-Victorian England was not confined to women's participation. There was also strong criticism of what was pejoratively called the "cult of athleticism." Although not as heated as the hysteria over the new sporting woman, skeptics warned of ill effects caused by the dramatic increase in sporting activities and preoccupations. Just as there was concern that sports dominated life at the public schools and universities, so also, opponents of the sporting revolution argued that, in the larger adult world, participation in sports, both as players and spectators, had been carried too far. Most critics agreed that England was a sporting nation, but they argued that the sporting life in late-Victorian England had been taken to an unhealthy and unnatural extreme. According to W. Beach Thomas, writing in the *Cornhill* in 1900, these critics were "people of by no means grandmotherly upbringing or unmasculine instincts who regard the progress of athleticism with dread, and . . . consider the exaggerated reverence for games as one of the many signs of a growing decadence."[1]

OPPOSITION TO THE SPORTING REVOLUTION

Unlike the evangelical opposition to sports in the early-nineteenth century, opposition to the sporting revolution was largely secular, although there was some religious concern about the increasing violation of the Sabbath with covert sporting activities. The early utilitarians had condemned all sporting fun as a waste of time, and there was still the echo of work ethic in the new criticisms, but the focus now was not against sports but against imbalance. Playing sports in moderation was fine, but having one's whole life wrapped up in one's team or in sporting competitions was counterproductive and unhealthy. It was acceptable for boys to be so involved, one critic argued, "but when you become a man you ought to put away childish things."[2]

There was particular concern that England's political leaders were spending too much time on the sporting fields or at the racetrack. With the increasingly aggressive nationalism in late-nineteenth century international relations, warnings that the British Empire might fall because of distractions from sports resonated with some nationalists. In rebuttal to these doomsayers, sporting enthusiasts argued that sports had always been important in English social life. The sports writer F. G. Aflalo, for example, pointed out with copious examples that most British statesmen from the eighteenth century on had been avid sportsmen, men who had presided over the rise of the British Empire to a position of world dominance.[3]

A more ominous and difficult argument to answer was that the sporting obsession was leading to the economic decline of the British Empire. The dominant commercial power in the eighteenth century and the industrial giant of the nineteenth century, Britain was experiencing keen economic competition by the end of the 1800s, particularly from the United States and Germany. Some critics placed the blame for the decline on sports, which they condemned as draining time and energy away from productive work. S. J. Jeyes, writing in the *Fortnightly Review* in 1897, complained that "the national need is all for longer hours and closer application, while the popular cry is for short hours, more holidays, and plenty of recreation." Jeyes hastened to explain that such criticism was not a suggestion for the end of the English sporting life.

> It is not to be hoped, nor need it be feared, that the manly type of young Englishmen, sound in wind and limb and clean in heart, will ever disappear. But it existed amongst us long before the present mania for athletics had set in, and will not become extinct when that craze has passed away.

Jeyes acknowledged that the United States was also preoccupied with sports, but it could remain economically strong because unlike the British adherence to free trade, American goods were protected by a tariff wall. The Germans, meanwhile, "our most formidable adversaries," were not sportsmen. They "have not yet been fascinated by an ideal which did very well for ancient Greeks, whose wants were simple, and who had no rivals to undersell them in their own markets."[4]

While Victorian capitalists were anxious lest sports undermine Britain's economic strength, the enemies of capitalism, the socialists who emerged as a political force in the late-nineteenth century, were concerned that workers focused too much on sports and especially football (soccer) rather than on overthrowing the exploitive economic system. (Middle-class sports promoters had used this argument from the French Revolution on as a reason to support sports for the working classes.) The gradualist Fabian Society, formed in 1884, and the revolutionary Marxist Social Democratic Federation, established in 1881, sought to arouse workers to resist rather than participate in the capitalist system. Socialists were concerned that, instead of nurturing revolutionaries, "we are in danger of producing a race of workers who can only obey their masters and think football."[5]

Not only did some socialists oppose sports as a distraction from revolution, but they also argued that modern sports were a toxic product of capitalism. As a member of the Social Democratic Federation wrote in 1891 in its journal *Justice*, "The truth is that sport, like every other thing, is demoralised and damned by capitalism. . . . Until capitalism is dead no real sport can have life. Sport in its present aspect must go too." Setting the agenda for the new Independent Labor Party, formed in 1893 by a coalition of socialists and trade unionists, the chairman of the North East Federation said that "difficult though the task may be to push football out of heads and push Socialism in, the task must be undertaken, for just as surely as football doesn't matter, Socialism matters a very great deal."[6] The difficulty with such arguments was that, by the late-nineteenth century, attachment to sports and one's team had too strong a hold on the working classes. Marx had underestimated the power of nationalism on workers' loyalties, and similarly, British socialists woefully misjudged the seductive power of sports on the working classes. The socialist critique of the sporting culture was also dampened by the fact that many socialist groups formed their own sports clubs, aimed at fostering camaraderie and providing recreation among members.

An argument against sports to which both capitalists and socialists could respond was that of damage to health. The healthful benefits of the sporting life had been one of the earliest and most repeated rationalizations for sports in Victorian England. This rationale was turned on its head by late-nineteenth century critics who maintained that, just as women who participate in any vigorous sport damaged their reproductive organs, so men who exercise their muscles strenuously suffer lasting injury to their heart and lungs. Thomas voiced the common belief that "violent muscular exertion beyond any doubt *does* produce heart disease." He accepted the importance of exercise and made the unpopular suggestion that, instead of competitive sports, the English should follow the German model of nonstrenuous, noncompetitive gymnastics. "We are as apt to despise gymnastics as much as the Germans exaggerate their importance. . . . Of course it is dull to swing your arms or try to touch your toes for even short daily periods. But if this short-lived dullness gives us good hearts, lungs and muscles fitted for any sudden call," it is foolish to neglect it.[7]

The novelist Wilkie Collins (1824–1889), in his 1870 novel *Man and Wife*, portrayed most dramatically the concerns about the physical and even more so the moral decline caused by excessive athleticism. Writing in the early stages of the sporting revolution, Collins voices his skepticism in the character of the wise lawyer, Sir Patrick, who admits that he holds "very unpopular opinions as to the athletic displays which are so much in vogue in England." He is concerned, however, that "there is far too much glorification in England, just now, of the mere physical qualities which an Englishman shares with the savage and the brute. And the ill results are beginning to show themselves already! We are readier than we ever were to practice all that is rough in our national customs, and to excuse all that is violent and brutish in our national acts." Collins argues that most crimes are committed by "out-of-doors men," although he hastened to add not all athletes are criminals.

> I am far from saying that the present rage for exclusively muscular accomplishments must lead inevitably downward to the lowest deep of depravity. . . . Thousands of the young gentlemen, devoted to the favorite pursuits of the present time, will get through existence with no worse consequences to themselves than a coarse tone of mind and manners, and a lamentable incapability of feeling. . . . [But] will the skill in rowing, the swiftness in running, the admirable capacity and endurance in other physical exercises . . . —will these physical attainments help him to win a purely moral victory over his own selfishness and his own cruelty?[8]

Collins's anti-hero, Geoffrey Delamayn, proves Sir Patrick's point. A star athlete in university and now the idol of society for his athletic feats, Delamayn is also coarse, selfish, and immoral. He seduces a young woman with promises of marriage, and then, to get rid of her, he attempts to kill her. His heart is, however, so weakened by his athletic exertions that when he attacks his wife, an old servant woman leaps to her defense—"The feeble old woman attacked the athlete!"[9]—and Delamayn suffers a fatal seizure. The erstwhile wife then marries the wise anti-athlete, Sir Patrick.

Man and Wife was an immediate success. Serialized first in *Cassell's Family Magazine*, the novel dramatically increased the magazine's circulation. It did not, however, stem the tide of the sporting revolution. Defenders of the new athleticism quickly rebutted what they saw as Collins's distorted caricature of the modern athlete. The mountaineering philosopher Leslie Stephen acknowledged that the athlete has his faults, but "he need not be painted with quite so black a brush. . . . Muscularity within due bounds is really a very excellent thing." It was natural and good, Stephen argued, that sports were giving relief from the pressures of the crowded urban world in which so many Englishmen lived. "Whilst the conditions of modern society remain what they are, it is likely that we shall every day feel more strongly the benefit of some strong unreasonable taste for healthy exercise on land or water as a natural corrective to the evils of a sedentary life."[10]

As is probably true in all eras, sentimental older sportsmen nostalgically looked back on sports in what they considered the good old days, when people played sports simply for fun, and they bemoaned that in their modern age, athletes were too focused on prizes, cup championships, and records. Gentlemen, they argued, do not expect such rewards when they compete in sports.[11] The most heated criticism, however, was not that players wanted medals and cups for their play, but that they wanted payment.

THE AMATEUR IDEAL AND THE OPPOSITION
TO PROFESSIONALISM

The debate over whether players should be paid for their participation was the most rancorous of all sporting controversies in late-nineteenth century England. The issue went to the heart of the meaning of sports in Victorian society and illuminated more clearly than perhaps in any other forum the class attitudes of the age. As long as sports were dominated by middle- and upper-class "gentlemen," the question of whether money changed hands was not a concern. In the late-nineteenth century, however, as more and more working-class men entered the sporting arena, the privileged classes, eager to defend what they saw as their special province, tried to limit access to sport. They did so by fervently insisting that no player receive compensation, especially in sports without an established and accepted tradition of professionalism.

The pressure for payment for players came as the competition between sporting teams grew more intense. Team owners and clubs wanted to increase their profits by attracting more spectators, which they could do by fielding the strongest and most successful teams. Many of the best players were from the working classes, especially in more physical sports like football, as evidenced by the victory of the historic working-class Blackburn Olympic football team over the Old Etonians in the FA Cup Championship in 1883. A working-class man, however, could not practice as much as needed, and certainly not as much as could a person of independent means. Workers had their half-Saturdays and bank holidays for games, but the only practice time was at night, after a long-

AMATEURS AND PROFESSIONALS.

Caddie (visiting): "WHAT KIND O' PLAYER IS HE?" *Caddie (engaged):* "IM? HE JUST PLAYS AS IF IT WAS FOR PLEESURE!"

day's work. As their participation in the clubs became more valuable, they began demanding compensation for "broken time," money replacement for wages lost due to team practice and games. Defenders of the old order saw such payments as the thin edge of the wedge of professionalism and fought it as bitterly as though it were the last bulwark defending the English class system. They were right about the thin wedge, because soon good players began demanding payment not just for lost work time but also for their play itself. If team owners could make profits, why should not the players share in those profits? Not ones to scorn payment for work, they had no reluctance to demand payment for their new sporting "work."

Opponents of professionalism in sports in whatever guise counterpoised professionalism with the class-based ideal of the amateur, from the Latin root *amo, amare,* to love. According to this surely illusory ideal, one played sports for love, not financial gain. A player could have the rewards of good health and camaraderie, but certainly not money. Amateurs played their best for their team, but they did not over-train, and winning was certainly not the point of the game. Praising the amateur ethic in England, a writer in the *Saturday Review* describes an American on a sporting pilgrimage in England, who was

> astonished at the equanimity of English sportsmen. In America, he assures us, it is no unusual thing to see members of a defeated team throw themselves on the ground, and even cry, in an agony of disappointment. . . . He had thought it impossible for men to be keen without giving up their faculty of enjoyment and their sense of proportion. But the 'master-bias' of the English athlete, as of the Happy Warrior, still leans towards an ideal which is not shattered by the mere accident of one defeat.[12]

This concept of amateurism overlooks the fact that many schools, universities, and amateur clubs hired professional coaches and trainers to increase their chances of winning. It also excuses the many amateur sportsmen, most notably the great W. G. Grace, who received large sums of money for inflated expenses and endorsement of products. Such men as Grace were gentlemen, and the padding of their bank accounts was therefore not seen as payment for play. That the concept of "amateur" was class based is evident in the fact that before the 1880s, the more common and synonymous term was simply "gentleman." "Professional" in the early-nineteenth century referred to a level of expertise, and, in the 1850s, it took on its modern meaning, with the term, a pejorative to many in the middle and upper classes, a clearly coded word for "working class."

The opposition to professionalization of sports was part of the larger resistance by people of property to the increasing democratization in late-Victorian England. Many of the same arguments against payment of sportsmen were used against the proposal to pay members of Parliament. The Reform Acts of 1867 and 1884 opened the franchise and the right to election to working-class men, but without payment, it was very difficult for them to serve in the parliamentary House of Commons. The argument that one should consider election to the Commons as honor without the need for rewards won out in late-Victorian England, and it was not until 1911 that members of Parliament received a stipend for their service. Distrust of payment of money for service was seen even in the compensation of barristers, the higher-status lawyers who could argue in court. They were not paid directly—their clerks took care of the tainted financial matters—but the robes of the barristers had pouches in the back for the discreet payment by clients of gratuities. Sportsmen did not have pouches in their uniforms, but there were many covert and, depending on the sport, overt ways of giving them compensation.

Critics of professionalization drew on a wide range of arguments. The common complaint was that if a man were paid to play, then the play became work, whereas sport was to be the antithesis of and antidote for the pressures of the everyday world of industrial capitalism. They also argued that if players were paid, then the pressures for the team to win would be intense, to maximize profits so the professionals could be paid. The emphasis on winning would destroy the ethic of fair play and gentlemanly behavior expected of sportsmen. Another argument, with ominous implications, linked professionalism and corruption. If a player were paid to win, then he could also be paid to lose.

The strong Victorian middle/upper-class resistance against class mixing fueled the opposition to professionalism in sports. Nevertheless, the English sportsman and sports journalist N. L. ("Pa") Jackson (1849–1937), an ardent defender of amateurism in sports, defensively insisted that the opposition to professionalism was not class prejudice. Similar to the arguments of defenders of racial segregation in the United States, Jackson argued that class separation was natural. For example, amateurs and professionals preferred to dine separately and "for two good reasons, namely that the professionals liked to dine earlier in order to be able to attend the music-hall or theatre and that they all felt a little constrained when with the amateurs, thinking that they could not talk among themselves so freely as they might wish." Servants, Jackson argued, "did not dine with their masters in the dining room, nor did they come and go through the front door," and professional sportsmen were nothing but "paid servants."[13]

The propertied classes usually couched their prejudice in terms of *noblesse oblige*. Treating the working classes as children, they patronizingly sought to protect them by keeping them from the false path of professional sports. Professional players could earn money in sports for only a short time in their lives, and after that, many then would be destitute. The more fortunate could become publicans, but only so many public houses were needed in a community. Much better that even talented working-class sportsmen continue in the reliable if hard life as manual workers, than following the illusory path of the professional sports.

Opponents of the professionalization of sports also voiced concern that it would turn the participatory healthful activity into a spectacle in which a few played, and the vast majority passively watched. "Spectatorism," as it was scornfully called, was seen as a sign of the decline of the vigorous manly Englishman. Spectatorism certainly became an important part of English social life, with large crowds flocking to watch especially the Saturday afternoon contests and matches. To accommodate them, grand pavilions and stadiums were built, constructed by the new engineering techniques and illuminated by the new energy sources of gas and electricity, which had been developed in the late-nineteenth-century "second industrial revolution." Just as the cathedral-style railway stations characterized the grand architecture of the early-nineteenth century, so these sports palaces were the iconic buildings in late-Victorian England. The concern that sports enthusiasts were watching rather than playing games could be alleviated to some extent by the observation that most spectators, including women and older men, were not fit to play anyway. For example, at a football game "very few outside the ropes are physically fitted to engage for an hour and a half in a game which requires stamina as well as resource, pluck as well as skill, and excellent bodily condition as well as fine speed, to play with success."[14] So they might as well watch the games as go to the pub or some other less desirable venue.

There was also the resurgence of fear of chaotic behavior by working-class spectators, attracted in even larger numbers to games and matches when the level of play was raised by professional athletes. After all, the word "fan," from the late-nineteenth-century American usage, is short for "fanatic." Certainly working-class sporting fans in England could be fanatic, but their behavior at games generally continued to be controlled. This was especially so in cricket matches. Well into the twentieth century, the Marxist revolutionary, C. L. R. James, a native of Trinidad who led the fight against British colonial rule of his homeland, combined his anti-imperial struggle with an avid love of the quintessentially British game of cricket. James was shocked when he attended an American baseball game and heard the "howls of anger and rage and denunciation" which his friends, all university educated, hurled at the players on the field. He was even more "filled with horror" when he heard of corruption in a U.S. basketball team. His friends were surprised that James, of all people, would have such reactions of propriety. He explained that "adults in Trinidad or in Britain, in the world of business or private life, could or would do anything, more or less. But in the adult world of sport, certainly in cricket ... I had never heard of any such thing and did not believe it possible."[15] Even less so would it have been in Victorian England.

The greatest concern was for fan behavior at professional football games, where passions and partisanship tended to run high. Viewing working-class people as children and also as wild animals, and as emotional volcanoes waiting to erupt, one skeptic wrote in 1894 that "the crowds are a great danger and disadvantage to football. A game is a very stirring sight to see, and the impetuous mob[s] are not always judicious observers of it: it is overmuch for their nerves sometimes. As a rule they do not go to see football: they go to see their own side win."[16] This class assumption that working-class spectatorship led to chaos and lawlessness was belied, however, by the usually controlled if partisan and emotional behavior of the working-class spectators, even after the acceptance of professionalism in association football.

TRADITIONAL PROFESSIONAL SPORTS AND THEIR TRANSFORMATIONS

England had a long history of professional sports, well before the revolutionary changes in the late-nineteenth century. One of the oldest and still most popular of sports, horseracing, depended since the eighteenth century on professional jockeys and on crowds of spectators to swell the coffers of the race promoters. The Jockey Club was able, with varying success, to control what some saw as the inevitable consequences of professionalism: gambling and corruption. Another traditional professional sport, prize-fighting, was not successfully regulated and was pushed underground by the weight of the vice associated with the sport. When boxing was resurrected in mid-century as a tool of muscular Christianity, it was strictly amateur.

Rowing as a sport began in the eighteenth century among professional watermen, whose races attracted enthusiastic gamblers. Introduced into the public schools and universities as an amateur sport in the late-eighteenth and early-nineteenth centuries, boat racing became the most popular organized athletic activity in the mid-Victorian elite educational institutions that had access to rivers. When the Henley Regatta was established in 1839, to differentiate itself from the old professional watermen races, it set strict rules for eligibility. All competitors were excluded who were not from the universities and public schools or who were officers of the Regatta. The universities similarly tightened restrictions on their boat races, disallowing the traditional practice of using professional watermen as coaches and as coxes (the member of the crew who sat in the stern facing the rowers and managing the rhythm of the rowers and direction of the boat).

Rowing clubs that were formed among Old Boys continued the strict criteria of excluding professionals. In 1878, fighting the pressures for the professionalization of sports, the major rowing clubs formed the Metropolitan Rowing Association, which issued a very narrow class definition of amateurism required for membership.

> An amateur oarsman or sculler must be an officer of her Majesty's Army, or Navy or Civil Service, a member of the Liberal professions, or of the Universities or Public Schools, or of any established boat or rowing club not containing mechanics or professionals; and must not have competed in any competition for either a stake, or money, or entrance fee, or with or against a professional for any prize; nor have ever taught, pursued, or assisted in the pursuit of athletic exercises of any kind as a means of livelihood, nor have ever been employed in or about boats, or in manual labour; nor be a mechanic, artisan, or labourer.

In 1879, the phrase was added "or engaged in any menial activity."[17]

The Metropolitan Rowing Association changed their title to the Amateur Rowing Association (ARA) in 1882 and functioned as the governing body for English rowing clubs and competitions. Its narrow class definition of amateurism was popular with those who considered the sport of boat racing as the province of the elites (working-class origins of the competitive sport notwithstanding). Others, and not just among the excluded manual workers, were uncomfortable with its class restrictions, including F. J. Furnivall (1825–1910). Best known for his work as honorary secretary of the Philological Society in conceiving and directing the early work on the *Oxford English Dictionary*, Furnivall was also, from his Cambridge days on, an avid rower. Becoming friends with Charles Kingsley, Thomas Hughes, and other muscular Christians, he helped found the Working Men's College in 1854. He believed in the democratic camaraderie that sports could foster and was therefore strongly opposed to the restrictions on participation of manual workers in his favorite sport:

> We feel that for a University to send its earnest intellectual men into an
> East-end or other settlement to live with and help working-men in their
> studies and sports, while it sends its rowing-men into the A.R.A., to say
> to these working-men, "You're labourers; your work renders you unfit
> to associate and row with us" is a facing-bothways, an inconsistency
> and contradiction which loyal sons of the University ought to avoid.[18]

A separate organization, the National Amateur Rowing Association, was founded in 1890, still barring professional rowers but without any restrictions on manual workers who wanted to row and compete in boating races for recreation.

Like rowing, the sport of athletics—track-and-field sports—popular in the public schools and universities from the 1860s on, had professional origins in the discredited sport of pedestrianism, a past from which athletics enthusiasts definitely wanted to disassociate. Therefore, the Amateur Athletic Club, founded in 1866 by university students and graduates to organize an athletic meet before the annual Oxford-Cambridge boat race and, thereafter, regular meets among public-school and university graduates, issued a code of rules in 1867, specifically excluding not just professional runners, but also all manual workers. That exclusion was dropped the next year, but they retained the definition of amateur as "any gentleman who has never competed."[19]

Amateur athletic clubs hotly debated what was called the "gentleman-amateur question." The London Athletic Club, for example, met in 1870 to consider adding to their rules the expulsion of any member who not only competed with manual workers but also anyone who willfully participates in any sport "wholly, or partially confined to tradesmen." One member spoke strongly against the rule, urging that "in these days when we were drifting towards universal suffrage, it did not do to draw any nice distinctions between the classes," and he urged instead "perfect freedom of action for every member." The proposed rule did not pass, although disgruntled supporters of the restriction said sarcastically that members who voted against it would themselves "never dream of competing with the sorts of a large firm of grocers or drapers." At a following meeting, a compromise resolution was passed, expressing the non-coercive sentiment that the governing committee "thinking that the position of the club may be affected if members compete at athletic meetings held by firms of tradesmen, express an earnest desire that members will not enter at such meetings."[20]

The more broad-based Amateur Athletic Association (AAA), formed in 1880, dropped the term "gentleman" from its definition of amateur, but it rigorously enforced the ban on participants who competed for money or against professionals. A founder of the AAA, Sir Montague Shearman (1857–1930), was nevertheless concerned about the admission of working-class men into competitive athletics. "Without casting any reflection upon the conduct of the masses as a whole, it is obviously impossible to expect that with many of them the money to be gained by betting or 'squaring' races will not offer irresistible temptations." With a coded reference to gentlemanly (meaning middle/upper-class) behavior, he described the "genuine amateurs" as "all of one kind; they run because the exercising of their bodies gives them delight, and because, being Englishmen, they find it pleasant to have beaten an honest adversary in an honest competition."[21]

CRICKET AS A BRIDGE BETWEEN AMATEURISM AND PROFESSIONALISM

Advocates of professional sports often cited the example of cricket as a game in which, from the eighteenth century on, amateur "gentlemen" played with and against professional working-class "players," without social chaos or the degradation of the sport. The seeming egalitarianism of cricket was deceiving, however, since the professional players were hired mainly to do the more arduous work of bowling, so that gentlemen could enjoy the easier and more refined batting. The social distinctions remained sharp, with the retention of the traditional practice of calling gentlemen with the honorary title of "sir" and the players just by their last names, and with the separate dressing rooms and separate entrances. Treated like servants, the players were supposed to do menial work in addition to bowling, such as keeping the grounds clean.

This social segregation in cricket was accepted without question in earlier days, but by the late-nineteenth-century age of democratization, apologists became increasingly defensive. W. J. Ford insisted that "only ignorance permits a man to apply such a word as 'snobbish' to the custom of providing separate accommodation for the two classes of players; worse is it when such a one hints at such a thing as stand-offishness on the part of the amateurs. There are certain differences in the education, and the social position of the two classes that makes the closer intimacy of the pavilion undesirable, and undesired also by both players."[22] Jackson, who had argued so strongly against fraternization in sports in general, was especially irritated that professional cricketers, abetted by trouble-making journalists, were beginning to resist staying in their assigned place:

> There is a danger that the happy relations which have so long existed between cricket amateurs and professionals may be interrupted owing to the irresponsible clamouring of a certain section of journalists who, knowing nothing of cricket, and being without those instincts which make a sportsman, endeavour to persuade the professional that he should be treated in exactly the same manner, and enjoy the same advantages, as the amateur. . . . As well might the workmen at a printing establishment insist upon passing through their employer's private office, when going to or from their work, instead of using the door provided for them. . . . The levelling up (and down) process has not yet removed all social distinctions in this country, and until these disappear the ordinary usages and observances should guide the conduct of professional cricketers as it does that of their peers in others walks of life.[23]

It was acknowledged that the professional cricketer tended to be well behaved—yes, even gentlemanly in conduct—but that was attributed to the good influence of the amateur cricketers. As a *Saturday Review* commentator explained in 1883, "it must be remembered that cricket brings them into association with men of the best manners and, above all, of unimpeachable character, whose tradition of the game, brought from school or college, make unfairness or even sharp practice as impossible to them as cheating at cards. It is from these men that cricket takes its tone in this country."[24] With the expansion of interest in cricket in the late-nineteenth century, including from working-class men wanting to play as professionals, there was urgent concern to maintain the dominance in numbers as well as in status of the amateur gentlemen. A. G. Steel, writing the cricket volume of the *Badminton Library of Sports and Pastimes* series, acknowledged that, although most professional cricketers are "honest, hard-working, and sober men," it is "not in the interests of cricket that any branch of the game should be left entirely in their hands. Your professional, as a rule, is the son of a small tradesman, or a person in that rank of life."[25] As an attempt to lessen reliance on professionals, there was a push to encourage more gentlemen to practice bowling. Another remedy was the invention of a machine to bowl the balls, but it did not catch on, and gentlemen were forced to rely on players whom they called, in dehumanizing terms, "bowling machines."[26]

THE PROFESSIONALIZATION OF ASSOCIATION FOOTBALL

The new sports that emerged in the late-nineteenth century were the least apt to resist the entry of professionals into their ranks. The National Cyclists'

Union, for example, from its founding in 1878, allowed professional cyclists to be members. Many competitive swimming clubs also accepted professionals. The new (or at least newly modernized) sport in which professionalism caused the greatest controversy and had the largest impact was association football. Reshaped in the mid-century public schools from its preindustrial popular origins, football attracted by the 1870s large numbers of working-class players and spectators, especially in the northern cities and towns. Working-class players were compensated at first for seemingly legitimate expenses and, more controversially, for broken time, when they missed work to play in games. By the early 1880s, the competitive pressures on teams to get the best players led to blatant payment for play. The FA tried to stop that practice, and in response, some northern teams threatened to secede. They formed a rival British National Football Association, which they said they would dissolve only if the FA accepted the practice of payment for play. To maintain its authority over football and to prevent a split in the game, the FA reluctantly agreed in 1885 to legalize professionalism.

To keep clubs from buying the best players from other teams, and to prevent players from selling their services to the highest bidder, the FA set strict residency requirements, similar to those in county cricket. A player had either to be born in the town he represented or to live at least two years within six miles of the club headquarters. This requirement also aimed at fulfilling the sentimental idea that, even though players were paid, they played primarily for their loyalty to their town or city. Even with residency requirements, the players' attachment to place was largely a myth. Many opponents of professionalization would agree with the novelist Jerome K. Jerome, author of the popular 1889 novel *Three Men in a Boat*, who complained that professional football was like a cattle market, where human beings were bought and sold. Jerome also voiced the common middle-class fear of working-class violence. Claiming that professional footballers were notoriously involved in cases of domestic violence (without putting the numbers in the larger context of domestic violence in Victorian England), he insisted that professionals were from a "low and savage class."[27]

Defenders of the old order repeatedly claimed that professionalization made football more dangerous and violent. Playing to win at any cost, the professional, it was argued, did not have the self-restraint and sense of fair play that was characteristic of a gentleman amateur. This fear was discounted most effectively through exaggeration by a proponent of professionalism. This advocate described a supposed Frenchman reporting to a Parisian journal about an English football game that he attended: "The players precipitated themselves furiously upon each other; arms and legs were instantly dislocated; collar-bones broken; children of tender years limped off the field with fatal injuries. . . . It was a spectacle terrible and affecting. I turned away with tears in my eyes." This account was, "Homeric in its vigour, and worthy of Munchausen for its veracity." (Munchausen was an eighteenth-century German baron known for his exaggerations and lies and after whom in the mid-twentieth century the syndrome of compulsive exaggeration especially of medical conditions was named.) What more effective defense of professionalism than to discount that report as "a dainty Gallic falsehood, designed to divert the wise, deceive the ignorant, and foster a distaste for English institutions across the Channel." The author acknowledged that there is risk in football, as in all sports, but that risk is not increased by the presence of professionals, even though they do not have a public-school education. "Discipline of mind and body may be obtained quite as satisfactorily in the football field as in class-rooms."[28]

Nevertheless, traditionalists continued to decry what they viewed as the evil effects of the professionalization of football. A recurrent lament was that the game was no longer a sport but simply an entertainment, and that "there is every reason why amateurs, who play for love of the game, for the sake of healthy exercise and the joy of battle, should refuse to take part in [professional football.]"[29] Frequent analogies were made to the gladiatorial contests in imperial Rome, always with the subtext that, just as Rome fell, so could the British Empire. The class argument remained paramount, although few expressed it as blatantly as did "Creston," writing in the *Fortnightly Review* in 1894. "Those pampered members of society, the British lower classes, can apparently only regard any form of sport as it assists them to make money. It was an ill day for the game when the northern labourer diverted his attention from quoits and rabbit coursing and pigeon flying, and turned it to football."[30]

Despite such denigrations, working-class professionals, often playing on mixed teams with amateurs, did not officially have a lower status, as they did in cricket. Some middle-class players did, however, refuse to mix with their fellow professionals teammates. Shocking at least to Jackson, some did not refuse. Blaming the FA for "endeavouring to remove all those social distinctions between amateurs and professionals which obtain in other sports," he cited with chagrin a recent match in Germany that the FA had arranged. The amateurs and the professionals "all travelled together, occupied the same hotels, accepted the same invitations to beer-drinking and other entertainments, and thus effectually adopted those democratising ideas which the Association has so long been endeavouring to introduce."[31]

Middle-class amateurs did remain in firm control of the game by disallowing professionals from the FA governing board or any of its other committees. The FA stayed headquartered in London, despite the rapid spread of association football in the north. The exclusion of professionals from the board was seen as fitting, for, in words very similar to those used to justify middle- and upper-class control of Parliament, "the average professional player is quite content to be represented by a good sportsmanlike amateur, with time and intelligence to spare to attend to the administration of the game."[32] Although the association did not split over the issue of professionalism, it did experience a *de facto* division based on geography, with the northern teams mainly professional, and the southern teams staunchly amateur.

As the critics had warned, the professionalization of association football meant that, to pay the players, the sport had to attract large crowds. One way of doing that was for the best teams to play each other in order to get the most exciting play. To achieve this, the Football League was established in 1888; it was composed of the 12 most successful teams who would play each other on a fixed schedule of home and away games (modeled on the American professional baseball leagues established in the 1870s). In the Football League and in the FA Cup championships, the professional teams dominated. The only amateur team that could successfully challenge the professional ones was the Corinthians. Founded in 1882 by Jackson, it consisted of the best players of public-school and university background, with the purpose of giving serious competition to the northern working-class teams. After the legalization of professionalism in 1885, the Corinthians became the nostalgic symbol of the best of amateur football. (The Corinthians amalgamated with the Casuals in 1939, and as the Corinthian Casuals, it remains the most famous amateur football club in England.) Also to protect amateur football, the FA established the Amateur Cup in 1893, with Jackson as the chairman. The Corinthians did not participate, because their rules forbade the club to compete for any cups or prizes.

CONSEQUENCES OF THE PROFESSIONALIZATION OF ASSOCIATION FOOTBALL

Professionalism in football allowed more working-class men to play the sport competitively. More importantly to the investors in the game, it raised the level of play, especially in the League games, thereby attracting large enthusiastic spectators. By the end of the century, football was "the major form of male entertainment in Britain."[33] It also, as its critics had warned, changed the game in significant ways. Seen as symptomatic of the new order was the necessity now of referees. Earlier amateur games were often played without outside referees, for it was assumed that gentleman players would follow the code of fair play, and police themselves. To soften amateur hostility, the analogy was made between the referee and the Speaker of the House of Commons, both necessary to regulate fair contests, the one of sports and the other of political debate.[34] This appeal to tradition and constitutional order probably had little effect on those who were convinced that professionalism meant the end of the game as a sport.

The change that caused the greatest controversy was the FA's introduction of the penalty kick in 1891, awarded if the opposing team committed a blatant foul within range of their goal. The penalty kick replaced the short-lived practice of the referee simply giving a goal to the team against which the foul was committed. Providing more of a contest rather than did the automatic award of a goal, the penalty kick is a free kick, taken 12 yards out from the goal, with only the goalkeeper of the defending team able to try to stop the ball entering the net and scoring. Its introduction aroused heated and acrimonious opposition, from those who saw it as symptomatic of the cutthroat, amoral play of professionals. A contributor to the *Saturday Review* in 1900 insisted that the FA, in instituting the penalty kick, "has legalised cheating: it has recognised the man who plays foul 'intentionally' and instead of turning him off the field, or treating him with the obloquy that falls to the detected swindler at cards, the new rule permits the referee to award a penalty kick to the other side!"[35] This theme was reiterated often, including again the next year in the *Saturday Review*. The penalty kick, the reviewer complained, is "a standing disgrace to the laws of any game supposed to be played as a sport." Amateurs have to follow the same rules as professionals.

> Consequently the former are obliged to submit to a rule which takes it for granted that players will commit intentional and grossly unfair breaches, not only of the laws, but of those rules of fair play which are, or should be, the foundation of all true sport. Among professional players less endowed with the sportsmanlike instincts, which make most of our athletic games so delightful, the penalty rule produces the impression that there is nothing mean or contemptible in outrageously breaking the laws because a "penalty" is provided.[36]

The Corinthians, that guardian of gentlemanly sporting ethic and amateur values, refused to accept the penalty kick. If they were awarded a kick, they would deliberately shoot wide to miss the goal. If they were penalized for a foul, they would withdraw their goalkeeper so the opposing team would have a free kick into the goal. After all, as their founder Jackson said, it was an insult to the honor of a gentleman to suggest that he would either deliberately commit a foul or go so low as to take advantage of an opponent's wrongdoings.[37]

While middle-class amateurs objected to the penalty kick, working-class professionals protested a new policy, set in the 1901–1902 season, of a maximum wage for players. Concerned that competition for good players was causing salaries to rise too high, team owners and amateur officials in the FA agreed that £4 a week would be the most a player could be paid. They also outlawed bonuses for match results, which they felt were detrimental to sportsmanship.[38] Many of those who supported this policy were committed advocates of a laissez-faire free-market economy, with free unrestricted competition. They would therefore have opposed a minimum wage for players as a violation of the free contract between employer and employee. They did not, however, seem to have a problem with setting a maximum wage to protect their own economic interests.

Even though this maximum wage was higher than most skilled workers could earn, professional footballers did protest. The wage limit was set at a time of increased unionization of workers, including what was known in the 1890s as the New Unionism, with unskilled workers forming mass unions and using strikes as a weapon of protest. The first effort towards unionization of football players was attempted in 1893, when a player circulated to the captains of the elite teams in the Football League a proposal that they form a union "to protect professional interests."[39] This effort did not lead to action, but in 1898 a National Union of Association Players was established, and a more effective Association Football Players' Union was formed in 1907. It was, however, not successful in getting the maximum wage abolished, which remained in effect until 1961.

HOCKEY AND RUGBY AS REFUGES FROM PROFESSIONALISM

Some amateur footballers, disgruntled with the professionalism "which is rapidly disgusting English gentlemen with the best game in the world," turned to the new game of field hockey instead. Strictly amateur, with the Hockey Association banning even the award of cups or prizes for any competition, hockey was tainted by its popularity in girls' schools. A promoter of the game insisted, however, that hockey is just like association football, except it was played "with a small ball and a stick instead of with a big one and the feet."[40] Despite such advocates, men never developed widespread interest in field hockey, and it remained in England sex-typed as a girls' and women's sport.

Rugby, considered a truly man's game, did receive middle-class converts disgruntled with the professionalization of association football. It is ironic, given their anxiety about professional footballers making football too dangerous, that middle-class more than working-class men were attracted to rugby, a much rougher sport. Despite the ban on hacking, rugby allowed almost unlimited body contact, with little or no padding. There was a popular saying, of unknown attribution, that rugby is a sport played like ruffians by gentlemen, and association football is a sport of the working classes played like gentlemen. By the late-nineteenth century, however, as part of the tremendous expansion in all sports across class lines, working-class men especially in the industrial north started playing rugby, and inevitably, wanting and needing payment for their play.

Anxious to keep their game to themselves, with the implicit assumption that violent games were only safe in respectable middle-class hands, and to resist the onslaught of the "hydra"[41] of invidious professionalism, the Rugby Football Union, in contrast to the FA, ruled in 1895 against any payment to players. All forms of remuneration were forbidden, including even payment for writing about the game. "If the working man cannot afford to play, he must do as other people have to do who want things they cannot afford—do without. Football is a luxury, not a necessity."[42]

After detailing the evils of professionalism in association football, the sportsman-educator Hely Hutchinson Almond proclaimed that it was a matter of highest importance for rugby to hold the line, for "the interests of a nation, the prosperity and even the existence of which depend upon the promotion of true manly sport and active habits." Almond said he has "never yet known a genuine Rugby forward who was not distinctively *a man*."[43] Harshly critical of professional football, "Creston" justified his attacks by saying that his words were "not too outspoken if they nerve the Rugby Union officials to maintain their admirable efforts in the cause of keeping their game at all hazards absolutely free from the taint."[44]

When the RFU voted to keep the ban on professionalism, northern working-class rugby clubs broke off and formed the Northern Union (renamed in 1921 as the Rugby League). The Northern Union insisted that they did not allow payment for play except for broken time. By 1898, this policy was relaxed, and outright professionalism was allowed, howbeit still with restrictions. No one could play as a professional who did not have full-time employment in another job other than during the rugby season, and, to protect the moral superiority of rugby even in the Northern Union, work in a public house or other unsavory jobs was not acceptable.[45]

To fortify the defenses of amateur rugby as a gentleman's game, the besieged RFU emphasized its public-school origins, reflected so prominently in the name of the game. To affirm the public-school roots of the game, as a counter to working-class demands to play, and to play for money, in 1895 Rugby School set up a committee of Old Rugbeans to investigate the origins of the of the distinctive characteristic of rugby, the carrying of the ball. The accepted story was that early in the history of the game, in 1823, a student at Rugby School, William Webb Ellis, "with a fine disregard for the rules of football as played in his time, first took the ball in his arms and ran with it, thus originating the distinctive feature of the Rugby game."[46] That the story of Ellis was just a myth was evidenced when even the most ardent advocate of Rugby sports, Hughes, testified that in his day running with the ball was uncommon. Nor could support be gained from any of the other witnesses. The verdict of the commission nevertheless confirmed the early public-school origins of the game, and a plaque to Ellis was placed in 1900 in a prominent site at Rugby School.[47] Despite this claim to historic (or at least early-nineteenth-century elite) origins and its repute as a bulwark against the flood of working-class professionalism, rugby remained a sport of secondary interest in England. In popular interest it was far behind association football, whose ardent supporters included not only the working classes, but also the respectable middle classes, who balanced their class attachment to amateurism with their love for what became known in England, as elsewhere, simply as "the people's game."

8

Sports and the Imperial Mission

With the modernization of traditional games and the creation of new ones, which were played across class and gender lines, using modern technology and expanding the business and the professionalization of play, sports transformed late-nineteenth-century English society. The story of sports in Victorian England is important and interesting in itself, but what gives it particular historical significance is that, with its vast empire and global economy, England spread its sports throughout the world. As Sir Charles Tennyson said, "They taught the world to play,"[1] or at least to play modernized, regulated, standardized sports. England has been known as the mother of parliaments, giving to other countries its model of parliamentary democracy. So also is it the mother of modern sports. Most of the sports played today in international contests, such as in the modern summer Olympic Games, are of English origin. Even when the colonies of the British Empire (after the 1707 union of England and Scotland created the political nation of Great Britain, the empire has been known as "British") separated from direct British rule, some peacefully, others violently, they held onto the legacy of English sports.

What makes the story of the global diffusion of sports especially interesting is that it was not just a one-way street, with English sports spreading outward through the world. Indigenous traditional games from colonized peoples, including lacrosse and polo, were also brought to England, where they were transformed into standardized and regulated modern games, enriching the sporting life of those most avid sports-loving people.

THE STRUCTURE OF VICTORIAN IMPERIALISM

The British overseas empire began in the late-sixteenth century, when, under the rule of the Virgin Queen, Elizabeth I, England turned from aspirations of conquest on the European continent to lands across the seas. Driven by economic motivations to find new markets and sources of raw materials, the English established trading ports and colonies in the Americas and Asia, and later in Africa. These colonies, especially on the North American seaboard, also served as a refuge for Englishmen and women who wanted to escape pressures such as religious conformity in their home country. Trade with these colonies as well as with Europe brought great wealth into eighteenth-century England. England suffered the blow of losing the American colonies in 1783, but they quickly compensated by establishing rule over Australia and New Zealand.

English power spread eastward when the East India Company, founded in 1600, established trading centers ("factories") in Calcutta (Kolkata), Bombay (Mumbai), and Madras (Chennai). Competing with the French over lucrative South Asian markets, the English established supremacy by defeating the French and their Indian allies in 1756. Ruling at first through the guise of the East India Company (under supervision of the British Parliament and its appointee, a governor-general), after the frightening Indian ("Sepoy") Revolt of 1857, Britain established direct rule in 1858 over about 60 percent of India, with the remaining lands semi-autonomous principalities, ruled by maharajahs and other princes loyal to the British Raj.

The colonization of Africa was more gradual. The English first established ports on the African west coast in the seventeenth century, to facilitate its trans-Atlantic slave trade. At the same time, the southern African territory known as the Cape Colony was conquered and settled by the Dutch (known in Africa in the nineteenth century as the Boers, and now as the Afrikaners), who enslaved or drove out the indigenous Africans. In 1806, during the Napoleonic Wars, the British conquered these lands, the possession of which was confirmed by the postwar treaty of 1815. In protest against the British rule, the Dutch Boers made a Great Trek northward in the 1830s and 1840s, to establish their own provinces in the Transvaal and the Orange Free State.

The danger of malaria kept the British and other Europeans mainly on the coast of Africa, until the discovery of quinine as a protection against the disease allowed, by the mid-nineteenth century, interior exploration and conquest. In especially the last decades of the nineteenth century, in the heat of the New Imperialism and in fierce competition with each other, European nations vied for lands in what was known as "the scramble for Africa." With their superior weapons and policies such as divide and rule, by the early-twentieth century Europeans had established colonial rule over almost all African peoples, with Britain as the dominant imperial power.

Cecil Rhodes (1853–1902), the governor of the Cape Colony, was one of the most ardent British imperialists in Africa. Aspiring to build a railway from the Cape to Cairo (with Britain necessarily controlling all the lands in the railway path), he believed that the Anglo-Saxons were a superior race, which gave them the right to rule Africa and elsewhere. As a means of bonding Anglo-Saxons in England with those in their original home of Germany and the

English descendents in the United States and the Empire, Rhodes, who made a fortune in African diamonds, created in 1902 the prestigious scholarship that still bears his name. Men (and now women) from those countries (including those of the Commonwealth) could apply to study at Oxford University for two years. To be eligible, the candidates had to show proficiency not just in intellectual areas but also in sports. Today, with British law prohibiting discrimination of the basis of disability, a candidate does not have to be active in sports but does have to show physical vigor.

Britain gained another important piece of land as a result of the infamous Opium Wars of 1839–1842 in which Britain forced the Chinese to buy opium that they had harvested in north India, and in so doing, they seized Hong Kong. Over the next decades, they acquired more colonies in Asia and the South Pacific, so that by the early-twentieth century, they ruled one-quarter of the world's population and had informal influence over many more. With its global reach, British imperialists could indeed accurately boast that "the sun never sets on the British Empire." In this vast empire, the British took not only their guns, language, law, and institutions but also, equally as important, their sports.

IMPERIAL RULE AND SPORTS: THE CELTIC NATIONS OF THE BRITISH ISLES

Before the English headed overseas to establish their vast empire, they honed their conquering skills on the peoples with whom they shared what are simply known as the "British Isles." In 1542, under the Tudor King Henry VIII, after long struggles, the Celtic lands of Wales were conquered and incorporated into England. The northern Celts, the Scots, were more difficult to subdue. It was not until 1707 that, with diplomatic negotiation rather than successful conquest, Scotland agreed to unite with England, forming Great Britain, a union bitterly resented by especially the Highland Scots. Easier to conquer but more difficult to rule were the Celtic Irish, separated from England as they were by ethnicity and also, after Henry VIII's break with the pope and the establishment of the Church of England, by religion. Although the English had established dominance over Ireland by the late-seventeenth century, the island was not politically united to Great Britain until the coercive and hated Act of Union in 1801, which lasted for southern Ireland until 1922, and for Northern Ireland into the present. Despite political devolution in 1998, granting internal self-government to the Celtic nations, the United Kingdom, composed of the four nationalities, is still dominated by England and by the British Parliament in Westminster.

For the Celtic peoples in the Victorian age, sports were a significant means of resistance to English domination. The Scots, Welsh, and Irish all played to some extent the sports of their colonizer and delighted in beating them at their own games. More importantly, especially in Scotland and Ireland, traditional Celtic sports and games were revived in the nineteenth century and played deliberately as statements of their distinctive cultural identities, as affirmation that they were not English.

Scotland was the strongest of the Celtic sporting nations, in its success against the English in their own sports, and in its own traditional games that it revived and developed, which then became part of the global world of sports. The Scots readily adopted the English game of association ("soccer") football, and in the first "international" football game in 1872, they played the English to a draw, and then, for the next 20 years, they dominated over their southern rivals. Many Scots also delighted in playing the gentler English lawn game of bowls, which had almost died out in nineteenth-century England. Bowling was reexported back into the home country in the 1890s, where it had renewed popularity. Characteristic of their impulse to organize and regulate, the late-Victorians founded in 1895 the governing London and Southern Counties Bowling Association, and in subsequent years other regional and then national associations.

As popular as football and bowling were, there was stronger sentimental if not spectator enthusiasm for indigenous games. As reprisal for the Scottish support for the Jacobite rebellion of 1745, when the Scots joined forces with English rebels to try to put on the British throne the Scottish Stuart "pretender," affectionately known as Bonnie Prince Charlie, and in fear of future revolts, the English tried to eradicate traditional Scottish culture. Included in their prohibitions were the wearing of the Highland dress, their dances and music, and their sports. By the early-nineteenth century, however, fears of rebellion ebbed, and with the romantic historical novels of Sir Walter Scott and the nationalistic poems of Robert Burns making Scottish culture seem more benign and appealing, the Scots could more freely celebrate their national identity through a revival of their traditional culture and sports.

Curling, still considered the Scottish "national game," became popular again in nineteenth-century Scotland. It is a fast-moving team sport played on ice, in which players slide stones with broom-like sticks towards a particular mark. Curling never migrated southward to England. As a Scottish curling enthusiast ruefully reported in 1896, "When recently extolling the virtues of this—my favourite—sport exercise to an unbelieving Englishman, I exclaimed as a finishing touch, 'But surely there must be something in a game over which a whole country goes mad!' Alas! I met with the dry retort, 'It depends on the country!'"[2] Queen Victoria, however, watching a game on a visit to Scotland in 1843, was interested enough in it to confer on the Caledonian Curling Club the title of "Royal."

The Highland Games were a more dramatic and a unique sporting assertion of Scottish identity. The Braemar Highland Society, founded in 1826 to restore such Scottish cultural markers as the wearing of the tartan (made in the English Lancashire mills) and playing the bagpipes, added athletic games to their annual festivals. The Highland Games were composed of stylized versions of traditional sports, including as its most distinctive, the "tossing of the caber." As Montague Shearman described the sport in the Badminton

Library series volume on athletics, "The caber is a beam or small tree, or trunk of a tree, heavier at one end than the other. The athlete holds this perpendicularly, with the small end downwards, balancing it in his hands against his chest. He then 'tosses' it so as to make it fall on the big end and turn over."[3] What better display of Scottish manhood, uncowed by long English domination? The Highland Games also include "putting" (throwing) the stone and throwing the hammer, as well as foot races and tugs of war, along with Highland dancing and bagpipes.

Although representing Scottish nationalism, the Braemar Highland Society and its games came under the patronage of Queen Victoria, after she bought her Scottish estate of Balmoral in 1848. She attended the games in that year and in 1859, and again in subsequent years, invited the Society to hold them at Balmoral. In 1866 she allowed the designation of "royal" to be added to the name of the society. The custom has remained to the present day for the monarch or a member of the royal family to attend the Braemar games in the role of Highland chieftain. As Scots emigrated to diverse parts of the world, they took their Highland Games with them, as a means of maintaining even in alien cultures their own ethic identity.

Most Scots, no matter how fervent their nationalistic feelings, could not toss the caber, but many could play the historic Scottish game of golf. Played mainly on the seacoasts of Scotland from the fifteenth century, golf was governed by the Golf Club of St. Andrews, founded in 1754, with "Royal and Ancient" added to its name in 1834 under Victoria's predecessor, King William IV. It is still the governing body of golf in all countries except the United States and Mexico. The club standardized the rules and regulations of the game for every aspect except the golf course itself, each of which is still quite different in size and difficulty.

Until the mid-nineteenth century, golf remained largely confined to Scotland, with the English dismissing the game as "Scottish croquet."[4] In the mid-century, technological improvements made the game much more accessible and playable, and therefore attracted interest in England. The ball, previously a leather pouch stuffed with feathers, was transformed when gutta-percha was invented. This substance, derived from latex and resistant to water, could be molded when heated but was hard when cold and so could be shaped into golf balls, which were much easier to hit than the leather ones. Clubs made with iron heads similarly made the game easier and more fun.[5]

From the 1850s on, golf spread throughout England, at first just on the seacoasts, and then inland, with artificial sand traps replicating the original beach sites. Requiring large tracts of land that were labor-intensive to maintain, the game appealed particularly to the affluent middle classes, eager to use games to demarcate their class status. In the 1870s, there were about 12 golf clubs in England, and by 1914, almost 1,200, dedicated primarily to the sport and not the more comprehensive "country clubs" as developed in the United States.[6] A non-sweating sport that does not require strenuous effort, golf could be played even by women without evoking much criticism. Crediting its Scottish origins, the golfing enthusiast Horace Hutchinson exclaimed that the English "have so safely buried the hatchet that we can even join her in Jacobite song," enjoy Highland pipes, drink her national beverage (scotch), and now, "as a crowning, no less insinuating boon, she bestows on us her national game of golf."[7]

Golf became so popular in England that there was fear that it might surpass cricket as the national game. Endless debates were waged over the relative merits of each game. In support of the most oft-iterated argument that, unlike cricket, golf could be played well into old age, a golf defender claimed that the sport had "transfigured the middle-aged citizen from the dull-eyed and pasty-faced obesity of sedentary life to the hale and hearty proportions of active maturity."[8] Some Scots objected to the English need to attribute healthful benefits to their games, saying that they turn sports into a kind of medicine.[9] On the other hand, an anti-golfer suggested that the game was making hearty Englishmen physically degenerate: "The bicycle-chest may be dreadful, but I think the golf-straddle, the golf-waggle, and the golf-twist are at least as alarming. Whenever I meet a friend coming along Pall Mall with his legs wide apart, his head and shoulders twisted round backwards, and his hands aimlessly swaying his umbrella, I know at once what has happened to him. The golf bacillus has got him."[10] In terms of moral benefits, cricket clearly had the weight of long eulogic tradition on its side, but as a compromise, Horace Hutchinson attributed different but equal merits to each: "Cricket teaches unselfishness and the lessons of the power of union. Golf teaches a self-reliance and a mastery over all temptations to irritation."[11] Whatever its healthful and moral benefits, golf became so popular that the English took the Scottish game with them as they roamed the globe, making it truly an international sport.

Scotland also became popular with English field sportsmen and some women not only for their games, but also for their game. As field sports in England increasingly became a matter of pursuit of animals, birds, and fish that were raised in captivity and carted to the hunt, sportsmen with more of a sense of adventure and challenge, as well as with the means, flocked to the Highlands in the last part of the nineteenth century, for such authentic contests with animals as stag shooting and wild salmon fishing.

Wales, with a much longer history of subordination to the English, sought to revive its indigenous culture with the establishment in 1880 of the National Eisteddfodd Association. The Eisteddfodd, a traditional Welsh competition among poets and musicians, was made in late-nineteenth century into an annual festival, celebrating the Welsh language, literature, and history. This cultural movement did not include any traditional Welsh sports. The dominant sport of Wales, and the one which became its national sport, was and is the English game of rugby football. A primarily middle-class game in England, in Wales it appealed to the broad masses and served to forge, more than any political boundaries could, a sense of Welsh national identity. One Englishman wrote of his puzzlement of Welsh rugby. Holding to the racial stereotype of

! ! ! ! !

Lily (from Devonshire, on a visit to her Scotch Cousin Margy in St. Andrews, N.B.). "WHAT A STRANGE THING FASHION IS, MARGY! FANCY A GAME LIKE GOLF REACHING UP AS FAR NORTH AS THIS!"

Celts as weak, he wrote that "as Celtic by descent as Ireland, Wales has made her own a game so little Celtic in conception and execution that it is admittedly difficult to reconcile her style of play with the racial idea."[12] As an assertion of their claim to the game, with what would be a common technique of peoples resisting English domination but loving their sports, Welsh nationals created the myth that rugby was originally a Welsh game—*cnappan*—played before the sixteenth-century English annexation of Wales.[13]

In Ireland, English sports, especially cricket and foxhunting, were popular with the anglicized wealthy Irish. As Irish nationalism grew in the late-nineteenth century, and as demands for home rule became more intense, the political movement was strengthened by resurgent cultural nationalism. Beginning in the 1880s, this Gaelic Renaissance stressed the use of the Irish instead of the English language, Irish theater and poetry, and the recovery of the vibrant early history of Ireland. Included in this renaissance was an emphasis on Gaelic sports. In 1884, Michael Cusack, active in the movement for the preservation of the Irish language, called a meeting "the purpose of which would be to concentrate on the development of Irish games and discourage the growth of English sports in which Irishmen 'can be easily beaten.'"[14] From this meeting and under his leadership, the Gaelic Athletic Association (GAA) was founded. Hosting games of Gaelic origin, the GAA had a long-lasting policy of banning the participation of all British players from their games.

The most important of these Gaelic games was hurling, a stick-and-ball sport that is a "combination of lacrosse and field hockey, in which a hard, leather ball (called a sliotar) is struck with a wooden, ax-like club (called a caman) toward an 'H'-shaped goal. When not passing the ball to teammates, who can catch the ball with bare hands, hurlers run with the sliotar balanced on the end of their caman." Called "still perhaps the most hazardous game in the Western world,"[15] hurling was especially important for the Irish, to counter the English degradation of Irish men as weak and womanish, and as an assertion of Irish physical strength after the devastating potato famine of the 1840s, which led to so much Irish starvation.

AUSTRALIA, CRICKET, AND THE ASHES

Of all the British colonies, Australia was probably the most Anglo-Saxon. Throughout the nineteenth century, seeking a better life and economic opportunities, English emigrants flocked to the colonies, with Australia as the most popular destination. A penal colony where English criminals were transported until 1868, after the discovery of gold in the 1850s Australia was seen as a desirable destination for non-convicts, a place to make one's fortune. The emigrants carried with them to this distant land their ethnic pride in being English and sought to recreate English culture even in the outback. An important means of cultural replication was the establishment of schools for their sons modeled on the English public schools, which inculcated in the male youth the love of sports, which they continued into adulthood.

Rugby was the most popular form of football played in Australia. In the southern province of Victoria, a new form of the game was developed, that was a mixture of rugby, association football, and other ball games. This hybrid game was known simply as Victorian football (from the province, not the queen), and later, after its spread throughout the continent, as Australian football. The most popular sport by far, however, was cricket. Playing cricket reinforced in Aussies their English heritage, with its values and ways of life. These ties were all the more strengthened when, with faster steamships and railroads facilitating long-distance travel, English cricket teams came to Australia for demonstrations and then more serious matches, and Australian teams journeyed to the mecca of cricketers, to Lord's in London, for matches to show the senior cricket country the skills of the colony.

The first English team to visit Australia came in 1860, and followed by three more teams between 1861 and 1878. The most memorable of the visits was in 1873–1874, when the great W. G. Grace was on the English team. Grace reported being surprised at the skills of the Aussies. "We had heard from time to time of the great strides which were taking place in Australian cricket, but we were not prepared to be beaten in three out of the first five matches. However, as soon as we became accustomed to the glare and light, we began to assert our superiority."[16] With this beginning of international cricket, the Marylebone Cricket Club awarded nations with sufficient level of skill "Test" status, with "Tests" referring to matches between countries with that designation. Although England remained dominant in the 1860s and 1870s, the

Australian teams showed sufficient skill and won enough games that they were given Test status in 1878.

Interestingly, the first Australian team to visit England, in 1868, was not of English background but was composed of black aborigines, who had been taught cricket in missionary schools as part of their "civilizing" mission. Treated as an exotic curiosity, the team startled the English with some victories over home teams. In addition to playing cricket, they gave demonstrations in their own games of throwing spears and boomerangs.[17]

As intriguing as the aborigine games were, much greater interest was aroused when Australian teams of English background came on tour to England. To the shock of the English, in a match played in August 1882, the visitors beat the mother country on their home field at the Kennington Oval cricket grounds. The *Sporting Life* published a mock obituary, "In affectionate Remembrance of ENGLISH CRICKET Which died at the Oval on 29th August, 1882, Deeply lamented by a large circle of sorrowing friends and acquaintances. R.I.P. N.B. The Body will be cremated and the ashes taken to Australia."[18] From then on, hotly contested "Ashes" matches have been played between England and Australia, with the winner symbolically winning the urn with ashes.

The English salvaged their pride from the 1882 defeat by claiming that, although the Australian players were not convicts, they were certainly not gentlemen and therefore that "disagreeable incidents are not uncommon, and that the game is played with a keenness, hardness, and greed very different from the good feeling which is almost invariable in England."[19] Nevertheless, these contests certainly intensified English popular interest in cricket. The poet, scholar, and avid sportsman Andrew Lang explained that "We tend not to care which county wins matches. But we do care, and we are depressed, when the Kangaroo defeats the British Lion. Australia v. England is even more exciting than Oxford v. Cambridge, or Eton v. Harrow."[20]

The 1882 Australia v. England match led not only to the annual Ashes matches but also to the last novel, *The Fixed Period*, by that sporting enthusiast, Anthony Trollope. A most "untrollopean" story, the novel is a grim futurist fantasy, set on a Pacific island, "Britannula," a former British colony that had achieved independence. Britannula had introduced a law which decreed that when a person reached 67 years of age, they would go to a "college" retreat to prepare to die. After one year, they would be put to death, saving the community the burden of supporting unproductive old people, and older people would not have to live out the indignities of declining strength and abilities. Trollope published this novel in 1882, just before his death at age 67.

As a subplot in the novel, the British send a cricket team to challenge that of their former colony. On the last day of the match, "feelings were carried to a pitch which was more befitting the last battle of a great war . . . than the finishing of a prolonged game of cricket." Britannula wins the match. "The game should have been regarded as no more than an amusement,—as a pastime, by which to refresh themselves between their work. But they regarded it as though a great national combat had been fought, and the Britannulians looked upon themselves as though they had been victorious against England." Losers in cricket, the British succeed in reestablishing imperial control over the island because of the hated Fixed Period law.[21]

CANADA AND LACROSSE

In the other major "white" British colony, Canada, cricket was played, but never with the interest as in Australia. Instead, Canadians enthusiastically adopted the Native-American sport of lacrosse. A team game which the Native-Americans called the "little brother of war," which they used to resolve conflicts in lieu of armed battle, lacrosse is played with sticks with nets at the end to catch, carry, and pass the ball, aiming at hurling it into the opponent's net. Granted semi-autonomous dominion status in 1867, Canada used lacrosse as their symbolic separation from Britain. Calling it their "national game," Canada incorporated lacrosse into their Dominion Day celebrations, with the motto, "Our country and our game."[22] The sport spread to England in the late 1860s, where it was standardized and regularized by the English Lacrosse Association, founded in 1892.

Like hockey, a new sport in England without long "manly" traditions, it was played chiefly, and without great objections, in the late-nineteenth-century girls' schools.

THE UNITED STATES, AMERICAN FOOTBALL, AND BASEBALL

The former colonies of the United States may have achieved independence from Britain, but they continued to play their games, howbeit several in dramatically different forms. Foxhunting and horse racing remained popular in southern states, which identified more with English aristocratic traditions. Schools and universities in the North played association football, except at Harvard University where a modified form of rugby was played. This "Boston game" spread to the other northeastern universities, and in 1879, rules were formulated for this game. In contrast to rugby and association football, American football uses chalk lines, giving the field a gridiron effect, and divides play into a series of downs, beginning with a scrimmage, which makes it a more static game than the mostly continuous play of association football and rugby.

Many English sportsmen were horrified at what one writer called this "perversion of the true spirit of the game." He particularly disliked the way the Americans, so unlike the English, tried to trick their opponents by frequently employing "'fake-runners' and 'fake-kicks' and other queer disguises." American football was also brutal, as visually shown in the padding the players have to play: "An American goes into battle (there is no other word for it) arrayed in almost as much armour as the medieval knight."[23] Some Americans, on the other hand, attached to their new form of football, considered English football and rugby as boring. Caspar Whitney, on a "sporting pilgrimage" to England, went to a rugby game and "candidly, I must confess I was disappointed. I could not help the feeling, as I stood on the side lines, that I was a spectator of an undeveloped game—that there were so many ignored opportunities. One who knows American football must, on first seeing a Rugby Union match, feel he is watching an elementary game."[24]

Cricket was played in some areas, but was soon superseded by the new American game of baseball. Baseball historians generally agree that the American ball game developed from the traditional English sport of rounders, a ball-and-bat game in which batters who hit the ball run around bases. Called "town ball" in North America, it was a popular ball sport in the eighteenth and nineteenth centuries. In the 1840s, young men in New York City started gathering in the suburbs to play a new version of this "base-ball" game, with rules for the game first drawn up in 1845. Spread by troops in the American Civil War, baseball quickly became what the United States considered their national game.

Eager to show their English elders their new game, two American baseball teams, the Boston Redstockings (now the Red Sox) and the Philadelphia Athletics (now the Oakland A's), travelled to England for demonstration games but did not make many converts. The *Illustrated Sporting and Dramatic News* reported pejoratively on the American game. "The reason of its popularity in America is no doubt that it is essentially suited to the American disposition—fretful of restraint and less tenacious of purpose than the English stock from which they spring.... It is probably that comparatively few of the youths of Great Britain will desert cricket, with its dignity, manliness and system, for a rushing helter-skelter game such as we are given to understand Base-ball is."[25] Americans, another writer suggested, are too busy to play a leisurely game like cricket. They are "far too fond of close application to business without any corresponding and necessary relaxation of a healthful nature.... In the towns you seldom see a healthy-looking young man ... all have a sallow broken-down look, and, aging before their time, generally die at years when a native of this country is in the prime of life."[26] Even the athletic talent shown in baseball was far inferior to that of cricket. The batting was seen as especially inferior.

> Cricketers are apt to despise what is called a full-pitched ball, that is, one which does not touch the ground before it reaches the bat.... Now the English cricketers saw none but full-pitched balls thrown in the baseball game they were watching, and yet to their astonishment quite a considerable proportion of these balls were missed! Here were the members of two trained teams, missing again and again a kind of ball which an English schoolboy would be ashamed to miss once in a score of trials.[27]

Americans responded to the English denigration of baseball with assertions of the superiority of their game, and by implication, of their society. The strongest advocate of American baseball was the sporting-goods magnate and baseball team owner Albert Spalding. In 1905 he commissioned a panel to investigate the origins of the game. Ignoring all historical data, the panel endorsed Spalding's claim that baseball was purely an indigenous sport, with no English roots. In reporting on the commission's conclusions, Spalding asserted that baseball

> owes its prestige as our National Game to the fact that as no other form of sport it is the exponent of American Courage, Confidence, Combativeness; American Dash, Discipline, Determination; American Energy, Eagerness, Enthusiasm; American Pluck, Persistency, Performance; American Spirit, Sagacity, Success; American Vim, Vigor, Virility.

In contrast, he described cricket as "a genteel game, a conventional game— our cousins across the Atlantic are nothing if not conventional." The English play cricket because "it is easy and does not overtax their energy or their thoughts.... Cricket would never do for Americans!"[28]

CRICKET IN THE WEST INDIES AND FOOTBALL (SOCCER) IN SOUTH AMERICA

As is suggested by the very name "Latin America," Britain did not have extensive direct colonial rule in Central and South America, except for important islands in the Caribbean and the colonies of British Honduras (Belize) in Central America and (British) Guinea (Guyana) in northern South America. In these British colonies, cricket was eagerly played by colonial administrators and white English emigrants, as a marker of racial superiority and as a tie to the mother country. Afro-Caribbeans also began playing cricket, but they were excluded from the more prestigious white teams until the white Trinidadian, Pelham Warner (1873–1963), an ardent but nonracist imperialist, insisted that blacks be allowed to play on especially the Trinidadian teams in matches between the West Indian islands and against English teams. "The admittance of black professionals into the best games," Warner argued, "cannot but do good, as they add considerably to the strength of a side, and their inclusion must instill a universal enthusiasm for the game amongst all colours and classes of the population."[29] As confirmation of this view, when a visiting English team beat a West Indian team in 1895, a black player told Warner that he was confident that "we shall yet propel our flag among the nations, as the colony which has humbled its mother."[30]

Even in South America, where the British had minimal direct rule but which was part of Britain's "informal" economic empire, English sports and especially association football predominated. British merchants, government officials, and missionaries introduced football to the South Americans. Importantly also in the spread of football to the local populace were the large number of British workers who built railroads in Latin America and throughout the world. Although the sports clubs remained race-segregated for many years, English football became in the twentieth century not just the most popular sport in Latin America, but also a sport that embodied the loyalty and released the passions of fans more than any other cultural or political institution.

SPORTS AND THE "WHITE MAN'S BURDEN" IN IMPERIAL RULE

Just as the British took their sports to the so-called "white" parts of their empire and to Latin America, so also sports were as important as guns and the Bible in British colonial rule in Asia and Africa. These "colored" colonies were more difficult to govern, requiring a much stronger military presence. The armies were accompanied by the legion of colonial administrators, merchants, and Christian missionaries, all of whom rationalized their work in the maintenance of British imperial power in terms of, to use the words of the English imperial poet Rudyard Kipling, the "white man's burden." Although especially the frontiers could be frightening and dangerous, colonial life was often boring, and sports provided a welcome diversion. Important in all parts of the empire but especially in India and Africa, games like cricket served to affirm the identity of the colonizers, that they, however alien their surroundings, were English. Even in the darkest heart of Africa, an Englishman could put on his "whites," play cricket, and know that he was English, and therefore superior with the right to rule.

As with soldiers back in the home country, sports in the colonies were also important as a means of maintaining military fitness during times of peace. The games could demonstrate to the colonized peoples the English sense of order, rules, and discipline. At first the English kept their games to themselves, to mark their separate and superior identity. Gradually, they came to realize that by including the native elites, they could co-opt them and affirm their loyalty. With British military, administrative, and technological (if not, as the British thought, also their moral and cultural) superiority so apparent, many of the colonized elites in the late-nineteenth century gladly adopted the British ways as a means of sharing in that superiority.

Reformers and missionaries, eager to westernize the "barbarian" peoples, used sports as a way of cultural and religious indoctrination. The drawback to teaching their sports, however, was that the colonized sportsmen then sometimes defeated the English at their own games. It was enough of a blow to national pride when the Australians defeated the English in cricket, but at least they were white. It became more difficult to maintain the myth of the superiority of the English when "colored" peoples could beat them in sports.

Less problematic, at least to sportsmen, was the English domination over animals in the empire. Eager to find new wild game, adventurous English hunters flocked to the colonies. Much more exciting than hunting foxes in England or wild stag in Scotland was the shooting of tigers in India and lions, elephants, and other exotic beasts in Africa. If not a primary motive for imperial expansion, certainly a benefit of great importance to English sportsmen and some sportswomen, the empire became a big playground for English hunters and shooters. English sporting adventurers could also enjoy the

"The Hunter's Dream."

conquest of the mountains in the colonial frontiers. After taming the major peaks in the Alps, mountaineers turned to the ranges not only in the Americas and New Zealand, but also the Caucasus, and, most thrilling of all, the Himalayas. Dramatic accounts of the hunting and climbing adventures filled the periodical press in the late-nineteenth century, arousing all the more interest in and enthusiasm for the New Imperialism.

ENGLISH SPORTS IN INDIA AND INDIAN SPORTS IN ENGLAND

In India, the "jewel of the crown" of the British Empire, the most popular English sport among the rulers and then also the ruled, was cricket. At first the Indian upper castes, and especially the Brahmins, were not impressed with the English game. The perhaps apocryphal story was often told in England of an upper-caste Indian watching English gentlemen playing cricket, and who said, when he was asked his opinion of the game, that he thought it "a very good one, but could not see why the rich men did not pay poor ones to play it for them, while they might sit by and watch it."[31]

The indigenous Indians who most quickly took to cricket were the westernized Parsees, living in the area of Bombay. Originally from Persia and of Zoroastrian rather than Hindu or Muslim faith, Parsees founded their own cricket club in 1848. The "Parsee eleven" toured England several times in the 1870s and 1880s, where they were generally welcomed as a sign of harmonious relations between the rulers and the ruled. As a cricket magazine pointed out,

"Anything which can tend to promote an assimilation of tastes and habits between the English and the native subjects of our Empress-Queen cannot fail to conduce to the solidity of the British Empire."[32] Using this same argument of strengthening the empire, in the late-nineteenth century, the Governor of Bombay, Lord George Harris, an avid cricketer and later president of the MCC, energetically promoted the sport among all Indian faiths.

Young elite Indian boys were also inculcated into the virtues and pleasures of the English sporting and especially cricketing life through the boarding schools that the English established in India, attempting to replicate the public school back home. Indian boys did not take to some of the English sports. Rowing, for example, was rejected because it seemed like the work that lower-caste boatmen did in transporting people and goods across rivers.[33] Cricket, however, despite its use of a leather ball that was problematic to Hindu youths, was readily embraced. One of the most notable of these schools was Rajkumar College, in Kathiwar, in what is today the state of Gujarat. The headmaster, Chester Macnaghten, believing strongly in the moral benefits of sports, made games a central part of the school curriculum. One of the students in this school went on to become one of the greatest cricketers in English history, ranked by many as second only to Grace, and a symbol of Anglo-Indian cricket—the extraordinary Prince Kumar Shri Ranjitsinhji (1872–1933), known affectionately by his friends and fans simply as "Ranji."

Ranjitsinhji was born to a family without great means, but as a boy he was designated by a distantly related childless prince as his successor as ruler, the "Jam Saheb," of his princely state of Nawanagar, in Kathiwar. When the ruling Jam Saheb then had his own son, Ranji was no longer needed as his heir, but the prince did pay for the boy's education at Rajkumar College. Ranji entered Trinity College, Cambridge in 1889, where he made a name for himself as a cricket star. Then, most remarkably for a brown-skinned Indian, he played first-class county cricket for Sussex from 1893 to 1920, setting amazing records as a batsman. When the Jam Saheb died in 1896, predeceased by his son, Ranji pressed his claim to be ruler of Nawanagar, which was finally confirmed in 1906, although Ranji continued during cricket season living and playing in England.

The English press labelled him the "black prince," a term resonate of romantic medieval English history, as well as an "oriental magician" for his unusual batting style. Despite his popularity, he did face racial prejudice in England. The MCC excluded him because of his color from the first Test match against Australia at Lord's. Speaking in support of Ranji, a member of the MCC said a fellow member threatened to have him expelled for "having the disgusting degeneracy to praise a dirty black."[34] The MCC did allow Ranji to play in the next Test match, when, after he showed his great skill with the bat, an English spectator reportedly "proudly clapped and turning to the Australian sitting next to him said 'He is a prince, you know. Do you have a prince in your team?' The Australian had to admit, defensively, that Australia did not. The very next ball Ranji was clean bowled [put out]. This time the Englishman muttered under his breath, 'bloody nigger.'"[35]

A PRINCE OF CRICKET.

Mr. Punch. "Bravo, Ranji! Plucky Performance!"

Ranjitsinhji's brilliant play in the 1897 cricket test match on the England team against Australia prompted this tribute not only from the hunchbacked Mr. Punch but also the Australian kangaroo.

Ranji nevertheless remained a loyal member of the British Empire. In honor of the old queen's Jubilee in 1897 celebrating her 60 years of rule, he wrote a *Jubilee Book of Cricket*, dedicated to Queen Victoria. Writing almost completely from the persona of an Englishman, Ranji says that he could understand that if a man did not have the opportunity to learn cricket, he might not like the game. Nevertheless, "there has never been a genuine Englishman but played cricket or wishes he did. Something must be very wrong with a boy or with the kind of cricket offered him if he does not care for the game."[36]

In a review of Ranji's book, the essayist and cricketer Andrew Lang, evoking the images of the cultural encounters in the medieval crusades, said that comparing Ranjitsinhji with Grace was like seeing "the Saladin as opposed to the Cœur de Lion of cricket."[37] The *Saturday Review* welcomed the book as "a hopeful sign of the times that an Indian aristocrat should in this Jubilee year produce a monumental work on the English national game: for nothing can more strongly conduce a cordial relations with our Oriental and Colonial fellow-subjects than the easy and manly associations of the cricket field."[38] When Ranji retired from county cricket in 1920, the journalist and editor A. G. Gardiner wrote emotionally, "We have said farewell to cricket. We have said farewell to cricket's king. The game will come again with the spring, but the king will come no more. . . . There were giants before the Jam Saheb, and yet, I think, it is undeniable that, as a batsman, the Indian will live as the supreme exponent of the Englishman's game."[39]

Through the work of cricketer administrators like Lord Harris, the public-school-type education of Indian elite youths, and most especially the fame of Prince Ranjitsinhji, cricket achieved and still has in India such popularity, among the masses as well as the Anglicized elites, that it can truly be called their national game. The Indian sociologist Ashis Nandy explained, probably only partly facetiously, that cricket "is an Indian game accidentally discovered by the English." It is more suited to Indian temperament. "Cricket does not deal with or satisfy the need for certitude; it excels in uncertainties and ambiguities." The apparent slowness of the game would also "tax the patience of most peoples except the *Gita*-devouring ahistorical Indians. . . . Cricket does not yield any ultimate truth; like everyday Hinduism, it only yields diverse constructions of truth."[40]

The cross-cultural diffusion of sports in the British Empire was not a one-way transmission but a two-way exchange. Just as the Indians played cricket, so the English took up the traditional Indian princely game of polo. Developed by the nomadic Mongols in central Asia for military training as much as sport, polo was brought to India with the invasion in 1526 of the Muslim Mughals, who ruled India for 300 years. Dying out by the time the British established direct rule in the mid-nineteenth century, polo as an equestrian ball game attracted the British soldiers and officials stationed in India. They began playing it among themselves and also with the Indian princes, who delighted in the resurrection of their game, and hosting their conquerors on fields that they had specially constructed for polo.

Although one English commentator described the game as one in which "wild shouts and clashing of sticks, and the thud of the galloping hoofs, mingle with strange music, and stir the pulses even of the self-possessed European onlooker, while they rouse the impulsive Easterns to a perfect frenzy," he also welcomed the cultural mixing it produced. It helped bridge "the yawning chasm that divides the Englishman and the native. . . . On the polo-field the native forgets to be stiff and the Englishman to be haughty, and under the influence of their common love for a manly exercise they each discover that their adversary is a good fellow and generous opponent, and thus a sure foundation for future friendly intercourse is laid."[41] When the game was introduced into England in 1870, it was at first a marginal sport, with one commentator expressing doubt "whether polo has excited any interest besides that of mere curiosity."[42] That writer was wrong. It quickly became a fashionable game, of course standardized and regulated by newly formed polo associations. By the end of the century, there were 56 polo clubs in the United Kingdom, and, as the British took the game throughout the empire and the Americas, many more polo clubs were formed worldwide.

ENGLISH SPORTS IN AFRICA

In much of Africa, football (soccer) became the most popular game not only of the colonizers but also of colonized peoples, who learned the game from the usual diffusers of sports: British missionaries, administrators, soldiers, and merchants. Today, on a continent composed of quite disparate and often conflicting nations, football has served as an important unifying force, with the biennial African Cup strengthening the sense of African identity, and the participation of African nations in the football World Cup, held every four years, bringing pride to peoples who had so long suffered under colonial and now often indigenous dictatorial rule.

The case of South Africa is different. When the British seized control of the Cape Colony and neighboring Natal from the Dutch Boers, they of course brought their games. Cricket was particularly popular among British settlers. Even though the Netherlands was one of the very few countries outside the British Empire where cricket was played, the Dutch Boers tended not to play the game. As the English imperialist writer John Buchan explained, "It is worth while considering the Boer in sport, for it is there he is seen at his worst. Without tradition of fair play, soured and harassed by want and disaster, his sport became a matter of commerce. . . . [The Boers] are not a sporting race."[43]

Tensions between the British and the Boers became especially tense in 1895, when a group of rogue British settlers, led by a colonial administrator, Leander Jameson, and secretly directed by the governor-general, Cecil Rhodes, attempted an abortive raid to seize the diamond- and gold-rich Boer state of the Transvaal. The failed and illegal raid, which led to Cecil Rhodes's resignation, was an embarrassment to the British in southern Africa and throughout the world.

In the midst of this crisis, an English cricket team came on a tour of southern Africa. A member of the team, the great cricketer C. B. Fry, recounted that they were sent from the Cape Colony to Johannesburg, in the Boer-ruled

Transvaal, "as an antidote to the inflamed melancholy of that distant city, then in the throes of not knowing what to do after the failure of the Jameson Raid." The team had little success in healing wounds in Johannesburg, so they were then sent to Pretoria, the capital of the Transvaal, where there were enough Boer cricketers to get together an eleven. As a tribute to the power of sports to transcend differences and conflicts, Fry reported that the English visitors played a match against a Boer team "without any feeling alien to the pleasant rivalry of an English cricket field."[44]

The good feelings of the cricket field did not last long. In 1899, still eager to gain control of the Boer states, the British declared war and invaded. Although the British expected it to be a short, easy conquest, the Anglo-Boer War lasted until 1902. As compensation for what was seen internationally as British aggression, in 1910 Britain united the four south African provinces into the Union of South Africa and granted it independence. A society with racial divisions between indigenous Africans and people of European descent, and also divisions between the Boer and British settlers, sports became a marker of those divisions. The black Africans played soccer. The British game was cricket. The Boers, restyled as Afrikaners, adopted the howbeit English but more elite game of rugby.

After World War II, the Afrikaners achieved political dominance in South Africa and established the system of total racial apartheid, with their rugby Springbok team as their defiant symbol of white supremacy. After the overthrow of the white supremist rule and the dismantlement of apartheid in the early 1990s, the new black South African president, Nelson Mandela, in a remarkable act of racial conciliation, went to a 1995 Rugby World Cup game held in South Africa. He wore a Springbok jersey and cap and cheered enthusiastically for the historically all-white Springbok team—the team, however racist, that represented his country. Mandela's conciliatory actions at this match were seen as a crucial step in healing the deep divisions in South Africa, a country today represented in rugby matches by a multiracial Springbok team.

THE REVIVAL OF THE OLYMPIC GAMES IN 1896

As evidenced ominously in the Anglo-Boer conflict, the war drums beat loudly in the late-nineteenth century, as nations in Europe and elsewhere raced more intensely and aggressively against each other for colonies, for allies, and for arms. In the effort to stem the tide of militarism and redirect towards peaceful means the energies and loyalties vested in national competition, an idealistic Frenchman, Baron Pierre de Coubertin (1863–1937), advocated in 1894 the idea of recreating the ancient Greek Olympic Games. An avid sportsman himself, Coubertin had originally been a strong nationalist who wanted France to adopt sports as a way to strengthen itself after its humiliating defeat in the 1870–1871 Franco-Prussian War. Coubertin was particularly inspired by the role of sports in English public schools. Based on his readings of his favorite book, *Tom Brown's School Days*, he accepted Hughes's credit of Thomas Arnold as the instigator of sports in schools. On a trip through England in 1886, he made a pilgrimage to Rugby School. "In the twilight, alone in the great Gothic chapel of Rugby, my eyes fixed on the funeral slab on which, without epitaph, the great name of Thomas Arnold was inscribed, I dreamed that I saw before me the corner-stone of the British Empire."[45]

By his early thirties, Coubertin had transformed his pedagogical interest in sports into the dream of sports as a force for international peace. The focus of the dreams was a revival of the ancient Greek Olympic games. Educated Europeans and especially the English, with their extensive classical education, were very familiar with the ancient games, in that accounts of the Olympics permeated Greek literature. The ancient Olympics were also of great current interest, with the late-nineteenth-century German archeological excavations of Olympus, including its sporting facilities.

Coubertin was especially drawn to the ideal of the Olympic Games as a hiatus from armed conflict. Exclusively pan-Greek though they were, they represented a time when, every four years, competitors were protected by the Olympic truce, which Coubertin hoped could be revived and extended in his modern age into a new world order. He thought that not only was such a sporting event necessary in the increasingly militaristic world, but also that the time was right for an international athletic gathering. Athletic sports, he said, had a new position of importance in the world. It was the moment in time when "the whole civilised world, from Petersburg to Madrid and from Tokio [sic] to Punta Arenas, is adopting Anglo-Saxon ideas on this point."[46]

Coubertin certainly deserves the credit as the instigator of the revival of the international Olympic Games in 1896, and its successful continuation as the premier international sporting contest was unquestionably due to his energetic and effective leadership. He was not, however, the first in the nineteenth century to advocate the re-creation of the games. That honor belongs to the largely unheralded Englishman, Dr. W. P. Brookes (1809–1895), a physician in the small Shropshire village of Wenlock. Concerned to promote physical exercise as a means to improve the health of his community, Brookes founded in 1850 the Wenlock Olympian Society, to hold annual contests, mainly in athletic games but also in literature and art.

Attempting unsuccessfully to get the Greek government to agree to revive Olympic games on an international basis, in 1865 Brookes helped establish the National Olympian Society, to hold games in England. These contests would be open only to amateurs, but, unlike the rival Amateur Athletic Association in its early years, it welcomed participants from the working classes. The first games were held in 1866. One of the contestants was the young 18-year-old Grace, who took time off from cricket to enter and win the hurdles race. These National Olympics continued for several years and then faded away. As the young Coubertin developed his ideas for the international Olympic revival, he consulted with the now elderly Brookes, and, in 1890, credited the doctor as the pioneer of modern Olympics: "If the Olympic Games that Modern Greece has not yet been able to revive still survives today, it is due, not to a Greek, but to Dr W. P. Brookes."[47] Later, however, when plans for the revival took shape, Brookes was never acknowledged.

A competing vision for international games, on a more limited scope, was also developed in the early 1890s by the Englishman J. Astley Cooper (ca. 1858–1930). Cooper envisaged athletic contests between the peoples of the British Empire and the United States. In the spirit of the imperialist Cecil Rhodes, Cooper at first intended the games to be only between Anglo-Saxons (e.g. whites) but then broadened the scope to include all English-speaking peoples, who shared the same language and cultural heritage (which still coded the games as for those of English backgrounds).

Cooper was skilled at conception but not at implementation. His proposed games received little interest in England. The *Saturday Review* mocked the plan, through which "the Hindoo would learn to appreciate the French Canadian, the New Zealander would clasp to his arm the faithful Fijian. ... Bengali would row in the same boat with the Australian, and the American politician would whisper his secrets into the appreciative ear of a negro from Jamaica."[48] When his proposed games were upstaged by Coubertin's plans for an internationalized revival of the Greek Olympics, Cooper was insistent that the Pan-Britannic games were quite different from Coubertin's Olympics. He repudiated "here once and for all the feeble insinuation and witless charge that we are trying to bring about a slavish and ridiculous imitation of the Greek institution."[49] Even though Cooper's Pan-Britannic games were never played as he conceived them, his idea of games linking the empire was realized in 1930, with the creation of the Empire Games (later renamed the Commonwealth Games) held every four years and providing today one of the few ties still linking the old British Empire now transformed as the Commonwealth of Nations.

In contrast to Brookes and Cooper, Coubertin had the organizing skills to see his dream fulfilled. An international committee (with two British representatives) that Coubertin formed in 1894 accepted his plan for a revival of the Greek Olympics and reorganized itself as the International Olympic Committee. It set April 1896 as the date for the games to be held in Athens. Since most countries that would be interested in competing were a long distance from Athens, even with travel aided by the railroad and steamship, only 311 athletes from 14 countries came to the games, 230 of whom were from Greece, 19 each from France and Germany, and only 8 from Great Britain. The events included the traditional Greek games (but not chariot racing) and also new sports such as swimming, weightlifting, fencing, and gymnastics. The most exciting new running event was the marathon, won appropriately by a Greek.

An English contestant reporting on his experience in the games explained that there were so few Britons at the Olympics because the games were not advertised effectively. He blamed, of course, the French, "who, we fear, were largely responsible for the mismanagement of the international arrangements."[50] Coubertin was disappointed by the sparse participation by England, that founder of modern sports. Once such an admirer of their sports, Coubertin blamed the English for thinking that only their sons had the right to play athletic games. Angry at this criticism, a writer in the *Graphic* denounced Coubertin for blaming England for not taking "the same romantic view of the revival as the Baron, and make a national affair of it. . . . The Baron has a perfect right to express regret that England was not able to take up the Olympic Games more enthusiastically than she has done, but he has no justification for attributing motives."[51] Nor was there much English interest in the Olympic Games held four years later, in Paris, and certainly not in the 1904 games in St. Louis. When the Olympic Games were held in London in 1908, however, there was great enthusiasm, which has marked British participation in the Olympics ever since.

ENGLISH SPORTS AT THE END OF VICTORIA'S REIGN

By the time good Queen Victoria died in January 1901, England's reputation as a sporting nation and as the mother of modern sports was firmly established. Its position in international politics was shakier, as it confronted across the Channel a continent divided into two hostile camps, while Britain still gloried in its now lonely splendid isolation. Economically, the country was also having trouble keeping up with the rising powerhouses of Germany and the United States. The English could take refuge, however, in their sports, modernized as they were with regulations, governing organizations, standardizations, and popular scheduled competitions. Wherever they went in the world, they could see their sports played—cricket in the Empire countries, association football almost everywhere, rugby (transformed as it was in the United States into American football and in Australia into their version), horseracing, track-and-field athletics, tennis, the Scottish and now English game of golf, cycling, badminton, handball and racquetball (from fives,) croquet, hockey, and foxhunting.

Even on the European continent, where nations tended to be resentful of England's long world dominance, English sports prevailed. The most popular sport was association football, played at first by English merchants and workers, then, as in other parts of the world, adopted by the populace. Germany tried to resist, exalting its gymnastic *turnen*, but to no avail. The Italians sought an indigenous origin from the Renaissance by naming the game "*calcio*." All knew, however, that football, as well as most other modern sports, were derived or developed in England. Ironically, however, it was the French and not the English who established in 1904 an international (soccer) football association, *Fédération Internationale de Football Association* (FIFA). England stayed aloof and did not join FIFA until after World War II nor participate in the football World Cup until 1950.

When Queen Victoria died in 1901, the increasingly unpopular Anglo-Boer War was still being fought, but those of her subjects discouraged by the war and by the apparent English slippage on the world scene could still take comfort in their guardianship of values as embodied in their sports. As that imperial poet Sir Henry John Newbolt said, in oft-quoted words written in his 1898 poem, "Vitaï Lampada" ("torch of life," from a Latin poem by Lucretius in which a torch is handed off in a relay race), evoking the image of a former schoolboy in battle applying the lessons of cricket:

> The river of death has brimmed his banks,
> And England's far, and Honour a name,
> But the voice of a schoolboy rallies the ranks:
> "Play up! play up! and play the game!"[52]

ILLUSTRATION SOURCES

1. "Women archers" from Hedley Peek, editor, *Poetry of Sport* (London: Longmans, Green, and Co., 1901).
2. "Cricket game, 1743" from Horace G. Hutchinson, editor, *Cricket* (London: The Offices of "Country Life," 1903).
3. "Bull-Baiting" from Nimrod (Charles James Apperley), *My Life and Times* (New York: Charles Scribner's Sons, 1927).
4. "Pedestrianism" from Montague Shearman, *Athletics and Football*, 3rd ed. (London: Longmans, Green, 1889).
5. "Historical parallel" from *Punch* 9 (1845).
6. "Lower-class man calls aristocrat out in cricket game" from *English Illustrated Magazine* 10 (1893).
7. "Swimming lesson" from Archibald Sinclair and William Henry, *Swimming*, 4th ed. (London: Longmans, Green, and Co., 1903).
8. "Wall game of football" from *English Illustrated Magazine* 7 (June 1890).
9. "Oxford-Cambridge boat race" from *Illustrated London News* 42 (1863).
10. "Inter-university athletics" from *Illustrated Sporting and Dramatic News* 1 (1874), courtesy of the Trustees of the Boston Public Library/ Rare Books.
11. "Association football" from *Illustrated Sporting and Dramatic News* 2 (1875), courtesy of the Trustees of the Boston Public Library/Rare Books.
12. "Dancing rugby player" from *Punch* 107 (1894).
13. "W. G. Grace" from Horace G. Hutchinson, editor, *Cricket* (London: The Offices of "Country Life," 1903).
14. "W. G. Grace leads charge to protect Lord's cricket field" from *Punch* 99 (1890).
15. "Water polo" from Archibald Sinclair and William Henry, *Swimming*, 4th ed. (London: Longmans, Green, and Co., 1903).

16. "Shooting tame game birds" from *Punch* 67 (1874).
17. "Women hunters" from *Punch* 66 (1873).
18. "Soft-hearted woman shooter" from *Punch* 87 (1879).
19. "Woman tricyclist" from *Cassell's Family Magazine* 2 (1885).
20. "Bicycle v. pony" from *Illustrated Sporting and Dramatic News* 2 (1874), courtesy of the Trustees of the Boston Public Library/Rare Books.
21. "Woman riding bicycle sidesaddle" from *Punch* 56 (1869).
22. "British Ladies Football Club," personal copy of reproduction, from *The Graphic* (1895).
23. "Amateurs and professionals" from *Punch* 111 (1896).
24. "English view of golf" from *Punch* 108 (1895).
25. "Hunting in the empire" from *Illustrated Sporting and Dramatic News* 2 (1874), courtesy of the Trustees of the Boston Public Library/Rare Books.
26. "Prince Ranjitsinhji" from *Punch* 113 (1897).

NOTES

CHAPTER 1

1. Mike Huggins, *The Victorians and Sport* (New York: Hambledon and London, 2004), ix.

2. Tim Blanning, *The Pursuit of Glory: Europe 1648–1815* (New York: Viking, 2007), 408.

3. Raymond Carr, *English Fox Hunting* (London: Weidenfeld and Nicolson, 1976), 36.

4. Pierce Egan, *Sporting Anecdotes* (London: Sherwood, Jones, and Co., 1825 [1807]), 392, 336.

5. Henry Fielding, *The History of Tom Jones* (New York: Heritage Press, 1952 [1749]), 97, 476.

6. Hester Lynch Piozzi, *Anecdotes of the Late Samuel Johnson*, edited by S. C. Roberts (Westport, CT: Greenwood Press, 1971), 133–34.

7. Izaak Walton, *The Compleat Angler, 1542–1676*, edited by Jonquil Bevan (Oxford: Clarendon Press, 1983), 371.

8. César de Saussure, *A Foreign View of England in the Reigns of George I & George II*, translated and edited by Madame Van Muyden (New York: E. P. Dutton and Company, 1902), 291.

9. [J. M. Hayman], "English Field Sports," *Bentley's Quarterly Review* 2 (October 1859): 281. The anonymous author of this article was identified in *The Wellesley Index to Victorian Periodicals, 1824–1900*, Vol. 2, edited by Walter Houghton (Toronto: University of Toronto Press, 1972), 29.

10. Carl Cone, editor, "Introduction," *Hounds in the Morning: Sundry Sports of Merry England: Selections from The Sporting Magazine, 1792–1836* (Lexington, KY: University of Kentucky Press, 1981), 7.

11. James Christie Whyte, "History of the British Turf," *New Sporting Magazine* 19 (November 1840): 285–86, in *ProQuest British Periodicals Collection* (online).

12. Egan, *Sporting Anecdotes*, 38, 36.

13. Ibid., 27.

14. Horace G. Hutchinson, "Some Points in Cricket History," in *Cricket*, edited by Horace G. Hutchinson (London: The Offices of "Country Life," 1903), 17.

15. Derek Birley, *A Social History of English Cricket* (London: Aurum Press, 1999), 33.

16. W. J. Ford, "Cricket Parlance," *Badminton Magazine of Sports and Pastimes* 9 (September 1899): 311, in *ProQuest*.

17. Quoted in Birley, *A Social History of Cricket*, 71.

18. Quoted in ibid., 72.

19. Saussure, *A Foreign View of England*, 295.

20. K. S. Ranjitsinhji, *The Jubilee Book of Cricket*, 4th ed. (London: William Blackwood and Sons, 1897), 268.

21. George M. Trevelyan, *English Social History: A Survey of Six Centuries* (New York: Longmans, Green and Co., 1942), 408.

22. Richard Holt, *Sport and the British* (Oxford: Oxford University Press, 1990), 25.

23. Charles Box, *The English Game of Cricket* (London: "The Field" Office, 1877), 349–50.

24. Paul Elledge, *Lord Byron at Harrow School* (Baltimore: Johns Hopkins University Press, 2000), 191, n. 7.

25. Saussure, *A Foreign View of England*, 293–94.

26. "Sports and Pastimes," *Monthly Visitor* 1 (1802): 394, in *ProQuest*.

27. "Bull-Baiting at Bristol," *Sporting Magazine* 59 (March 1822), reprinted in *Hounds in the Morning*, edited by Cone, 138–42.

28. "Billy the Rat-Killer," *Sporting Magazine* 61 (October 1822), reprinted in *Hounds in the Morning*, edited by Cone, 137.

29. Henry Mayhew, *London Labour and the London Poor*, Vol. 3 (New York: Dover Publications, 1968 [1861]), 7.

30. 'Discriminator,' "On Humanity to Beasts, Popular Sports, and Pugilism," *Weekly Entertainer* 46 (July 1806): 567, in *ProQuest*.

31. Pierce Egan, *Boxiana*, Vol. I (London: George Virtue; 1830), iv, 254–55, facimile reprint (n.p.: Elibron Classics, 2006).

32. Quoted in M. Dorothy George, *London Life in the Eighteenth Century* (London: Kegan Paul, Trench, Trubner & Co., 1930), 132.

33. "Fight between Crib [sic] and Molineaux, by An Amateur," *Sporting Magazine* 37 (December 1810), reprinted in *Hounds in the Morning*, edited by Cone, 144–45.

34. Bob Mee, *Bare Fists: The History of Bare-Knuckle Prize-Fighting* (New York: The Overlook Press, 2001), 71.

35. "Pedestrianism," *Sporting Magazine* 61 (October 1822), reprinted in *Hounds in the Morning*, edited by Cone, 45–46.

36. Egan, *Boxiana*, xiii, i–iv.

37. C. A. Wheeler, ed. *Sportascrapiana: Cricket and Shooting, Pedestrianism, Equestrian, Rifle and Pistol Doings. Lion Hunting and Deer Stalking, by Celebrated Sportsmen* (London: Simpkin, Marshall, & Co., 1867), 66, 103.

38. James I / Charles II, "The Declaration of Sports," reprinted in *Constitutional Documents of the Puritan Revolution, 1625–1660*, edited by Samuel Rawson Gardiner (Oxford: Clarendon Press, 1906), 99–103.

39. Emma Griffin, *Blood Sport: Hunting in Britain since 1066* (New Haven: Yale University Press, 2007), 98.

40. *Annals of Sporting and Fancy Gazette* 1 (January 1, 1822): 1.

41. Sir Derek Birley, *Sport and the Making of Britain* (Manchester: Manchester University Press, 1993), 166.

CHAPTER 2

1. Oliver Goldsmith, "The Deserted Village," in *The Restoration and the 18th Century* edited by Stuart Sherman, in *The Longman Anthology of British Literature*, Vol. 1, edited by David Damrosch (New York: Longman, 1999), 2845–46.

2. L. C. B. Seaman, *Victorian England* (New York: Methuen, 1973), 28.

3. Peter Bailey, *Leisure and Class in Victorian England* (New York: Methuen, 1978), 28.

4. Ibid., 23.

5. Adrian Harvey, *The Beginnings of a Commercial Sporting Culture in Britain, 1793–1850* (Burlington, VT: Ashgate Publishing Ltd., 2004), 209.

6. Quoted in Emma Griffin, *Blood Sport: Hunting in Britain since 1066* (New Haven: Yale University Press, 2007), 142.

7. Quoted in Richard Holt, *Sport and the British* (Oxford: Oxford University Press, 1990), 33.

8. "On Mr. Martin's Bill for Animal Protection and on the Subject Generally," *The Sporting Magazine* 61 (October 1822), reprinted in *Hounds in the Morning*, edited by Carl Cone, 174, 176.

9. "Observations upon Cruel Sports, and the Laws Relating to the Subject," *Imperial Magazine* 6 (July 1824), 626, in *ProQuest British Periodicals Collection* (online).

10. Harvey, *The Beginnings of a Commercial Sporting Culture in Britain*, 71.

11. Quoted in Lord William Lennox, "Here's Sport Indeed," *Sporting Magazine* 15 (1869): 21.

12. "On Due Discrimination between Barbarous and Fair Sporting," *The Sporting Magazine* 60 (April 1822), reprinted in *Hounds in the Morning*, edited by Cone, 171.

13. Hoary Frost, "National Sports, Ancient and Modern, Article II," *New Sporting Magazine* 189 (September 1856): 214, in *ProQuest*. The name "Hoary Frost" sounds like a pseudonym, but I have been unable to confirm that.

14. "Vindication of Cocking," *Sporting Magazine* 61 (March 1823), reprinted in *Hounds in the Morning*, edited by Cone, 142.

15. Harvey, *The Beginnings of a Commercial Sporting Culture in Britain*, 87.

16. Henry Mayhew, *London Labour and the London Poor*, Vol. 3 (New York: Dover Publications, 1968 [1861]), 5–7.

17. Ibid., 38.

18. Alfred E. T. Watson, "Steeple-chasing," *Longman's Magazine* 3 (April 1884): 604.

19. Quoted in Sir Derek Birley, *Sport and the Making of Britain* (Manchester: Manchester University Press, 1993), 231.

20. "Sports," *Moral Reformer* 3 (October 1833), 306, in *ProQuest*.

21. [J. M. Hayman], "English Field Sports," *Bentley's Quarterly Review* 2 (October 1859): 292.

22. [Francis Lawley], "On Horseracing," in *British Sports and Pastimes*, edited by Anthony Trollope (London: Virtue, 1868), 19–20. This and the other essays collected in *British Sports and Pastimes* were originally published in *St. Paul's Magazine*, which

Trollope edited. The author of this essay was anonymous, in *St. Paul's* and in *British Sports and Pastimes*, but was identified in *The Wellesley Index to Victorian Periodicals, 1824–1900*, Vol. 3, edited by Walter Houghton (Toronto: University of Toronto Press, 1979), 367.

23. G. Herbert Stutfield, "Modern Gambling and Gambling Laws," *Nineteenth Century* 26 (November 1889): 841–43.

24. Harry R. Sargent, *Thoughts upon Sport* (London: n.p., 1894), 406.

25. Alice M. Hayes, *The Horsewoman: A Practical Guide to Side-Saddle Riding*, 2nd ed. (New York: Charles Scribner's Sons, 1903 [1893]), 1.

26. Ibid., 304–5.

27. "Sports," *Moral Reformer*, 305–6.

28. "Vindication of Cocking," *Sporting Magazine* 61 (March 1823), reprinted in *Hounds in the Morning*, edited by Cone, 143.

29. L. R., "Sports of the Field," *New Sporting Magazine* 228 (December 1859): 413–14, in *ProQuest*.

30. "Field Sports in Foreign Lands,"*Fraser's Magazine* 51 (January 1855): 15–16.

31. [Hayman], "English Field Sports," 269–70.

32. Harry Hieover, *The Sporting World* (London: T. C. Newby, 1858), 1.

33. Raymond Carr, *English Fox Hunting* (London: Weidenfeld and Nicolson, 1976), 107.

34. Harvey, *The Beginnings of a Commercial Sporting Culture in Britain*, 103.

35. Col. J. R. Hamilton, *Reminiscences of an Old Sportsman*, Vol. 1 (London: Longman, Green, Longman, and Roberts, 1860), 9.

36. Lord William Lennox, "Sporting Incidents at Home and Abroad," *New Sporting Magazine* (May 1849): 349–51, in *ProQuest*.

37. Derek Birley, *A Social History of English Cricket* (London: Aurum Press, 1999), 70.

38. 'Rambler', "The Field Sports of England," *New Sporting Magazine* 319 (July 1867): 54–55, in *ProQuest*.

39. Herbert Maxwell, "Odd Volumes," *Blackwood's Edinburgh Magazine* 164 (August 1898): 266.

40. E. D. Cuming, "Additional Chapters," in Nimrod (Charles James Apperley), *My Life and Times*, edited by E. D. Cuming (Edinburgh: William Blackwood & Sons, Ltd., 1927), 318.

41. Quoted in Raymond Carr, "Country Sports," in *The Victorian Countryside*, Vol. 2, edited by G. E. Mingay, (Boston: Routledge & Kegan Paul, 1981), 478.

42. Quoted in Bonnie Rayford Neumann, *Robert Smith Surtees* (Boston: Twayne Publishers, 1978), 44.

43. Anthony Trollope, *An Autobiography* (n.p., Filiquarian Publishing, 2007 [1883]), 54.

44. [Anthony Trollope], "On Hunting," in *British Sports and Pastimes*, edited by Trollope, 71–74. Although Trollope was named as the editor of this volume, his essay was anonymous (see above, note 22), but was identified in *The Wellesley Index to Victorian Periodicals, 1824–1900*, Vol. 3, edited by Houghton, 365.

45. [James Glass Bertram], "On Fishing," in *British Sports and Pastimes*, edited by Trollope, 160. The anonymous author was identified in *The Wellesley Index to Victorian Periodicals, 1824–1900*, Vol. 3, edited by Houghton, 367.

46. Ibid., 185, 184.

47. "Manly Sports: Their Use and Their Abuse," *Universal Review*, 2 (November 1859): 734–35.

48. A. Lang, "Cricket," *English Illustrated Magazine* 12 (September 1884): 747.

49. [Charles Merewether], "On Cricket," in *British Sports and Pastimes*, edited by Trollope, 319–22. The anonymous author was identified in *The Wellesley Index to Victorian Periodicals, 1824–1900*, Vol. 3, edited by Houghton, 368.

50. Quoted in Birley, *A Social History of English Cricket*, 94.

51. "The Morale of Cricket," *Chambers's Journal* 54 (May 12, 1877): 298–300.

52. Charles Box, *The English Game of Cricket* (London: "The Field" Office, 1877), 78.

53. Quoted in W. K. R. Bedford, "A Chat about Cricket," *English Illustrated Magazine* 117 (June 1893), 683.

54. Box, *The English Game of Cricket*, 77–78.

55. "Reminiscences of a Cricketer," *London Society* 8 (September 1865): 250.

56. A. G. Steel, "Bowling," in *Cricket*, edited by A. G. Steele and R. H. Lyttelton (London: Longmans, Green, and Co., 1901), 222–23.

57. "Cricket Reform," *Blackwood's Edinburgh Magazine* 169 (February 1901): 197.

CHAPTER 3

1. Quoted in [W. Lucas Collins], "School and College Life: Its Romance and Reality," *Blackwood's Edinburgh Magazine* 89 (February 1861): 148. The anonymous author of this article was identified in *The Wellesley Index to Victorian Periodicals, 1824-1900*, Vol. 1, edited by Walter Houghton (Toronto: University of Toronto Press, 1966), 112.

2. J. A. Mangan, *Athleticism in the Victorian and Edwardian Public School* 1981 (London: Falmer Press, 1986), 31.

3. Thomas Hughes, *Tom Brown's School Days* (London: Blackie, n.d. [1857]), 66.

4. Ibid., 119.

5. Ibid., 104–5.

6. Ibid., 103–4.

7. Charles Box, *The English Game of Cricket* (London: "The Field" Office, 1877), 330.

8. Hoary Frost, "National Sports, Ancient and Modern, Article I," *New Sporting Magazine* 188 (August 1856): 96, in *ProQuest British Periodicals Collection* (online).

9. Richard Holt, *Sport and the British* (Oxford: Oxford University Press, 1990), 81–82.

10. Hughes, *Tom Brown's School Days*, 104.

11. Quoted in Bruce Haley, *The Healthy Body and Victorian Culture* (Cambridge: Harvard University Press, 1978), 207.

12. Alfred Lubbock, *Memories of Eton and Etonians* (London: John Murray, 1899), 15–18, 224.

13. Ibid., 19.

14. "The Game of Cricket," *New Sporting Magazine* 298 (October 1865): 292, in *ProQuest*.

15. Box, *The English Game of Cricket*, 330–31.

16. Hughes, *Tom Brown's School Days*, 280–81.

17. "The Public School Matches," *Saturday Review* 4 (August 8, 1857): 128.

18. James Pycroft, "Fifty Years a Cricketer," *London Society* 30 (August 1877): 148.

19. R. Russell, "'Eton and Harrow' at Lord's," *Belgravia* 24 (July 1874): 128–31.

20. Lubbock, *Memories of Eton and Etonians*, 246, 221–22.

21. "The 'Cricket Derby'—Cricket Legislation—Pt. II." *London Society* 6 (August 1864): 136–37.

22. Quoted in Holt, *Sport and the British*, 75.

23. Philip H. Martineau, "Harrow School," *English Illustrated Magazine* 91 (April 1891): 521.

24. Lees Knowles, M.P., "Rugby School III. Games," *English Illustrated Magazine* 98 (November 1891): 90.

25. Hughes, *Tom Brown's School Days*, 77, 85, 121.

26. Anthony Trollope, "Preface," in *British Sports and Pastimes*, edited by Trollope (London: Virtue, 1868), 3.

27. Hamish Stewart, "The Football Nations," *Blackwood's Edinburgh Magazine* 169 (April 1901), 492.

28. Knowles, "Rugby School III. Games," 91.

29. Hughes, *Tom Brown's School Days*, 104.

30. "The Wall Game," *Saturday Review* 56 (December 1, 1883): 697.

31. [John Wilson], "Gymnastics," *Blackwood's Edinburgh Magazine* 20 (August 1826): 136. The anonymous author of this article was identified in *The Wellesley Index to Victorian Periodicals, 1824–1900*, Vol. 1, edited by Houghton, 20.

32. Trollope, *British Sports and Pastimes*, 4.

33. Frederick Gale, *Modern English Sports: Their Use and Abuse* (London: Sampson Low, Marston, Searle, & Rivington, 1885), 58.

34. Quoted in J. A. Mangan and Callum McKenzie, "The Other Side of the Coin: Victorian Masculinity, Field Sports and English Elite Education," in *A Sport-Loving Society: Victorian and Edwardian Middle-Class England at Play*, edited by J. A. Mangan (New York: Routledge, 2006), 54.

35. Gale, *Modern English Sports*, 37–39.

36. [Leslie Stephen], "On Rowing," in *British Sports and Pastimes*, edited by Trollope, 243–49, 238–39. The anonymous author was identified in *The Wellesley Index to Victorian Periodicals, 1824–1900*, Vol. 3, edited by Walter Houghton (Toronto: University of Toronto Press, 1979), 365.

37. "Athletes at Ease," *All the Year Round* 39 (August 11, 1877): 17–8.

38. Quoted in [Stephen], "On Rowing," 239.

39. "Manly Sports: Their Use and Their Abuse," *Universal Review* 2 (November 1859): 735.

40. Quoted in J. A. Mangan, "'Oars and the Man': Pleasure and Purpose in Victorian and Edwardian Cambridge," in *A Sport-Loving Society*, edited by J. A. Mangan, 110.

41. Charles Kingsley, *Alton Locke* (London: The Co-operative Publication Society, 1898 [1849]), 311–12.

42. "University Boat-Race," *Saturday Review* 31 (April 8, 1871): 435.

43. Montague Shearman, "Athletic Sports at Oxford and Cambridge Universities," *English Illustrated Magazine* 102 (March 1892): 441–42.

44. [W. Lucas Collins], "Light and Dark Blue," *Blackwood's Edinburgh Magazine* 100 (October 1866): 448. The anonymous author was identified in *The Wellesley Index to Victorian Periodicals, 1824–1900*, Vol. 1, edited by Houghton, 125.

45. Ibid., 448, 452.

46. "The Public School Matches," *Saturday Review* 4 (August 8, 1857): 128.

47. Quoted in Tony Money, *Manly & Muscular Diversions: Public Schools and the Nineteenth-Century Sporting Revival* (Avon: The Bath Press, 2001), 123–24.

48. Mangan, *Athleticism in the Victorian and Edwardian Public School*, 122.

49. "Athletics," *Saturday Review* 27 (March 27, 1869): 414.

50. *Illustrated Sporting and Dramatic News* 1 (June 27, 1874): 418.

51. "Athletics at the University," *Punch* 56 (March 20, 1869): 112.

52. Frost, "National Sports, Ancient and Modern, Article I," 95.

53. Thomas Case, "Oxford University Cricket," supplemental essay, in K. S. Ranjitsinhji, *The Jubilee Book of Cricket*, 4th ed. (London: Wm. Blackwood and Many, 1897), 339.

54. B. Fletcher Robinson, "Kings of the Playing-Fields," *Cassell's Family Magazine* 13 (1896): 366.

55. Quoted in Haley, *The Healthy Body*, 166.

56. Ibid., 167.

57. Hely Hutchinson Almond, "Football as a Moral Agent," *Nineteenth Century* 34 (December 1893): 903.

58. A. W. Ready, "Public School Products," *New Review* 15 (October 1896): 424.

59. H. H. Almond, "The Public School Product (A Rejoinder)," *New Review* 16 (January 1897): 87, 88–89, 91–92.

60. Edward Lyttelton, "Athletics in Public Schools," *Nineteenth Century* 7 (January 1880): 44.

61. Haley, *The Healthy Body*, 167.

62. E. Lyttelton, *Memories and Hopes* (London: John Murray, 1925), 5–6.

CHAPTER 4

1. John Stuart Mill, *Autobiography*, edited by Jack Stillinger (New York: Houghton Mifflin Co., 1969 [1873]), 6.

2. George J. Romanes, "Recreation," *Nineteenth Century* 6 (September 1879): 402.

3. R. W. Dale, "Amusements," *Good Words* 8 (May 1, 1867): 332, in *ProQuest British Periodicals Collection* (online).

4. Hoary Frost, "National Sports, Ancient and Modern: Article I," *New Sporting Magazine* 188 (August 1856): 95–96, in *ProQuest*.

5. "Manly Sports: Their Use and Their Abuse," *Universal Review* 2 (November 1859): 729, 734–35, in *ProQuest*.

6. "The Influence of Field Sports on Character," *London Society* 2 (August 1872): 127.

7. "Athletics," *Saturday Review* 27 (March 27, 1869): 414.

8. *New Sporting Magazine* 333 (September 1868): 230, in *ProQuest*.

9. C. A. Wheeler, ed., *Sportascrapiana: Cricket and Shooting: Pedestrian, Equestrian, Rifle and Pistol Doings: Lion Hunting and Deer Stalking* (London: Simpkin, Marshall, & Co., 1867), iv, 109.

10. James Paget, "Recreation," *Nineteenth Century* 14 (December 1883): 984.

11. Romanes, "Recreation," 407, 423.

12. Samuel Smiles, *Self-Help*, edited by Peter W. Sinnema (New York: Oxford University Press, 2002 [1859]), 263.

13. Romanes, "Recreation," 409.

14. Charles Box, *The English Game of Cricket* (London: "The Field" Office, 1877), 72.

15. Archibald Sinclair and William Henry, *Swimming* (London: Longmans, Green and Co., 1901), 325.

16. Ibid., 107–8.

17. Edmund Routledge, ed., *Every Boy's Book: A Complete Encyclopedia of Sports and Amusements* (London 1868), 325, in *Defining Gender, 1450–1910: Five Centuries of Advice Literature Online* (Marlborough, England: Adam Matthews Publications, 2003).

18. "Manly Sports: Their Use and Their Abuse," 735.

19. Sinclair and Henry, *Swimming*, 34, 35, 44.

20. Montague Shearman, *Athletics* (London: Longmans, Green and Co., 1901), 283.

21. Frost, "National Sports, Ancient and Modern, Article I," 96.

22. Hoary Frost, "National Sports, Ancient and Modern, Article III," *New Sporting Magazine* 191 (November 1856): 370.

23. Quoted in Derek Birley, *A Social History of English Cricket* (London: Aurum Press, 1999), 86.

24. W. J. Ford, "County Cricket," in *Cricket*, edited by Horace G. Hutchinson (London: The Offices of "Country Life," 1903), 140–41.

25. "Athletes at Ease," *All the Year Round* 39 (August 11, 1877): 19–20.

26. Frederick Gale, *Modern English Sports: Their Use and Abuse* (London, Sampson Low, Marston, Searle, & Rivington, 1885), xviii.

27. "A Model Boxer, by 'One Who Knew Him,'" *Fores's Sporting Notes & Sketches* 10 (1893): 167.

28. [G. C. Swayne], "Mountaineering.—The Alpine Club," *Blackwood's Edinburgh Magazine* 86 (October 1859): 456. The anonymous author was identified in *The Wellesley Index to Victorian Periodicals, 1824–1900*, Vol. 1, edited by Walter Houghton (Toronto: University of Toronto Press, 1966), 110.

29. Quoted in Bruce Haley, *The Healthy Body and Victorian Culture* (Cambridge, MA: Harvard University Press, 1978), 258.

30. Alan Bell, "Stephen, Sir Leslie (1832–1904)," *Oxford Dictionary of National Biography*, Oxford University Press, September 2004, online edition, May 2007.

31. [Leslie Stephen], "On Alpine Climbing," in *British Sports and Pastimes*, edited by Trollope, 267. The anonymous author was identified in *The Wellesley Index to Victorian Periodicals, 1824–1900*, Vol. 3, edited by Walter Houghton (Toronto: University of Toronto Press, 1979), 366.

32. Ibid., 264, 288.

33. [Swayne], "Mountaineering.—The Alpine Club," 470.

34. [Frederic Harrison], "Mountaineering," *Westminster Review* 26 (October 1864): 276–80. The anonymous author was identified in *The Wellesley Index to Victorian Periodicals, 1824–1900*, Vol. 3, edited by Houghton, 636.

35. Quoted in Peter H. Hansen, "Albert Smith, The Alpine Club, and the Invention of Mountaineering in Mid-Victorian Britain," *Journal of British Studies* 34 (July 1995): 317.

36. Quoted in Arnold Lunn, *Switzerland and the English* (London: Eyre & Spottiswoode, 1944), 110.

37. "Hardihood and Foolhardihood," *All the Year Round* 14 (August 19, 1865): 86.

38. Ibid.

39. Ibid.

40. "Foreign Climbs," *All the Year Round* 14 (September 2, 1865): 135–37.

41. W. T. Mainprise, "The Pleasures of Mountaineering," *Cassell's Family Magazine* 3 (1886): 527.

42. "Athletics," 413.

43. [T. C. Sandars], "Two Years Ago," *Saturday Review* 3 (February 21, 1857): 176. The anonymous author was identified in Merle Mowbray Bevington, *The Saturday Review, 1855-1868: Representative Opinion in Victorian England* (New York: Columbia University Press, 1941), 370.

44. A. K. H. B. [Andrew Kennedy Hutchinson Boyd], "Charles Kingsley," *Fraser's Magazine* 15 (February 1877): 257. The anonymous author was identified in *The Wellesley Index to Victorian Periodicals, 1824–1900*, Vol. 2, edited by Walter Houghton (Toronto: University of Toronto Press, 1972), 504.

45. Quoted in Haley, *The Healthy Body*, 117.

46. Charles Kingsley and Frances Eliza Grenfell Kingsley, *Charles Kingsley: His Letters and Memories of His Life*, abridged from the London ed. (New York: Charles Scribner's Sons, 1899 [1877]), 271.

47. Quoted in [Boyd], "Charles Kingsley," 258.

48. Ibid., 263.

49. Quoted in Haley, *The Healthy Body*, 109, 215.

50. "Manly Sports: Their Use and Their Abuse," 721.

51. R. W. Dale, "Amusements," 334.

52. R. W. Dale, "The Discipline of the Body," *Good Words* 8 (June 1, 1867): 375.

53. Quoted in [Boyd], "Charles Kingsley," 263.

54. Thomas Hughes, *Tom Brown at Oxford*, 1862 (New York: A. L. Burt Company, n.d.), 112–13.

55. Thomas Hughes, *The Manliness of Christ* (Boston: Houghton, Osgood and Company, 1880), 4, 19–20, 126.

56. Quoted in Haley, *The Healthy Body*, 152.

57. "The Great Fight," *Saturday Review* 9 (February 25, 1860): 239.

58. "The Fight for the Championship," *Saturday Review* 9 (April 21, 1860): 498–99.

59. Baptist Wriothesley Noel, *The Fight between Sayers and Heenan. A Letter to the Noblemen and Gentlemen Who Attended the Fight* (London: James Nisbet, 1860), 6, 10, in *Defining Gender, 1450–1910: Five Centuries of Advice Literature Online*.

60. Ibid., 9, 14.

61. Mike Huggins, *The Victorians and Sport* (New York: Hambledon and London, 2004), 187.

62. Gale, *Modern English Sports*, 74.

63. G. Bernard Shaw, *Cashel Byron's Profession* (New York: Brentano's, 1899), 191.

64. Lord William Lennox, "The Fistic Tournament—1847. With a Few Remarks upon the Prize-Ring of the Present and Past Times," *New Sporting Magazine* (June 1848): 444, in *ProQuest*.

65. Harry Hieover, *The Sporting World* (London: T. C. Newby, 1858), 251–52.

66. *Cassell's Complete Book of Sports and Pastimes* (London: Cassell & Company, Ltd., 1892), 163.

67. William J. Baker, "To Pray or to Play? The YMCA Question in the UK and the US, 1850–1900," in *A Sport-Loving Society: Victorian and Edwardian Middle-Class England at Play*, edited by J. A. Mangan (New York: Routledge, 2006), 199.

68. Quoted in ibid., 212.

69. Keith A. P. Sandiford, *Cricket and the Victorians* (Aldershot, UK: Scolar Press, 1994), 36.

CHAPTER 5

1. N. L. Jackson, "Professionalism and Sport," *Fortnightly Review* 73 (January 1900): 154.

2. "Mind and Muscle," *Saturday Review* 6 (April 21, 1860): 493.

3. Walter Pater, *The Renaissance: Studies in Art and Poetry*, edited by Donald Hill (Berkeley: University of California Press, 1980 [1873]), 190.

4. Quoted in Tony Mason, *Association Football and English Society, 1863–1915* (Sussex: The Harvester Press, 1980), 229.

5. E. Gambier-Parry, "Sport and Sportsmen," *New Review* 11 (September 1894): 309.

6. Alfred Lubbock, *Memories of Eton and Etonians* (London: John Murray, 1899), 142–43.

7. "Football," *Every Boy's Book* (1868), 225, in *Defining Gender, 1450–1910: Five Centuries of Advice Literature Online* (Marlborough, England: Adam Matthews Publications, 2003).

8. "Football," *Chambers's Journal* 11 (March 12, 1864): 174.

9. Quoted in Tony Money, *Manly & Muscular Diversions: Public Schools and the Nineteenth-Century Sporting Revival* (Avon: The Bath Press, 2001), 114.

10. W. J. Oakley & G. O. Smith, "The Association Game," in Montague Shearman, *Football* (London: Longmans, Green, and Co., 1901), 89–90.

11. Montague Shearman, "Football History," in *Football*, 33.

12. 'A Lover of Football', "Football, A Comparison of the Principal Rules as Played in the Leading Codes of Laws," *The Sporting Gazette*, November 28, 1863, 901, in *19th Century UK Periodicals* (Gale Digital Collections).

13. Quoted in J. A. Mangan, *Athleticism in the Victorian and Edwardian Public School: The Emergence and Consolidation of an Educational Ideology* (Cambridge: Cambridge University Press, 1986), 196–97.

14. Montague Shearman, "Athletic Sports at Oxford and Cambridge Universities: Oxford," *English Illustrated Magazine* 102 (March 1892): 442.

15. "Football in the Field," *Saturday Review* 57 (April 26, 1884): 534.

16. Shearman, "Football History," 1.

17. Montague Shearman, *Athletics and Football* (Boston: Little, Brown, and Co., 1887), 368.

18. Frederick Gale, *Modern English Sports: Their Use and Abuse* (London: Sampson Low, Marston, Searle, & Rivington, 1885), 50–51.

19. "Football in the Field," 535.

20. E. B. Osborn, "A Gallery of Athletes," *New Review* 12 (March 1895): 451.

21. Charles Dickens, *Sunday under Three Heads*, 1836, excerpt in *The Portable Victorian Reader*, edited by Gordon Haight (New York: Penguin Books, 1972), 326.

22. John Lubbock (Lord Avebury), *Essays and Addresses, 1900–1903*, reprint (Freeport, NY: Books for Libraries Press, 1966), 117, 120.

23. Quoted in Tony Collins, *Rugby's Great Split: Class, Culture and the Origins of Rugby League Football* (London: Frank Cass, 1998), 36.

24. Mason, *Association Football*, 62.

25. J. F. Ramsay, "The Growth of Association Football," *Windsor Magazine* 2 (July 1895): 451, in *ProQuest British Periodicals Collection* (online).

26. Quoted in Matthew Taylor, *The Association Game: A History of British Football* (Harlow, UK: Pearson Education Limited, 2008), 43.

27. Quoted in Mason, *Association Football*, 234–35.

28. C. W. Alcock, "Association Football," *English Illustrated Magazine* 88 (January 1891): 285.

29. Mike Huggins, *The Victorians and Sport* (New York: Hambledon and London, 2004), 165.

30. Alfred E. T. Watson, "The Badminton Library: Preface," in *The Poetry of Sport*, edited by Hedley Peek (London: Longmans, Green, and Co., 1901), xxii, xxvii.

31. [Harry Jones], "Tournaments and Matches," *Cornhill* 21 (July 1893): 91. The anonymous author was identified in *The Wellesley Index to Victorian Periodicals, 1824–1900*, Vol. 1, edited by Walter Houghton (Toronto: University of Toronto Press, 1966), 395.

32. B. Fletcher Robinson, "Kings of the Playing-Fields," *Cassell's Family Magazine* 13 (1896): 363.

33. W. G. Grace, *Cricket* (London: Simpkin, Marshall, Hamilton, Kent, & Co. Ltd., 1891), 71. Like most of Grace's writings, this book was ghost-written, but presumably the memories are his own.

34. A. G. Steel, "Bowling," in *Cricket*, edited by A. G. Steel and R. H. Lyttelton (London: Longmans, Green, and Co., 1901), 109.

35. Sir Charles Tennyson, "They Taught the World to Play," *Victorian Studies* 2 (March 1959): 214–15.

36. Derek Birley, *A Social History of English Cricket* (London: Arum Press, 1999), 111–12.

37. Frederick Gale, "Recollections of Cricket," *English Illustrated Magazine* 93 (June 1891): 637.

38. Robert H. Lyttelton, "W. G.," *New Review* 13 (August 1895): 135.

39. K. S. Ranjitsinhji, *The Jubilee Book of Cricket*, 4th ed. (London: William Blackwood and Sons, 1897), 460.

40. "The Ojibbeway Indians," *Times* (London), April 22, 1844.

41. Quoted in Archibald Sinclair and William Henry, *Swimming*, reissue (London: Longmans, Green and Co., 1901), 87.

42. Quoted in Ralph Thomas, *Swimming* (London: Sampton Low, Marston & Co., 1904), 140.

43. Charles Sprawson, "Webb, Matthew [*known as* Captain Webb] (1848–1883)," *Oxford Dictionary of National Biography* (Oxford: Oxford University Press, 2004), online edition.

44. "Drowning of Captain Webb," *Times* (London), July 26, 1883.

45. John Lowerson, "Brothers of the Angle: Coarse Fishing and English Working-Class Culture, 1850–1914," in *Pleasure, Profit, Proselytism: British Culture and Sport at Home and Abroad, 1700–1914*, edited by J. A. Mangan (London: Frank Cass and Company, Limited, 1988), 107.

46. "Laws and Customs of Sport," *Quarterly Review* 134 (January 1873): 30.

47. Raymond Carr, "Country Sports," in *The Victorian Countryside*, Vol. 2, edited by G. E. Mingay (Boston: Routledge & Kegan Paul, 1981), 476.

48. 'Dooker' [James Moray Brown], "Frauds of Sport," *Blackwood's Edinburgh Magazine* 148 (December 1890): 845. The anonymous author was identified in *The Wellesley Index to Victorian Periodicals, 1824–1900*, Vol. 1, edited by Houghton, 179.

49. W. Bromley Davenport, "Covert-Shooting," *Nineteenth Century* 14 (December 1883): 1090.

50. Oscar Wilde, *Woman of No Importance* (1893), in *The Plays of Oscar Wilde* (New York: Modern Library, n.d.), 141.

51. Edward A. Freeman, "The Morality of Field Sports," *Fortnightly Review* 34 (October 1, 1869): 370, 373.

52. Anthony Trollope, "Mr. Freeman on the Morality of Hunting," *Fortnightly Review* 12 (December 1869): 616, 623–25; Edward A. Freeman, "The Controversy on Field Sports," *Fortnightly Review* 14 (December 1870): 680, 689.

53. T. E. Kebbel, "English Love of Sport," *Fortnightly Review* 13 (April 1886): 540.

54. 'Rockwood', "The Future of British Sports and Pastimes," in *Fores's Sporting Notes & Sketches* 40 (1894): 55.

55. W. Bromley Davenport, "Fox-Hunting," *Nineteenth Century* 13 (June 1883): 982.

CHAPTER 6

1. George J. Romanes, "Recreation," *Nineteenth Century* 6 (September 1879): 414–16, 420.

2. [T. Pilkington White], "Modern Mannish Maidens," *Blackwood's Edinburgh Magazine* 147 (February 1890): 254. The anonymous author was identified in *The Wellesley Index to Victorian Periodicals, 1824–1900*, Vol. 1, edited by Walter Houghton (Toronto: University of Toronto Press, 1966), 176.

3. Kathleen E. McCrone, *Sport and the Physical Emancipation of English Women 1870–1914* (London: Routledge, 1988), 220.

4. "The Game of Croquet and Its Laws," *London Society* 9 (June 1866): 507.

5. Anthony Trollope,"Preface," in *British Sports and Pastimes*, edited by Anthony Trollope (London: Virtue, 1868), 3–4.

6. H. G. Wells, *The Croquet Player* (New York: The Viking Press, 1937), 10–11, 13.

7. George H. Powell, "The Psychology of Croquet," *Temple Bar* 124 (September 1901): 59–61.

8. Helen Walker, "Lawn Tennis," in *Sport in Britain: A Social History*, edited by Tony Mason (New York: Cambridge University Press, 1989), 245.

9. Miss C. Cooper, "Lawn Tennis," *Cassell's Family Magazine* 15 (1897): 325.

10. Richard Holt, *Sport and the British* (Oxford: Oxford University Press, 1990), 127.

11. Ibid., 126.

12. [White], "Modern Mannish Maidens," 256–57.

13. Jeffrey Pearson, *Lottie Dod, Champion of Champions: The Story of an Athlete* (Birkenhead, England: Countyvise Ltd., 1988), 10–95 passim.

14. "Tennis Twins, Some Famous Lawn-Tennis Players," *Cassell's Family Magazine* 17 (1898): 204.

15. [White], "Modern Mannish Maidens," 257.

16. Sir Charles Tennyson, "They Taught the World to Play," *Victorian Studies* 2 (March 1959): 217.

17. Ibid.

18. Quoted in Peter Bailey, *Leisure and Class in Victorian England: Rational Recreation and the Contest for Control, 1830–1885* (New York: Methuen, 1978), 88.

19. Constance Everett-Green, "Swimming for Ladies,"*Badminton Magazine of Sports and Pastimes* 7 (August 1898): 227, 229, in *ProQuest British Periodicals Collection* (online).

20. Alice M. Hayes, *The Horsewoman: A Practical Guide to Side-Saddle Riding*, 2nd ed. (New York: Charles Scribner's Sons, 1903 [1893]), 96–98.

21. Ardern Holt, "The Evolution of the Riding Habit," *Cassell's Family Magazine* 14 (1897): 325.

22. Quoted in Dorothy Middleton, *Victorian Lady Travellers* (Chicago: Academy Chicago, 1982), 22.

23. Mrs. Alec Tweedie, *A Girl's Ride in Iceland*, 1889, extract in *Unsuitable for Ladies, An Anthology of Women Travellers*, edited by Jane Robinson (Oxford: Oxford University Press, 2001), 73–74.

24. Quoted in Nannie Power O'Donoghue, *Ladies on Horseback: Learning, Park-Riding, and Hunting* (London: W. H. Allen & Co., 1881), 244–45.

25. Ibid., 278–79.

26. Emma Griffin, *Blood Sport: Hunting in Britain since 1066* (New Haven: Yale University Press, 2007), 166.

27. Hayes, *The Horsewoman*, 312.

28. Lady Boynton, "Shooting," in *Ladies in the Field*, edited by Lady Greville (London: Ward & Downey, Limited, 1894), 199–200, in *Defining Gender, 1450–1910: Five Centuries of Advice Literature Online* (Marlborough, England: Adam Matthews Publications, 2003).

29. 'A Lady Cyclist', "Women on Wheels," *Cassell's Family Magazine* 2 (1885): 590.

30. [White], "Modern Mannish Maidens," 255.

31. *Punch* 110 (June 6, 1896): 268.

32. 'Creston', "Cycling and Cycles," *Fortnightly Review* 61 (May 1894): 669.

33. T. P. W. [T. Pilkington White], "The Cycling Epidemic," *Scottish Review* 29 (January 1897): 61, in *ProQuest*. The anonymous author was identified in *The Wellesley Index to Victorian Periodicals, 1824–1900*, Vol. 2, edited by Walter Houghton (Toronto: University of Toronto Press, 1972), 804.

34. G. Lacy Hillier, "The Development of Cycling," *Longman's Magazine* 3 (March 1884): 493.

35. B. Fletcher Robinson, "Kings of the Playing-Fields," *Cassell's Family Magazine* 13 (1896): 366.

36. Mrs. Lynn Linton, "Cranks and Crazes," *North American Review* 161 (December 1895): 671–72.

37. Quoted in C. Willet Cunnington and Phillis Cunnington, *Handbook of English Costume in the Nineteenth Century* (Boston: Plays, Inc., 1970), 24.

38. White, "The Cycling Epidemic," 69–70.

39. Mrs. Lynn Linton, "A Counterblast," *English Illustrated Magazine* 121 (October 1893): 85.

40. Lady Jeune, "Cycling for Women," *Badminton Magazine* 1 (October 1895): 411, in *ProQuest*.

41. [White], "The Cycling Epidemic," 63–64.

42. Quoted in David Rubenstein, "Cycling in the 1890s," *Victorian Studies* 21 (1977): 68.

43. Grant Allen, *The Typewriter Girl* (New York: Street and Smith, 1900 [1897]), 43.

44. J. Hamilton Fletcher, "Athletics for Ladies," *Cassell's Family Magazine* 13 (1896): 340.

45. W. H. Fenton, "A Medical View of Cycling for Ladies," *Nineteenth Century* 39 (May 1896): 801.

46. H. G. Wells, *Wheels of Chance: A Bicycling Idyll* (New York: Charles Scribner's Sons, 1925 [1896]), 234.

47. Quoted in Catriona M. Parratt, *"More than Mere Amusement": Working-Class Women's Leisure in England, 1750–1914* (Boston: Northeastern University Press, 2001), 204.

48. McCrone, *Sport and the Physical Emancipation of English Women*, 27, 37.

49. Sir Derek Birley, *Land of Sport and Glory: Sport and British Society, 1887–1910* (Manchester: Manchester University Press, 1995), 100.

50. White, "Modern Mannish Maidens," 260.

51. McCrone, *Sport and the Physical Emancipation of English Women*, 128–29.

52. Quoted in Keith A. P. Sandiford, *Cricket and the Victorians* (Aldershot, England: Scolar Press, 1994), 45.

53. Birley, *Land of Sport and Glory*, 99–100.

54. E. Lynn Linton, "The Wild Women as Social Insurgents," *Nineteenth Century* 30 (October 1891): 598.

55. Fletcher, "Athletics for Ladies," 343.

56. Birley, *Land of Sport and Glory*, 99; and Holt, *Sport and the British*, 129.

57. Ibid., 98.

58. "The Ladies' Football Match," *The Ladies' Treasury* 1 (June 1895), in *19th Century UK Periodicals* (Gale Digital Publications).

59. Lady Florence Dixie, "The Horrors of Sport," *Westminster Review* 137 (January 1892): 49–52.

60. Lady Florence Dixie, *Gloriana, or the Revolution of 1900* (London: Henry and Company, 1890), 25.

61. Lady Florence Dixie, "Football for Women," *Pall Mall Gazette*, February 8, 1895, in *19th Century British Library Newspapers* (Gale Digital Publications).

62. Quoted in Nancy Fix Anderson, *Woman against Women in Victorian England: A Life of Eliza Lynn Linton* (Bloomington, IN: Indiana University Press, 1987), 205.

63. Arabella Kenealy, "The Talent of Motherhood," *National Review* 16 (December 1890): 446–57.

64. Arabella Kenealy, "Woman as an Athlete," *Nineteenth Century* 45 (April 1899): 636–45.

65. L. Ormiston Chant, "Woman as an Athlete, A Reply to Dr. Arabella Kenealy," *Nineteenth Century* 45 (May 1899): 752.

66. A. Kenealy, "Woman as an Athlete, A Rejoinder," *Nineteenth Century* 45 (June 1899): 927.

CHAPTER 7

1. W. Beach Thomas, "Athletics and Health," *Cornhill* 8 (April 1900): 538.

2. Dr. Miller Maguire, "A Diatribe against the Curse of Games," *Journal of the Royal United Service Institution*, summarized in *Review of Reviews* 26 (September 1902): 267.

3. F. G. Aflalo, "Statesmen Who Were Sportsmen," *Fortnightly Review* 75 (May 1904): 864–79.

4. S. J. Jeyes, "Our Gentlemanly Failures," *Fortnightly Review* 67 (March 1897): 394–98.

5. Quoted in Tony Mason, *Association Football and English Society, 1863–1915* (Sussex: Harvester Press, 1980), 237.

6. Quoted in Stephen G. Jones, *Sport, Politics and the Working Class: Organised Labour and Sport in Inter-War Britain* (Manchester: Manchester University Press, 1988), 29.

7. Thomas, "Athletics and Health," 542, 548.

8. Wilkie Collins, *Man and Wife*, 1870, facsimile repr. (Ann Arbor: University of Michigan University Library, n.d.), 81, 28, 83–84.

9. Ibid., 237.

10. Leslie Stephen, "Athletic Sports and University Studies," *Fraser's Magazine* 2 (December 1870): 693, 694.

11. "Athletics," *Saturday Review* 27 (March 27, 1869): 414.

12. "The Happy Athlete," *Saturday Review* 91 (March 30, 1901): 398–99.

13. Quoted in Mason, *Association Football and English Society*, 77.

14. J. F. Ramsay, "The Growth of Association Football," *Windsor Magazine* 2 (July 1895): 453–54, in *ProQuest British Periodicals Collection* (online).

15. C. L. R. James, *Beyond a Boundary* (Durham, NC: Duke University Press, 1993 [1963]), 43–44.

16. 'Creston', "Football," *Fortnightly Review* 61 (January 1894): 33.

17. Quoted in John Lowerson, *Sport and the English Middle Classes, 1870–1914* (Manchester: Manchester University Press, 1993), 159.

18. Quoted in Eric Halladay, "Of Pride and Prejudice: The Amateur Question in English 19th-Century Rowing," in *A Sport-Loving Society: Victorian and Edwardian Middle-Class England at Play*, edited by J. A. Mangan, ed., (London: Routledge, 2006), 249.

19. Jeremy Crump, "Athletics," in *Sport in Britain: A Social History*, edited by Tony Mason (New York: Cambridge University Press, 1989), 50–51.

20. *Sporting Magazine* 156 (1870): 395–97.

21. Montague Shearman, *Athletics* (London: Longmans, Green and Co., 1901), 268, 278.

22. W. J. Ford, "Country Cricket," in *Cricket*, edited by Horace G. Hutchinson (London: The Offices of "Country Life," 1903), 148.

23. N. L. Jackson, "Professionalism and Sport," *Fortnightly Review* 73 (January 1900): 156.

24. "Professional Cricket," *Saturday Review* 56 (July 14, 1883): 47–48.

25. A. G. Steel, "Bowling," in *Cricket*, edited by A. G. Steel and the Hon. R. H. Lyttelton (London: Longmans, Green, and Co., 1901), 98.

26. "Professional Cricket," 47.

27. Quoted in John Bale, *Anti-Sport Sentiments in Literature: Batting for the Opposition* (New York: Routledge, 2008), 71–73.

28. "Professional Football," *All the Year Round* 10 (December 9, 1893): 558, 562.

29. "Professionals in English Sports," *Saturday Review* 65 (April 14, 1888): 438.

30. 'Creston', "Football," 30.

31. Jackson, "Professionalism and Sport," 157.

32. 'X. Y.,' "Football in '96-'97," *New Review* 16 (May 1897): 577.

33. Richard Holt, *Sport and the British* (Oxford: Oxford University Press, 1990), 161.

34. Charles Edwardes, "The New Football Mania," *Nineteenth Century* 32 (October 1892): 628.

35. "Association Football: A Retrospect and a Lament," *Saturday Review* 89 (March 3, 1900): 261.

36. "The Football Association and an Incident," *Saturday Review* 91 (February 23, 1901): 232.

37. Sir Derek Birley, *Land of Sport and Glory: Sport and British Society, 1887–1910* (Manchester: Manchester University Press, 1995), 36.

38. Wray Vamplew, *Pay Up and Play the Game: Professional Sport in Britain, 1875–1914* (Cambridge: Cambridge University Press, 2004), 129.

39. Ibid., 244.

40. Francis Prevost, "Hockey," *English Illustrated Magazine* 98 (November 1891): 107.

41. Montague Shearman, *Athletics and Football* (Boston: Little, Brown, and Co., 1887), 267.

42. Quoted in Tony Collins, *Rugby's Great Split: Class, Culture and the Origins of Rugby League Football* (London: Frank Cass, 1998), 122.

43. Hely Hutchinson Almond, "Football as a Moral Agent," *Nineteenth Century* 34 (December 1893): 911.

44. 'Creston', "Football," 30.

45. Vamplew, *Pay Up and Play the Game*, 195–96.

46. Quoted in Collins, *Rugby's Great Split*, 6.

47. William J. Baker, "William Webb Ellis and the Origins of Rugby Football: The Life and Death of a Victorian Myth," *Albion* (Summer 1981): 120–24.

CHAPTER 8

1. Sir Charles Tennyson, "They Taught the World to Play," *Victorian Studies* 2 (March 1959): 211–22.

2. E. H. Lawson Williams, "Curling," *Badminton Magazine of Sports and Pastimes* 2 (January 1896), 40, in *ProQuest British Periodicals Collection* (online).

3. Montague Shearman, *Athletics* (London: Longmans, Green, and Co., 1901), 177.

4. Horace Hutchinson, "Cricket v. Golf, A Comparison," *Blackwood's Edinburgh Magazine* 147 (April 1890): 510.

5. Sir Derek Birley, *Sport and the Making of Britain* (Manchester: Manchester University Press, 1993), 218–19; and Tennyson, "They Taught the World to Play," 218.

6. John Lowerson, *Sport and the English Middle Classes, 1870–1914* (Manchester: Manchester University Press, 1993), 125.

7. Hutchinson, "Cricket v. Golf, A Comparison," 510–11.

8. Leonard B. Williams, "Golfers: Some Mortals and the Game of Croquet," *Badminton Magazine* 7 (October 1898): 452, in *ProQuest*.

9. Lowerson, *Sport and the English Middle Classes*, 127.

10. R. C. Lehmann, "Are Our Oarsmen Degenerate?" *New Review* 2 (November 1892): 619.

11. Horace Hutchinson, "Golf and Golfing," *English Illustrated Magazine* 109 (October 1892): 58.

12. Hamish Stuart, "The Football Nations," *Blackwood's Edinburgh Magazine* 169 (April 1901): 495.

13. Gareth Williams, "From Popular Culture to Public Cliché: Image and Identity in Wales, 1890–1914," in *A Sport-Loving Society: Victorian and Edwardian Middle-Class England at Play*, edited by J. A. Mangan (New York: Routledge, 2006), 136.

14. Quoted in W. F. Mandle, *The Gaelic Athletic Association & Irish Nationalist Politics, 1884–1924* (London: Christopher Helm, 1987), 5.

15. Patrick F. McDevitt, *"May the Best Man Win": Sport, Masculinity, and Nationalism in Great Britain and the Empire, 1880–1935* (New York: Palgrave Macmillan, 2004), 14–15, 19.

16. W. G. Grace, "Cricket. A Review of the Game, Past and Present, in Australia, Canada, the United States, India, and England," *English Illustrated Magazine* 81 (June 1890): 641.

17. Charles Box, *The English Game of Cricket* (London: "The Field" Office, 1877), 323, 328–29.

18. Quoted in Derek Birley, *A Social History of English Cricket*, (London: Aurum Press, 1999). 137.

19. "Professional Cricket," *Saturday Review* 56 (July 14, 1883): 48.

20. A. Lang, "Cricket," *English Illustrated Magazine* 12 (September 1884): 755.

21. Anthony Trollope, *The Fixed Period* (n. p.: Elibron Classics, 2007 [1882]), 114, 120–21.

22. Allen Guttmann, *Games & Empires: Modern Sports and Cultural Imperialism* (New York: Columbia University Press, 1994), 22.

23. Theodore Andrea Cook, "American Football," *Cassell's Family Magazine* 18 (1899): 313, 316.

24. Caspar W. Whitney, *A Sporting Pilgrimage* (New York: Harper & Brothers, 1895), 192.

25. *Illustrated Sporting and Dramatic News* 1 (1874): 491, 510.

26. John C. Hutcheson, "Transatlantic Sports and Sporting Matters," *Belgravia* 7 (June 1872): 478.

27. R. A. Proctor, "Baseball and Cricket," *Longman's Magazine* 10 (June 1887): 181–82.

28. Albert G. Spalding, *America's National Game* (Lincoln, NE: University of Nebraska Press, 1992 [1911]), 4–6.

29. P. F. Warner, "Foreign Cricket," in *Cricket*, edited by Horace G. Hutchinson (London: The Offices of "Country Life," 1903), 385.

30. P. F. Warner, *Cricket in Many Climes* (London: William Heinemann, 1900), 52.

31. James Paget, "Recreation," *Nineteenth Century* 14 (December 1883): 979.

32. Quoted in Guttmann, *Games and Empires*, 32–33.

33. Satadru Sen, "Schools, Athletes and Confrontation: The Student Body in Colonial India," in *Confronting the Body: The Politics of Physicality in Colonial and Post-Colonial India*, edited by James H. Mills and Satadru Sen (London: Anthem Press, 2004), 69.

34. Quoted in Birley, *A Social History of English Cricket*, 166.

35. Ashis Nandy, *The Tao of Cricket* (New York: Penguin Books, 1989), 57.

36. K. S. Ranjitsinhji, *The Jubilee Book of Cricket*, 4th ed. (London: William Blackwood and Sons, 1897), 24.

37. Andrew Lang, "The 'Jubilee Cricket Book,'" *Longman's Magazine* 30 (October 1897): 499.

38. "Prince Ranjitsinhji on Cricket, The Jubilee Book of Cricket," *Saturday Review* 14 (August 14, 1897): 170.

39. Quoted in Nandy, *The Tao of Cricket*, 67.

40. Ibid., 1, 21, 51.

41. T. F. Dale, "Polo and Politics," *Blackwood's Edinburgh Magazine* 165 (June 1899): 1032–34.

42. E. N. A., "Polo," *London Society* 26 (September 1874): 214.

43. Quoted in André Odendaal, "South Africa's Black Victorians: Sport and Society in South Africa in the Nineteenth Century," in *Pleasure, Profit, Proselytism: British Culture and Sport at Home and Abroad, 1799–1914*, edited by J. A. Mangan (London: Frank Cass and Company, Limited, 1988), 203.

44. C. B. Fry, *Life Worth Living, Some Phases of an Englishman* (London: Eyre & Spottiswoode, 1941), 109–13.

45. Quoted in Richard Holt, *Sport and the British* (Oxford: Oxford University Press, 1990), 1.

46. Pierre de Coubertin, "Why I Revived the Olympic Games," *Fortnightly Review* 84 (July 1908): 110.

47. Quoted in Helen Clare Cromarty, "Brookes, William Penny (1809–1895)," *Oxford Dictionary of National Biography* (Oxford: Oxford University Press, 2004), online edition.

48. "Imperial Jinks," *Saturday Review* 72 (October 17, 1891): 439.

49. J. Astley Cooper, "Americans and the Pan-Britannic Movement," *Nineteenth Century* 38 (September 1895): 427.

50. G. S. Robertson, "The Olympic Games by a Competitor and Prize Winner," *Fortnightly Review* 59 (June 1896): 944–45.

51. 'Vanderdecken', "Sports and Pastimes, Our French Critics Again," *Graphic* (April 11, 1896), in *19th Century British Library Newspapers* (Gale Digital Collections).

52. Sir Henry Newbolt, "Vitaï Lampada," in *The Victorian Age*, edited by Heather Henderson and William Sharpe, in *The Longman Anthology of British Literature*, Vol. 2, edited by David Damrosch (New York: Longman, 1999), 1629.

BIBLIOGRAPHY

PRIMARY SOURCES

Electronic Resources (available online by subscription)

Defining Gender, 1450–1910: Five Centuries of Advice Literature Online. Marlborough, England: Adam Matthews Publications, 2003. www.amdigital.co.uk/collections/Defining-Gender/Default.aspx.

19th Century British Library Newspapers. Gale Digital Publications. www.gale.cengage.com/pdf/facts/BritLibNewspapers.pdf.

19th Century UK Periodicals Online, 1800–1900. Gale Digital Publications. www.gale.cengage.com/DigitalCollections/products/ukperiodicals.

ProQuest British Periodicals Collections. http://britishperiodicals.chadwyck.com.

Periodicals (many of which are in the electronic resources named above)

All the Year Round
Annals of Sporting and Fancy Gazette: A Magazine
Badminton Magazine of Sports and Pastimes
Belgravia: A London Magazine
Bentley's Quarterly Review
Blackwood's Edinburgh Magazine
Cassell's Family Magazine
Chambers's Journal of Popular Literature, Science and Art
Cornhill Magazine
English Illustrated Magazine
Fores's Sporting Notes & Sketches: A Quarterly Magazine
Fortnightly Review
Fraser's Magazine for Town and Country
Good Words
Graphic

Illustrated Sporting & Dramatic News
Imperial Magazine
The Ladies' Treasury
London Society: An Illustrated Magazine of Light and Amusing Literature for the
        Hours of Relaxation
Longman's Magazine
The Monthly Visitor and New Family Magazine
Moral Reformer and Protestor against the Vices, Abuses and Corruptions of the Age
National Review
New Review
New Sporting Magazine
The Nineteenth Century: A Monthly Review
North American Review
Pall Mall Gazette
Punch, or the London Charivari
Quarterly Review
The Review of Reviews
Saturday Review
Scottish Review
The Sporting Gazette
The Sporting Magazine
Temple Bar
The Times (London)
Universal Review
Weekly Entertainer: or Agreeable and Instructive Repository
Westminster Review
Windsor Magazine: An Illustrated Monthly for Men and Women

Books

Allen, Grant. *The Typewriter Girl*. New York: Street and Smith, 1900 [1897].
Box, Charles. *The English Game of Cricket, Comprising a Digest of Its Origin, Charac-*
        ter, History, and Progress, Together with an Exposition of Its Laws and
        Language. London: "The Field" Office, 1877.
Cassell's Complete Book of Sports and Pastimes, Being a Compendium of Out-Door
        and Indoor Amusements. London: Cassell & Co., 1892.
Collins, Wilkie. *Man and Wife*. 1870. Facsimile reprint, Ann Arbor: University of
        Michigan Library, n.d.
Dixie, Lady Florence. *Gloriana, or the Revolution of 1900*. London: Henry and Company,
        1890.
Egan, Pierce. *Boxiana; or Sketches of Ancient & Modern Pugilism from the Days of the*
        Renowned Broughton and Slack, to the Championship of Cribb. London:
        George Virtue, 1830 [1812]. Facsimile reprint of Vol. I, n.p.: Elibron Classics,
        2006.
———. *Sporting Anecdotes, Original and Selected*. London: Sherwood, Jones, and Co.,
        1825 [1807].
Fielding, Henry. *The History of Tom Jones, A Foundling*. New York: Heritage Press,
        1952 [1749].

Fry, C. B. *Life Worth Living: Some Phases of an Englishman.* London: Eyre & Spottiswoode, 1939.

Gale, Frederick. *Modern English Sports: Their Use and Their Abuse.* London: Sampson Low, Marston, Searle, & Rivington, 1885.

Gardiner, Samuel Rawson, ed. *Constitutional Documents of the Puritan Revolution, 1625–1660.* Oxford: Clarendon Press, 1906.

Grace, W. G. *Cricket.* London: Simpkin, Marshall, Hamilton, Kent & Co. Ltd., 1891.

Hamilton, Col. J. R. *Reminiscences of an Old Sportsman.* 2 vols. London: Longman, Green, Longman, and Roberts, 1860.

Hayes, Alice M. *The Horsewoman: A Practical Guide to Side-Saddle Riding.* 2nd ed. New York: Charles Scribner's Sons, 1903 [1893].

Hieover, Harry. *The Sporting World.* London: T. C. Newby, 1858.

Hughes, Thomas. *The Manliness of Christ.* Boston: Houghton, Osgood and Company, 1880.

———. *Tom Brown at Oxford.* 1862. New York: A. L. Burt Company, n.d.

———. *Tom Brown's School Days.* 1857. London: Blackie, n.d.

Hutchinson, Horace G., ed. *Cricket.* London: The Offices of "Country Life," 1903.

James, C. L. R. *Beyond a Boundary.* Durham, NC: Duke University Press, 1993 [1963].

Kingsley, Charles. *Alton Locke.* London: The Co-operative Publication Society, 1898 [1849].

Kingsley, Charles, and Frances Eliza Grenfell Kingsley. *Charles Kingsley: His Letters and Memories of His Life.* Abridged from the London ed. New York: Charles Scribner's Sons, 1899 [1877].

Lubbock, Alfred. *Memories of Eton and Etonians, Including My Life at Eton, 1854–1863 and Some Reminiscences of Subsequent Cricket, 1864–1874.* London: John Murray, 1899.

Lubbock, John (Lord Avebury). *Essays and Addresses, 1900–1903.* Reprint, Freeport, NY: Books for Libraries Press, 1966.

Lyttelton, E. *Memories and Hopes.* London: John Murray, 1925.

Mayhew, Henry. *London Labour and the London Poor.* 4 vols. New York: Dover Publications, 1968 [1861].

Mill, John Stuart. *Autobiography,* edited by Jack Stillinger. New York: Houghton Mifflin Co., 1969 [1873].

Nimrod (Apperley, Charles James). *My Life and Times.* Edited with Additions by E. D. Cuming. Edinburgh: William Blackwood & Sons, Ltd., 1927.

O'Donoghue, Nannie Power. *Ladies on Horseback: Learning, Park-Riding, and Hunting.* London: W. H. Allen & Co., 1881.

Pater, Walter. *The Renaissance: Studies in Art and Poetry,* edited by Donald Hill. Berkeley: University of California Press, 1980 [1873].

Peek, Hedley, ed. *Poetry of Sport, with a Chapter on Classical Allusions to Sport by Andrew Lang, and a Special Preface to the Badminton Library by A. E. T. Watson.* London: Longmans, Green, and Co., 1901.

Piozzi, Hester Lynch. *Anecdotes of the Late Samuel Johnson, LL.D., During the Last Twenty Years of His Life,* edited by S. C. Roberts. Westport, CT: Greenwood Press, 1971.

Ranjitsinhji, K. S. *The Jubilee Book of Cricket.* 4th ed. London: William Blackwood and Sons, 1897.

Sargent, Harry R. *Thoughts upon Sport; A Work Dealing Shortly with Each Branch of Sport, and Showing that as a Medium for the Circulation of Money SPORT Stands Unrivaled among the Institutions of the Kingdom*. London: n.p., 1894.

Saussure, César de. *A Foreign View of England in the Reigns of George I & George II. The Letters of Monsieur César de Saussure to His Family*, translated and edited by Madame Van Muyden. New York: E P. Dutton and Company, 1902.

Shaw, G. Bernard. *Cashel Byron's Profession*. New York: Brentano's, 1899.

Shearman, Montague. *Athletics and Football, with a Contribution on Paper-Chasing by W. Rye and an Introduction by the Sir Richard Webster*. Boston: Little, Brown, and Co., 1887.

———. *Athletics, with Chapters on Athletics at School by W. Beach Thomas: Athletic Sports in America by C. H. Sherrill: A Contribution on Paper-Chasing by W. Rye: and an Introduction by Sir Richard Webster*. London: Longmans, Green, and Co., 1901.

———. *Football, with Chapters by W. J. Oakley & G. O. Smith, "The Association Game," and by Frank Mitchell, "The Rugby Union Game," and Others*. New edition. London: Longmans, Green and Co., 1901.

Sinclair, Archibald, and William Henry. *Swimming*. London: Longmans, Green and Co., 1901.

Smiles, Samuel. *Self-Help*, edited by Peter W. Sinnema. New York: Oxford University Press, 2002 [1859].

Spalding, Albert G. *America's National Game*. Lincoln: University of Nebraska Press, 1992 [1911].

Steel, A. G., and Hon. R. H. Lyttelton, eds. *Cricket, with Contributions by A. Lang, W. G. Grace, R. A. H. Mitchell, and F. Gale*. London: Longmans, Green, and Co., 1901.

Thomas, Ralph. *Swimming*. London: Sampton Low, Marston & Co., 1904.

Trollope, Anthony. *An Autobiography*. N.p.: Filiquarian Publishing, 2007 [1883].

———, ed. *British Sports and Pastimes*. London: Virtue, 1868.

———. *The Fixed Period*. N.p.: Elibron Classics, 2007 [1882].

Walton, Izaak. *The Compleat Angler, 1542–1676*, edited by Jonquil Bevan. Oxford: Clarendon Press, 1983.

Warner, P. F. *Cricket in Many Climes*. London: William Heinemann, 1900.

Wells, H. G. *The Croquet Player*. New York: Viking Press, 1937.

———. *Wheels of Chance: A Bicycling Idyll*. New York: Scribner's Sons, 1925 [1896].

Wheeler, C. A., ed. *Sportascrapiana: Cricket and Shooting, Pedestrianism, Equestrian, Rifle and Pistol Doings. Lion Hunting and Deer Stalking. By Celebrated Sportsmen*. London: Simpkin, Marshall, & Co., 1867.

Whitney, Caspar W. *A Sporting Pilgrimage, Riding to Hounds, Golf, Rowing, Football, Club and University Athletics. Studies in English Sport, Past and Present*. New York: Harper & Brothers, 1894.

Wilde, Oscar. *Woman of No Importance*. 1893. In *The Plays of Oscar Wilde*. New York: Modern Library, n.d.

SECONDARY WORKS

Anderson, Nancy Fix. *Woman against Women in Victorian England: A Life of Eliza Lynn Linton*. Bloomington: Indiana University Press, 1987.

Bailey, Peter. *Leisure and Class in Victorian England: Rational Recreation and the Contest for Control, 1830–1885*. New York: Methuen, 1978.

Baker, William J. "William Webb Ellis and the Origins of Rugby Football: The Life and Death of a Victorian Myth." *Albion* 13 (Summer 1981): 117–30.

Bale, John. *Anti-Sport Sentiments in Literature: Batting for the Opposition*. New York: Routledge, 2008.

Bevington, Merle Mowbray. *The Saturday Review, 1855–1868: Representative Opinion in Victorian England*. New York: Columbia University Press, 1941.

Birley, Sir Derek. *Land of Sport and Glory: Sport and British Society, 1887–1910*. Manchester: Manchester University Press, 1995.

———. *A Social History of English Cricket*. London: Aurum Press, 1999.

———. *Sport and the Making of Britain*. Manchester: Manchester University Press, 1993.

Blanning. Tim. *The Pursuit of Glory: Europe 1648–1815*. New York: Viking, 2007.

Brailsford, Dennis. *British Sport: A Social History*. Cambridge: Lutterworth Press, 1992.

Carr, Raymond. *English Fox Hunting: A History*. London: Weidenfeld and Nicolson, 1976.

Collins, Tony. *Rugby's Great Split: Class, Culture and the Origins of Rugby League Football*. London: Frank Cass, 1998.

Cone, Carl, ed. *Hounds in the Morning: Sundry Sports of Merry England: Selections from The Sporting Magazine, 1792–1836*. Lexington: University of Kentucky Press, 1981.

Cunnington, C. Willet, and Phillis Cunnington. *Handbook of English Costume in the Nineteenth Century* Boston: Plays, Inc., 1970.

Damrosch, David, ed. *The Longman Anthology of British Literature*. 2 vols. New York: Longman, 1999.

Elledge, Paul. *Lord Byron at Harrow School*. Baltimore: Johns Hopkins University Press, 2000.

George, M. Dorothy. *London Life in the Eighteenth Century*. London: Kegan Paul, Trench, Trubner & Co., 1930.

Griffin, Emma. *Blood Sport: Hunting in Britain since 1066*. New Haven: Yale University Press, 2007.

Guttmann, Allen. *Games & Empires: Modern Sports and Cultural Imperialism*. New York: Columbia University Press, 1994.

Haight, Gordon, ed., *The Portable Victorian Reader*. New York: Penguin Books, 1972.

Haley, Bruce. *The Healthy Body and Victorian Culture*. Cambridge, MA: Harvard University Press, 1978.

Hansen, Peter H. "Albert Smith, the Alpine Club, and the Invention of Mountaineering in Mid-Victorian Britain." *Journal of British Studies* 34 (July 1995): 300–24.

Harvey, Adrian. *The Beginnings of a Commercial Sporting Culture in Britain, 1793–1850*. Burlington, VT: Ashgate Publishing Ltd., 2004.

Holt, Richard. *Sport and the British: A Modern History*. Oxford: Oxford University Press, 1990.

Houghton, Walter E., and Jean Slingerland, eds. *The Wellesley Index to Victorian Periodicals, 1824–1900*. 5 vols. Toronto: University of Toronto Press, 1966–1989.

Huggins, Mike. *The Victorians and Sport*. New York: Hambledon and London, 2004.

Jones, Stephen G. *Sport, Politics and the Working Class: Organised Labour and Sport in Inter-War Britain*. Manchester: Manchester University Press, 1988.

Lowerson, John. *Sport and the English Middle Classes, 1870–1914*. Manchester: Manchester University Press, 1993.

Lunn, Arnold. *Switzerland and the English*. London: Eyre & Spottiswoode, 1944.

Mandle, W. F. *The Gaelic Athletic Association & Irish Nationalist Politics, 1884–1924*. London: Christopher Helm, 1987.

Mangan, J. A. *Athleticism in the Victorian and Edwardian Public School: The Emergence and Consolidation of an Educational Ideology*. London, Falmer Press, 1986 [1981].

———, ed. *Pleasure, Profit, Proselytism: British Culture and Sport at Home and Abroad, 1700–1914*. London: Frank Cass and Company, Limited, 1988.

———, ed. *A Sport-Loving Society: Victorian and Edwardian Middle-Class England at Play*. New York: Routledge, 2006.

Mason, Tony. *Association Football and English Society, 1863–1915*. Sussex: The Harvester Press, 1980.

———, ed. *Sport in Britain: A Social History*. New York: Cambridge University Press, 1989.

McCrone, Kathleen E. *Sport and the Physical Emancipation of English Women, 1870–1914*. London: Routledge, 1988.

McDevitt, Patrick F. *"May the Best Man Win": Sport, Masculinity, and Nationalism in Great Britain and the Empire, 1880–1935*. New York: Palgrave Macmillan, 2004.

Mee, Bob. *Bare Fists: The History of Bare-Knuckle Prize-Fighting*. New York: The Overlook Press, 2001.

Middleton, Dorothy. *Victorian Lady Travellers*. Chicago: Academy Chicago, 1982.

Mills, James H., and Satadru Sen, eds. *Confronting the Body: The Politics of Physicality in Colonial and Post-Colonial India*. London: Anthem Press, 2004.

Mingay, G. E., ed. *The Victorian Countryside*. 2 vols. Boston: Routledge & Kegan Paul, 1981.

Money, Tony. *Manly & Muscular Diversions: Public Schools and the Nineteenth-Century Sporting Revival*. Avon: The Bath Press, 2001.

Nandy, Ashis. *The Tao of Cricket: On Games of Destiny and the Destiny of Games*. New York: Penguin Books Ltd., 1989.

Neumann, Bonnie Rayford. *Robert Smith Surtees*. Boston: Twayne Publishers, 1978.

Oxford Dictionary of National Biography, edited by Colin Matthew, Brian Harrison, and Lawrence Goldman. Oxford: Oxford University Press, 2004. Online edition: www.oxforddnb.com.

Parratt, Catriona M. *"More than Mere Amusement": Working-Class Women's Leisure in England, 1750–1914*. Boston: Northeastern University Press, 2001.

Pearson, Jeffrey. *Lottie Dod, Champion of Champions: Story of an Athlete*. Birkenhead, England: Countyvise Ltd., 1988.

Robinson, Jane, ed., *Unsuitable for Ladies, An Anthology of Women Travellers*. Oxford: Oxford University Press, 2001.

Rubenstein, David. "Cycling in the 1890s." *Victorian Studies* 21 (1977): 47–71.

Sandiford, Keith A. P. *Cricket and the Victorians*. Aldershot, England: Scolar Press, 1994.

Seaman, L. C. B. *Victorian England*. New York: Methuen, 1973.

Stoddart, Brian, and Keith A. P. Sandiford. *The Imperial Game: Cricket, Culture and Society*. Manchester: Manchester University Press, 1998.

Taylor, Matthew. *The Association Game: A History of British Football*. Harlow, England: Pearson Education Limited, 2008.

Tennyson, Sir Charles, "They Taught the World to Play." *Victorian Studies* 2 (March 1959): 211–22.

Tranter, Neil. *Sport, Economy and Society in Britain, 1750–1914*. Cambridge: Cambridge University Press, 1998.

Trevelyan, George M. *English Social History: A Survey of Six Centuries: Chaucer to Queen Victoria*. New York: Longmans, Green and Co., 1942.

Vamplew, Wray. *Pay Up and Play the Game: Professional Sport in Britain, 1875–1914*. Cambridge: Cambridge University Press, 1988.

INDEX

About the Author

NANCY FIX ANDERSON is professor emerita of history at Loyola University New Orleans. She has written *Woman against Women in Victorian England: A Life of Eliza Lynn Linton* (1987), and edited *Lives of Victorian Political Figures: Annie Besant* (2008).